Public Sector Collective Bargaining

A Practical Guide To Obtaining A Fair Contract

Will Aitchison

LRIS PUBLICATIONS
PORTLAND, OREGON

Published by Labor Relations Information System
3021 NE Broadway
Portland OR 97232
503.282.5440
www.LRIS.com

PUBLIC SECTOR COLLECTIVE BARGAINING: A Practical Guide to Obtaining A Fair Contract. Copyright 2016 by Will Aitchison. All rights reserved. Printed in the United States of America. No part of this book may be used or reproduced in any manner whatsoever without written permission except in the case of brief quotations embodied in critical articles and reviews.

Aitchison, William Bruce, 1951 -

ISBN 978-1-880607-31-2

Library of Congress Control Number: 2016934981

ABOUT THE AUTHOR

Will Aitchison is a Portland, Oregon attorney who has, over the course of his career, represented over 100 law enforcement and firefighter labor organizations in five western states. He is the veteran of hundreds of collective bargaining negotiations and arbitration hearings, and has handled FLSA litigation involving tens of thousands of public safety employees, recovering in excess of $100 million in unpaid overtime compensation.

Aitchison graduated from the University of Oregon (Honors College) in 1973, and received his Doctor of Jurisprudence Degree from Georgetown University Law Center in Washington, D.C. in 1976. After two years of clerking for Chief Judge Herbert Schwab of the Oregon Court of Appeals, Aitchison entered private practice and has been representing labor organizations since that time. In addition to his private practice, Aitchison has served as both an arbitrator and a pro tem district court judge, and has contributed numerous articles to various periodicals.

Aitchison is the author of *The Rights Of Law Enforcement Officers (7th Edition)*, *The FMLA: Understanding the Family & Medical Leave Act*, *Interest Arbitration (2nd Edition)*, *The FLSA – A User's Manual (5th Edition)*, *The Rights of Firefighters (4th Edition)*, *A Model Law Enforcement Contract: A Labor Perspective (3rd Edition)*, and *A Model Firefighter's Contact: A Labor Perspective*, all published by Labor Relations Information System.

Aitchison has lectured on many occasions throughout the country on FLSA issues and topics concerning labor relations and personnel issues, and has served as an expert witness and consultant in a variety of employment matters.

Aitchison lives in Portland, Oregon with his wife Valerie. Aitchison is the father of four sons, Michael, Matthew, and twins Alex and Luke.

TABLE OF CONTENTS

Chapter 1
Public Employee Bargaining — 1

Chapter 2
What Must Be Bargained — 13

What Makes A Topic Mandatory For Bargaining? — 15

What Are The "Wages" That Are Mandatory For Bargaining? — 17

What Are The "Hours" That Are Mandatory For Bargaining? — 17

What Are The "Working Conditions" That Are Mandatory For Bargaining? — 18

- Safety Issues. — 19
- Working Conditions With A Monetary Impact. — 19
- Working Conditions With An Off-Duty Impact. — 20
- Working Conditions Impacting Employee Discipline. — 21
- Working Conditions With Implications On Job Security. — 21
- Working Conditions Involving Union Activities. — 21

Management Rights Clauses. — 22

Notes — 23

Chapter 3
When Bargaining Must Occur — 27

What Amounts To A Past Practice? — 29

Waivers By Inaction – How A Union Forfeits Its Right To Bargain Over Changes In Past Practice By Not Acting In A Timely Fashion. — 31

Waivers By Contract And Management Rights Clauses. — 33

The Continuing Duty To Bargain And Maintenance Of Benefits Clauses.	36
Notes	37

Chapter 4
Long-Range Bargaining Preparation — 39

Continuous Bargaining Preparation And The Negotiations "Binder" – The Single Most Important Tool In Preparing For Bargaining.	41
Trying Your Arbitration Case, Even If You Don't Have Arbitration.	43

Chapter 5
The Bargaining Team — 45

When To Select The Bargaining Team.	50
Training The Bargaining Team.	50
Selecting The Chief Negotiator.	52
The Pros Of Hiring An Outside Negotiator.	53
The Cons Of Hiring An Outside Negotiator.	53
Notes	55

Chapter 6
Writing Bargaining Proposals — 57

Determining What Is Important To Constituents.	59
Brainstorm The Contract.	60
Anticipate The Issues The Other Party May Bring To The Table.	60
Research Bargaining History.	60
Gather Contract Language From Comparable Jurisdictions.	61

Write Proposals.	61
Remember The Basic Rules Of Contract Interpretation.	62
Proposals Will Be Construed Against Whoever Wrote Them.	62
Technical Words Will Be Interpreted In Light Of The Employer's Business.	62
Specific Contract Language Will Control Over General Language.	63
The Agreement Will Be Interpreted As A Whole.	63
The *Expressio Unius Est Exclusio Alterius* Rule.	63
Contract Language Will Be Interpreted Using The Ordinary Meaning Of Words.	64
Lawyers And Drafting Contract Language.	64
Prioritize Proposals.	64
How Many Proposals Should Be Made?	65
Is There An Obligation That Proposals Be Reasonable?	65
Pre-Bargaining Discussions With The Other Party.	66
Notes	67

Chapter 7
Costing Proposals

	69
The Most Accurate Way To Cost Proposals.	71
Estimating Costs.	74

Chapter 8
Ground Rules For Bargaining

	75
Bargaining Sessions.	77

Proposals.	78
Negotiators.	78
Bargaining Sessions.	79
Reaching Agreement.	80
Breaches of Ground Rules.	81
Notes	82

Chapter 9
Sharing Bargaining Information — 83

Categories Of Information Considered Relevant To The Bargaining Process.	86
Wage and Benefit Comparisons.	86
Health Insurance Information.	87
Budgetary Information.	87
Vacation, Sick Leave, Holidays, and Other Leave.	87
Contract Administration.	87
Work Schedule Information.	88
Promotional Information.	88
Disciplinary Information.	88
Retirement Information.	88
Other Information.	88
What Should Happen When An Information Request Is Received.	89
Notes	91

Chapter 10
The Bargaining Process — 93

The Stages Of Bargaining. — 97

Tentative Agreements. — 98

The Need For An Integrated Approach To Negotiations. — 99

Keeping Records Of Negotiations. — 101

The Process Of Contract Ratification. — 106

Relationship With Other Labor Organizations. — 107

Notes — 109

Chapter 11
Unfair Labor Practices During Bargaining — 111

Bad-Faith Bargaining. — 115

Regressive Bargaining. — 118

Changing The *Status Quo* During Bargaining. — 118

Interest Arbitration Unfair Labor Practices. — 119

Other *Per Se* Bargaining Unfair Labor Practices. — 120

Direct Dealing. — 120

Blocking Charges. — 121

Remedies For Bargaining Unfair Labor Practices. — 122

Notes — 124

Chapter 12

Interest-Based Bargaining — 129

Is Interest-Based Bargaining For You? — 133

Notes — 135

Chapter 13

Bargaining In Hard Times and Concessionary Bargaining — 137

When Contracts Are In Effect. — 139

Notes — 143

Chapter 14

Selecting Comparable Jurisdictions — 145

Statistical Means Of Selecting Comparable Jurisdictions. — 150

Notes — 152

Chapter 15

Comparisons Of Wages And Total Compensation — 153

Performing Wage Comparisons. — 155

What Should Be Included In Total Compensation Comparisons? — 157

How To Calculate Total Compensation. — 158

Calculating Total Compensation. — 160

Where Should Total Compensation Be Set? — 162

Notes — 164

Chapter 16

The Cost of Living — 165

Getting Started – The Types Of Cost Of Living Indices. — 167

Which Index Should Be Used, The CPI Or The PCE Deflator?	168
Which CPI To Use – The CPI-U Or The CPI-W?	169
Which CPI-W to Use?	170
Using The Consumer Price Index – Selection Of A "Base Year."	171

Should The CPI Be Discounted Or Augmented? — 171

Arguments in Favor of Discounting the CPI.	172
The Substitution Argument.	172
The Housing Component Argument.	173
The Medical Component Argument.	173
Arguments in Favor of Augmenting the CPI.	174

Adjustments to the CPI – A Conclusion. — 175

Analyzing The Cost of Living. — 175

Regional Costs Of Living. — 176

Notes — 179

Chapter 17
An Employer's Ability To Pay — 181

The Most Important Financial Documents Bearing Upon An Employer's Ability To Pay.	184
The Twelve Questions To Ask About An Employer's Ability To Pay.	184
1. What About Total Compensation, Comparability, The Cost Of Living, And Other Factors?	184
2. What Are The Budget Impacts Of Compensation Adjustments?	185
3. Has Revenue Growth Matched Expenses?	185

4. How Have The Employer's Reserves Been Faring?	185
5. Have There Been Layoffs Or Program Reductions?	186
6. Has The Pain Been Shared?	186
7. What Is The Community's Overall Economic Condition?	187
8. Are There Untapped Revenue Streams Available?	187
9. What Are The Revenue Projections For The Future?	187
10. How Well Has The Employer Done At Budgeting In The Past?	188
11. Are There "Me-Too" Implications To A Settlement?	188
12. Did the Union Meaningfully Participate in the Budget Process?	189
Notes	190

Chapter 18
The "Other Factors" Element Of Wage Analysis — 193

Interests And Welfare Of The Public.	195
Workload And Productivity.	196
Internal Comparability.	197
Wage Increases For Other Employees.	198
The Level Of Turnover And Employment Application Rates.	199
Public Opinion.	200
The Local Labor Market.	200
Notes	201

Chapter 19

Interest Arbitration	203
Selecting An Arbitrator.	205
Scheduling The Hearing.	206
Developing Final Offers.	207
The Interest Arbitration Hearing.	208
The Evidence You Should Submit In Interest Arbitration.	210
The Use Of Experts In Interest Arbitration.	210
Technology – Use It Effectively.	211
Recording The Hearing.	212
After The Hearing But Before The Decision.	212
The Finality Of The Arbitrator's Decision.	213
What Will Likely Result From Arbitration?	213
Notes	215

Chapter 20

On-Line Negotiations Resources	217
The Law.	219
Employment Law Newsletters and Blogs.	219
How To Negotiate.	220
Demographic and Economic Data.	220
Regional Cost of Living Calculators.	221
Medical Information.	222

National Labor Organizations.	222
National Employer Organizations.	223
News Article "Trawlers."	224
Index	227

CHAPTER 1

PUBLIC EMPLOYEE BARGAINING

The National Labor Relations Act (NLRA) is the federal law which governs private sector labor relations. The NLRA excludes state governmental bodies and their political subdivisions such as cities, counties, and special districts from its definition of "employers." As a result, non-federal public sector collective bargaining laws have developed on a state-by-state and, occasionally, a local basis. Though public employee collective bargaining laws differ, they follow three general models: "Binding Arbitration," "Meet and Confer," and "Bargaining Not Required."

Binding Arbitration Model. Most states with collective bargaining laws follow the binding arbitration model, at least with respect to their public safety employees. In this model, public employees are granted the right to select exclusive representatives for the purposes of collective bargaining with their employers. Bargaining must occur over "mandatory" subjects of bargaining. When an impasse is reached, unresolved disputes are submitted to a process known as "interest arbitration," where a neutral third party selected by the parties makes a final and binding resolution of the disputed issues.

There are three general types of binding arbitration laws, reflecting differences in the latitude given arbitrators to render decisions. "Issue-by-issue" arbitration allows an arbitrator the ability to render a decision on each issue independently, and to craft whatever award on each issue the arbitrator believes is most appropriate. For example, if an employer is proposing a wage freeze and a union a 5.0% raise, an arbitrator in an issue-by-issue setting is free to award a freeze, a 5.0% raise, or anything in between that the arbitrator believes is fair.

"Final offer, issue-by-issue" arbitration also involves an arbitrator looking at each open issue independently, but the arbitrator must award the final offer made by one of the parties, and is not free to craft a compromise position which has not been specifically proposed by either party. In the example from the previous paragraph, the arbitrator must award a wage freeze or 5.0%, and is not free to award a compromise position.

"Total package" arbitration requires the arbitrator to select the most reasonable of the total packages submitted by each party, even if selected elements of that party's total package might not have been awarded by the arbitrator on an issue-by-issue basis. For example, if eight issues are sent to binding arbitration, including wages, health insurance, overtime and seniority, the arbitrator must award one side or the other's complete eight-issue package, even if the arbitrator might not agree with that party's position on one or more issues.

All states with binding arbitration require an arbitrator to analyze a set of criteria established by the collective bargaining statute, usually including factors such as the wages and benefits paid in comparable jurisdictions, the cost of living, and an employer's ability to pay.

Meet-And-Confer Model. Collective bargaining following a meet-and-confer model creates much the same structure as with binding arbitration, but with one notable exception. When negotiations end in impasse in a meet-and-confer setting, the employer is allowed to unilaterally implement its last best offer, or at least that portion of the offer that contains mandatory subjects of bargaining.[1] This leaves employees in the position of either accepting the employer's last offer of settlement, taking whatever form of job action is permissible under the laws of the state, or attempting political or other measures to resolve the collective bargaining dispute.

Bargaining Not Required Model. The last model for public sector collective bargaining laws is found in those states that do not statutorily require, or in some cases, even allow collective bargaining for some or all classes of public employees. In some of these states, bargaining laws have been enacted by the state legislature only to later be declared unconstitutional by the courts. In the majority of "bargaining not required" states, a statewide collective bargaining statute covering public employees has simply never been enacted.

Individual Exceptions To Statewide Models. There are some local exceptions to the "meet-and-confer" and "bargaining not required" models. In California, for example, though the state statutes generally follow the "meet-and-confer" model, a number of cities and counties have enacted ordinances or charter provisions calling for binding arbitration for at least some employees. Along similar lines, though Arizona follows a "bargaining not required" model at the state statute level, individual cities have enacted ordinances or charter provisions requiring collective bargaining with their employees.

What follows is a general summary of statewide collective bargaining laws across the nation.

Alabama

Alabama has no statewide public employee collective bargaining laws.

Alaska

In 1972, Alaska passed the Public Employment Relations Act (PERA), which extended collective bargaining to employees of the state and its political subdivisions.[2] The Alaska PERA calls for binding arbitration as the last step in the bargaining process, but only for public safety employees.[3] When it was adopted, the Alaska PERA allowed local employers to opt out of its coverage under limited circumstances.[4] Several municipalities chose to opt out of the coverage of the Alaska PERA; some, such as Anchorage, enacted local collective bargaining ordinances, while others operate without collective bargaining.

Alaska's public employment collective bargaining statutes are administered by the Alaska Labor Relations Agency (ALRA).

Arizona

Arizona has not enacted a public employee collective bargaining statute. Some local governmental bodies, including Phoenix, Tucson, and most of Arizona's larges cities, have adopted collective bargaining systems through a local ordinance or charter.

Arkansas

Arkansas has no statewide public employee collective bargaining laws.

California

California has a variety of laws allowing public employees to collectively bargain.[5] The laws generally follow a meet-and-confer model. Though the laws once called for binding arbitration for public safety employees, the California Supreme Court struck down the arbitration provisions as conflicting with "home rule" provisions in the California constitution.[6] A number of local governmental bodies, including the cities of San Francisco, San Jose and Oakland, have adopted binding arbitration through their ordinances or charters. California's hodge-podge of collective bargaining laws are administered in different ways, but largely by California's Public Employment Relations Board (PERB).[7]

Colorado

Colorado has only one statewide public employee collective bargaining law, one that covers firefighters. A number of cities, counties, and special districts, including the City of Denver, bargain under local ordinance or charter provisions.

Connecticut

Connecticut has three basic statewide collective bargaining laws.[8] The Municipal Employee Relations Act, adopted in 1965, follows a binding arbitration model, using total-package arbitration. The law allows local governmental bodies to reject an arbitration decision by a 2/3 vote; if this occurs, a second arbitration panel is convened, with the award of the panel being final and binding. The Teacher Negotiation Act also follows a similar binding arbitration model for school employees.[9] Connecticut's statutes are administered by the Connecticut State Board of Labor Relations.

Delaware

Delaware's Public Employment Relations Act, supplemented by the Police Officers' and Firefighters' Employment Relations Act and the Public Schools Employment Relations Act, provides a comprehensive collective bargaining scheme for Delaware employees.[10] The laws call for total package binding arbitration for public safety employees. Delaware's Public Employment Relations Board administers the statutes.

Florida

In 1974, Florida adopted the Public Employees Relations Act (PERA), a comprehensive collective bargaining bill covering most public employees.[11] The PERA follows a meet-and-confer model, though public safety employees have access to a non-binding "special magistrate" process that produces a recommendation for a resolution of opening bargaining issues. The PERA is administered by the Florida Public Employees Relations Commission.

Georgia

Georgia has no statewide collective bargaining laws.

Hawai'i

The Hawai'i Employment Relations Act (ERA), adopted in 1970, creates an issue-by-issue binding arbitration system for most public employees.[12] The ERA is administered by the Hawai'i Labor Relations Board.

Idaho

Idaho's state laws allow collective bargaining for teachers and firefighters, but not for general employees or law enforcement personnel.[13]

Illinois

The Illinois Public Labor Relations Act (PLRA) was a relative late-comer to the scene, enacted in 1983.[14] The PLRA calls for a complicated system of binding arbitration for public safety employees. The Act is administered by the Illinois Labor Relations Board.

Indiana

Indiana's state laws provide only for collective bargaining for some educational employees.[15] Some cities and counties collectively bargain on a local-option basis.

Iowa

Iowa's Public Employment Relations Act is a relatively unusual collective bargaining law, with a truncated list of topics that are negotiable.[16] The Act calls for issue-by-issue final offer arbitration for public safety employees. The Iowa Public Employment Relations Board administers the law.

Kansas

The Kansas Public Employer-Employee Relations Act establishes collective bargaining rights for those public employees whose employers elected to be bound by the Act.[17] The Act, which calls for a meet-and-confer process, is administered by the Kansas Department of Labor.

Kentucky

Kentucky has no mandatory system of collective bargaining for public sector employees. Some larger cities and counties have adopted meet-and-confer bargaining systems with their public safety employees.

Louisiana

Louisiana has no statewide public employee collective bargaining laws. Through local option, some cities have entered into collective bargaining agreements with public safety employees.

Maine

Maine has a system of four laws that calls for public sector collective bargaining.[18] The laws are administered by the Maine Labor Relations Board. The laws give municipal employees the right to binding arbitration on all issues except "salary, pensions, and insurance," and includes the right to advisory arbitration on those three issues.

Maryland

Maryland's laws grant teachers and state employees collective bargaining rights.[19] Many cities and counties in Maryland bargain under a local option, occasionally with binding arbitration rights.

Massachusetts

Massachusetts' long-standing public sector collective bargaining statutes call for binding arbitration for many employees, including public safety employees.[20] The statutes are administered by the Massachusetts Division of Labor Relations.

Michigan

The heart of Michigan's Public Employment Relations Act dates to 1947.[21] Through a statute often referred to as Act 312, Michigan's laws call for issue-by-issue interest arbitration for public safety employees. The statutes are administered by the Michigan Employment Relations Commission.

Minnesota

Minnesota's Public Employment Labor Relations Act was adopted in 1984, and provides for collective bargaining for most public employees.[22] The Act calls for issue-by-issue interest arbitration for many public employees, including public safety employees. The Act is administered by the Minnesota Bureau of Mediation Services.

Mississippi

Mississippi has no statewide public employee collective bargaining laws.

Missouri

Missouri's collective bargaining system is still in a state of flux. Missouri has statutes covering some public employees, and Missouri courts have held that other local jurisdictions have an obligattion to engage in bargaining.[23] The state statutes, which call for meet-and-confer negotiations, are administered by the Missouri Department of Labor.

Montana

Montana's statutes provide meet-and-confer collective bargaining rights for most public employees.[24] The statutes are administered by the Montana Labor Standards Bureau.

Nebraska

Through a series of statutes, Nebraska has granted most public employees the right to collectively bargain.[25] The statutes are administered by the Nebraska Commission on Industrial Relations. The statutes give public safety employees the right to issue-by-issue interest arbitration.

Nevada

Nevada's statutes give local governmental employees (but not state employees) the right to collectively bargain.[26] The statutes, which call for total-package interest arbitration for public safety employees, are administered by Nevada's Local Government Employee-Management Relations Board.

New Hampshire

New Hampshire's Public Employee Labor Relations Act grants most public employees meet-and-confer collective bargaining rights.[27] New Hampshire's Public Employee Labor Relations Board administers the statutes.

New Jersey

New Jersey's Employer-Employee Relations Act, passed in 1968, establishes an issue-by-issue system of interest arbitration for public employees.[28] The Act is administered by the New Jersey Public Employment Relations Commission.

New Mexico

New Mexico's Public Employee Bargaining Act (PEBA) was passed in 2003.[29] The PEBA created a bargaining system that ends with a total-package form of binding arbitration. The PEBA is administered by the New Mexico Public Employee Labor Relations Board.

New York

New York's basic public employee collective bargaining statute is known as the Taylor Law, and was enacted in 1967.[30] New York City employees bargain under a different system.[31] The statutes call for issue-by-issue interest arbitration for public safety employees, and are administered by New York's Public Employment Relations Board.

North Carolina

North Carolina has enacted a statute that makes collective bargaining illegal for public employees.[32]

North Dakota

North Dakota has no statewide public employee collective bargaining laws.

Ohio

Ohio's basic collective bargaining law is the Public Employees' Collective Bargaining Act (PECBA).[33] The PECBA calls for issue-by-issue binding arbitration for public safety employees. The PECBA is administered by the State Employment Relations Board.

Oklahoma

Oklahoma grants many of its public employees the right to collectively bargain.[34] The laws are administered by Oklahoma's Public Employees Relations Board. The last step in the bargaining process for public safety employees is binding arbitration.

Oregon

Oregon adopted the Public Employee Collective Bargaining Act (PECBA) in 1973.[35] The PECBA follows a "total package" binding arbitration approach for public safety employees. The law is administered by Oregon's Employment Relations Board.

Pennsylvania

Pennsylvania's long-standing Public Employment Relations Act grants most public employees the right to collectively bargain.[36] A separate statute, usually referred to as Act 111, sets binding arbitration as the last step in the bargaining process for law enforcement officers and firefighters.[37] Pennsylvania's labor laws are administered by the Pennsylvania Labor Relations Board.

Rhode Island

Rhode Island's panoply of collective bargaining laws date to 1968, and create a binding arbitration process for many employees.[38] Rhode Island's statutes are administered by the State Labor Relations Board.

South Carolina

South Carolina has no statewide public employee collective bargaining laws.

South Dakota

South Dakota's statutes establish a meet-and-confer bargaining system for public employees. The laws are administered by the South Dakota Department of Labor.[39]

Tennessee

Tennessee's state statutes do not provide for collective bargaining by public employees, with the exception of teachers, who are covered by the Education Professional Negotiations Act.[40] Some cities and counties in Tennessee, including Memphis, bargain on a local-option basis.

Texas

Texas has no statewide laws that mandate public employee collective bargaining. The Texas Fire and Police Employee Relations Act does allow the voters of a local governmental body the ability to call for an election as to whether a system of collective bargaining should be adopted.[41] A number of cities in Texas, including Houston, Austin, San Antonio and Fort Worth, have adopted bargaining by local option.

Utah

Utah has no statewide public employee collective bargaining laws. Some jurisdictions, including Salt Lake City, bargain on a local-option basis.

Vermont

Vermont has a series of laws enacted in the late 1960s and early 1970s granting public employees the right to collectively bargain.[42] The laws create a meet-and-confer system, with a non-binding fact-finding process as the last articulated step in the bargaining process. The laws are administered by the Vermont Labor Relations Board.

Virginia

Virginia not only has no statewide public employee collective bargaining laws, but a long-standing decision of the Virginia Supreme Court holds that any voluntarily-adopted public employee collective bargaining agreement is void.[43]

Washington

Washington has a breathtaking array of collective bargaining laws, the core of which were adopted in 1967.[44] The laws are administered by Washington's Public Employment Relations Commission. The laws grant most public safety employees the right to issue-by-issue binding arbitration as the last step in the bargaining process.

West Virginia

West Virginia has no statewide public employee collective bargaining laws.

Wisconsin

Wisconsin's public employee collective bargaining laws are among the earliest in the country, dating to 1959.[45] Wisconsin's bargaining laws were significantly amended in the last few years, removing whole swaths of topics from the scope of negotiations for non-public safety employees. The system, which is administered by the Wisconsin Employment Relations Commission, calls for total package binding arbitration for public safety employees.

Wyoming

The only public employee collective bargaining law in Wyoming covers firefighters.[46] The law calls for an unusual type of binding arbitration.

NOTES

[1] *City of Cocoa*, 15 NPER FL-23235 (Fla. PERC 1993)(employer may not unilaterally implement management rights clause).

[2] Alaska Statutes Title 23, Ch. 40, § 23.40.070 *et seq.*

[3] *Alaska Public Employees Ass'n v. City of Fairbanks*, 753 P.2d 725 (Alaska 1988).

[4] *State v. City of Petersburg*, 538 P.2d 263 (Alaska 1975).

[5] State employees are covered by the Dills Act, Government Code §§ 3512-3524. Cities, counties, and other subordinate governmental bodies are covered by the Meyers-Milias-Brown Act, Government Code §§ 3500-3510. Teachers are covered by the Public Educational Employer-Employee Relations Act, Government Code §§ 3540 - 3549.3, and higher education employees are covered by Government Code §§ 3560-3599. Firefighters are covered by Labor Code §§ 1960-1964.

[6] *County of Riverside v. Superior Court*, 66 P.3d 718 (Cal. 2003).

[7] The decisions of PERB are available through http://www.perb.ca.gov/.

[8] Municipal employees are covered by Municipal Employee Relations Act, Conn. Gen. Stats., Title 7, § 7-467 *et seq.* State employees are covered by the State Employee Collective Bargaining Act, Conn. Gen. Stats., Title 5, § 5-270 *et seq.*, and teachers are governed by Conn. Gen. Stats., Title 10, Ch. 166, § 10-153a *et seq.*

[9] *See* http://www.cga.ct.gov/2005/pridata/Studies/pdf/Binding_Arbitration_Final_Report.pdf.

[10] Del. Code Ann. Title 19, §§ 1301-1318; Del. Code Ann. Title 19, §§ 1601-1618; Del. Code Ann. Title 14, §§ 4001-4018.

[11] Fla. Stats., Ch. 447, § 447.201 *et seq.*

[12] Hawai'i Rev. Stats., Ch. 89.

[13] Idaho Code §§ 33-1271 to 33-1276; Idaho Code §§ 44-1801 to 44-1811.

[14] 5 Ill. Comp. Stat. Ann. 315/1 - 315/27 ; 115 Ill. Comp. Stat. Ann. 5/1 - 5/20.

[15] Ind. Code Ann. §§ 20-7.5-1-1 to 20-7.5-1-14.

[16] Iowa Code §§ 20.1 - 20.26.

[17] Kan. Stat. Ann. §§ 75-4321 to 75-4337; *see* Kan. Stat. Ann. §§ 72-5410 to 72-5437 (teachers).

[18] Me. Rev. Stat. Ann., Title 26, §§ 1281-1294 (judicial employees); Me. Rev. Stat. Ann., Title 26, §§ 979 (state employees); Me. Rev. Stat. Ann., Title 26, §§ 1021-1035 (university employees); Me. Rev. Stat. Ann., Title 26, §§ 961-974 (municipal employees).

[19] Md. Code Ann., State Personnel and Pensions § 3-101 *et seq.* (state employees); Md. Code Ann., Educ. §§ 6-501 - 6-510 (school employees other than teachers); Md. Code Ann., Educ. §§ 6-401 - 6-411 (teachers).

[20] Mass. Ann. Laws, Ch. 150E, §§ 1-15.

[21] The Public Employment Relations Act is codified at Mich. Comp. Laws Ann. §§ 423.201 to 423.216. A special law for state troopers is at Mich. Comp. Laws Ann. §§ 423.271 to 423.286, and what is usually referred to as Act 312 is found at Mich. Comp. Laws Ann. § 423.231 to 423.246.

[22] Minn. Stat. §§ 179A.01 – 179A.25.

[23] Mo. Rev. Stat. §§ 105.500 – 105.530.

[24] Mont. Code Ann. §§ 39-31-101 to 39-31-409.

[25] Nebraska Const. Article 13, Ch. 81, § 81-1369 *et seq.*; Nebraska Const. Article 8, Ch. 48, § 48-801 *et seq.*

[26] Nev. Rev. Stat. Ann. §§ 288.010-288.280.

[27] N.H. Rev. Stat. Ann. §§ 273-A.1 to 273-A.17.

[28] N.J. Stat. Ann. §§ 34:13A-1 to 34:13A-13.

[29] New Mexico Statutes Annotated 10-7E-1 to 10-7E-26.

[30] N.Y. Civ. Serv. Law §§ 200-214.

[31] N.Y. City Charter Ch.54; N.Y. Admin. Code, Sec. 1173-1.0 *et seq.*

[32] General Statute (GS) 95-98.

[33] Ohio Rev. Code Ann. §§ 4117.01-4117.23. *See also Rocky River v. State Emp. Relations Bd.*, 43 Ohio St.3d 1, 13, 539 N.E.2d 103 (1989).

[34] Okla. Stat. Ann., Title 70, Ch. 70, §§ 509.1 - 509.10; Okla. Stat. Ann., Title 11, Ch. 256, §§ 51-101 to 51-112.

[35] O.R.S. § 243.650 *et seq.*

[36] 43 Pa. Stat. Ann. §§ 1101.101 ¬ 1101.2301.

[37] 43 Pa. Stat. Ann. §217.1.

[38] RIGL 28-9.1, Firefighters' Arbitration Act; RIGL 28-9.2, Municipal Police Arbitration Act; RIGL 28-9.3, Certified School Teachers' Arbitration Act; RIGL 28-9.4, Municipal Employees' Arbitration Act; RIGL 28-9.5, State Police Arbitration Act; RIGL 28-9.6 911, Employees' Arbitration Act; RIGL 28-9.7, Correctional Officers' Arbitration Act; RIGL 36-1,1 State Employees' Arbitration Act.

[39] S.D. Codified Laws §§ 3-18-1 to 3-18-17.

[40] Tenn. Code. Ann. §§ 49-5-601 to 49-5-613.

[41] Tex. Loc. Gov't Code Ann. § 174.001 *et seq.*

[42] *See* Vt. Stat. Ann., Title 3, Ch. 27, §§ 901-1006; Vt. Stat. Ann., Title 21, Ch. 22, §§ 1721-1735; Vt. Stat. Ann., Title 21, Ch. 19, §§ 1501-1623; Vt. Stat. Ann., Title 16, Ch. 57, §§ 1981-2010.

[43] *Commonwealth v. County Board of Arlington*, 217 Va. 558 (1977).

[44] State employees bargain under Was. Rev. Code § 41.06.150 *et seq.*, city, county and special district employees under Was. Rev. Code § 41.56.010 *et seq.*, educational employees under Was. Rev. Code § 41.59.010 *et seq.*, academic employees in community colleges under Was. Rev. Code § 28B.52.010 *et seq.*, marine employees under Was. Rev. Code § 47.64.011 *et seq.*, and port district employees under Was. Rev. Code § 53.18.010 *et seq.*

[45] State employees bargain under Wis. Stat. Ann. §§ 111.80 - 111.97; other employees do so under Wis. Stat. Ann. §§ 111.70 - 111.77.

[46] Wyo. Stat. Ann. §§ 27-10-101 to 27-10-109.

CHAPTER 2

WHAT MUST BE BARGAINED

Often, one of the first questions in a collective bargaining environment is "what's negotiable?" Bargaining topics are usually organized in three categories: mandatory, permissive, and prohibited subjects of bargaining. *Mandatory* subjects are those that must be negotiated if either party raises the issue. *Prohibited* subjects are illegal topics for bargaining. *Permissive* subjects lie in the middle, with the parties permitted but not required to negotiate over a permissive topic.

The categorization of a topic has three primary levels of significance. First, it defines whether a party is compelled to negotiate over the issue. Second, only mandatory subjects of bargaining can be referred to interest arbitration or can form the basis for a strike. Third, as discussed at length in the following chapter, unless a union waives the right to negotiate, an employer is not free to make unilateral changes in a mandatory subject of bargaining, even if the topic is not referenced in the parties' collective bargaining agreement.

Permissive subjects of bargaining can be incorporated into a collective bargaining agreement, and if they are, they become as enforceable as any other contract clause. However, incorporating a permissive topic into a contract does not convert it into a mandatory subject of bargaining for purposes of subsequent negotiations. So, for example, if parties who ordinarily would not end their bargaining with interest arbitration choose to include in their contract a clause requiring that future bargaining disputes be resolved by interest arbitration, the clause is enforceable. However, when the contract is next open for bargaining, either party is free to designate the continuation of the contract clause as a permissive subject of bargaining and refuse to bargain over the issue. When that occurs, the permissive subject simply falls out of the contract. This seemingly unusual result strongly suggests that no party should ever exchange much of value to include a permissive subject of bargaining in a contract lest the entire value of the trade vanish when the contract is next open for bargaining.

One other point about the three basic bargaining categories is important to keep in mind. Some permissive subjects of bargaining may have mandatorily negotiable impacts, giving rise to what is known as "impact bargaining." For example, the decision to lay off employees is typically a permissive subject of bargaining. However, an employer may well have to bargain over the impact of layoffs on employees,[1] such as safety, hours of work, and other working conditions.[2] Negotiable impacts of layoffs might include the order of layoff, how long laid-off employees would have the right to be recalled from layoff status, and the continuation of health insurance during a layoff.[3]

What Makes A Topic Mandatory For Bargaining?

Most states tend to define mandatory subjects of bargaining using some version of the definition that mandatorily negotiable topics include "wages, hours, and terms and conditions of employment." Washington's collective bargaining statute is a good example.

> Collective bargaining means the performance of the mutual obligations of the public employer and the exclusive bargaining representative to meet at reasonable times, to confer and negotiate in good faith, and to execute a written agreement with respect to grievance procedures and collective negotiations on personnel matters, **including wages, hours and working conditions**, which may be peculiar to an appropriate bargaining unit of such public employer, except that by such obligation neither party shall be compelled to agree to a proposal or be required to make a concession unless otherwise provided in this chapter.[4]

What are the "wages, hours, and working conditions" that are mandatory topics for negotiations? This inquiry is often phrased as the "scope of bargaining" question. Once again, there is a good deal of uniformity among the states, with all but a few following the general law developed under the National Labor Relations Act on scope of bargaining issues. To be sure, there are exceptions. New Jersey, for example, has been quite conservative in labeling topics as mandatory for bargaining; Washington has been at the other end of the continuum. However, it can usually be safely assumed that if one state has found a topic to be mandatorily negotiable, the same reasoning and result will be produced in another state.

Some states list the topics that are mandatory for bargaining, excluding other potential topics from the negotiations process. Nevada, for example, limits negotiations to the following topics:

(a) Salary or wage rates or other forms of direct monetary compensation.

(b) Sick leave.

(c) Vacation leave.

(d) Holidays.

(e) Other paid or nonpaid leaves of absence.

(f) Insurance benefits.

(g) Total hours of work required of an employee on each workday or workweek.

(h) Total number of days' work required of an employee in a work year.

(i) Discharge and disciplinary procedures.

(j) Recognition clause.

(k) The method used to classify employees in the bargaining unit.

(l) Deduction of dues for the recognized employee organization.

(m) Discrimination because of union activities.

(n) No-strike provisions consistent with the provisions of this chapter.

(o) Grievance and arbitration procedures.

(p) General savings clauses.

(q) Duration of collective bargaining agreements.

(r) Safety of the employee.

(s) Teacher preparation time.

(t) Materials and supplies for classrooms.

(u) The policies for the transfer and reassignment of teachers.

(v) Procedures for reduction in workforce.

(w) Procedures in fiscal emergencies.[5]

What Are The "Wages" That Are Mandatory For Bargaining?

Of "wages, hours, and working conditions," it is easiest to identify the "wages" that are mandatory for bargaining. Of course, an employee's salary constitutes wages, and must be negotiated. However, wages is given wide scope by labor boards, and includes pretty much anything that is included in an employee's taxable income and how an employee is paid. For example, all of the following topics have been found to be mandatory for bargaining:

- Callback pay.[6]
- Longevity pay.[7]
- Merit pay steps.[8]
- Overtime, how it is calculated, and whether it is paid in the form of cash or compensatory time off.[9]
- Pay days,[10] pay periods,[11] and whether employees are paid by direct deposit.[12]
- Pay rates for part-time work.[13]
- Pay rates for working out of classification.[14]
- Pay reductions for certain types of work.[15]
- Weekend work, and whether it is compensable at the overtime rate.[16]

What Are The "Hours" That Are Mandatory For Bargaining?

Mandatorily negotiable "hours," like "wages," are fairly easy to identify. Broadly defined, negotiable hours include when and how long an employee must be at work, and the rules governmng an employee's meal periods and other rest periods. All of the following are usually held to be negotiable "hours":

- Bereavement leave.[17]
- Business hours for the employer.[18]
- Compensatory time off.[19]
- Length of work shifts.[20]
- Meal periods, when and how they are taken, whether meal periods are paid time, and the length of meal periods.[21]

- On-call time policy, the impact of changes.[22]
- Shift configurations, including starting and stopping times.[23]
- Sick leave practices,[24] including compensation for unused sick leave.[25]
- Trades of shifts or tours.[26]
- Vacations and holidays in general,[27] the maximum number of employees permitted to take leave on any day, and the minimum increments of leave time employees are required to use.[28]
- Whether shifts are fixed or rotating.[29]
- Whether time in a fire department is "active" or "stand down."[30]

What Are The "Working Conditions" That Are Mandatory For Bargaining?

The "working conditions" that are mandatory for bargaining are usually more difficult to identify than wages or hours. Almost every employer decision has *some* impact on working conditions.[31] Obviously, not every working condition is mandatory for bargaining. For example, whether an employer provides an employee a pen versus a pencil to make notes would not be negotiable. The usual approach taken by labor boards is to engage in a "balancing test" in determining whether a particular working condition is mandatory for bargaining.

Though there have been different phrasings of the balancing test over time, the United States Supreme Court's rulings have provided general guidance in the area. In the seminal case of *Fibreboard Paper Products Corporation v. National Labor Relations Board,* the Court stated that the NLRA's phrase "other terms and conditions of employment" should be construed in light of prevailing industry practices. In a concurring opinion in *Fibreboard*, an opinion that has perhaps become more important than the Court's majority opinion, Justice Potter Stewart observed that "core entrepreneurial activities" were not subject to collective bargaining. In a later case, the Supreme Court stated more explicitly that "bargaining over management decisions that have a substantial impact on the continued availability of employment should be required only if the benefit, for labor-management relations and the collective-bargaining process, outweighs the burden placed on the conduct of the business."[32]

State labor boards have generally followed the Supreme Court's benefit/burden balancing test. The balancing test is often described as assessing whether a particular bargaining topic has a great impact on an employer's operations or on the working conditions of employees.[33] As that test has been applied, the usual result is that if a working condition falls in one of six areas, it is likely to be mandatory for bargaining. Those six areas are workplace safety, working conditions with a monetary impact, rules that impact off-duty life, discipline, job security, and union activities.

Safety Issues.

The following working conditions have all been found to be mandatorily negotiable, in whole or in part because of the safety implications of the working conditions:

- Air quality in the employer's facilities.[34]
- Whether ballistic vests are provided by the employer.[35]
- Eye examinations for employees engaged in long-term video display terminal use, and whether the employer should provide them.[36]
- Reconfiguration of prison population.[37]
- "Ride-along" policies, regarding whether citizens can ride along with employees on the job.[38]
- The creation and authority of safety committees.[39]
- The use and condition of employer vehicles, including "home car" programs.[40]

Staffing is a working condition with potential safety implications that has a curious bargaining status, with labor boards more than occasionally issuing conflicting decisions. Most states start with the proposition that staffing is a management right that is a permissive subject of bargaining. Thus, the number of police officers per shift[41] or the number of students per teacher[42] would usually be permissive subjects of bargaining.[43] However, those same states may find keener safety implications when equipment is involved, and can reach the conclusion that the number of firefighters per piece of apparatus is mandatory for bargaining[44] (even though the number of police officers per patrol car might not be negotiable).[45] And if a proposal looks like a staffing proposal but is really a monetary proposal – for example, for additional premium pay if staffing falls below certain levels – then the proposal may be mandatorily negotiable as a wage issue.[46]

A few states allow more bargaining about staffing, even finding that the number of employees per shift is mandatory for bargaining.[47] Some states are at the other end of the spectrum, and find all staffing decisions to be management rights, no matter the safety implications. For example, New York's Public Employment Relations Board has written that "while we conclude that a demand in general terms for firefighter safety is a mandatory subject of negotiation, we determine that the specific demand for a 'minimum number of men that must be on duty at all times per piece of firefighting equipment' is not."[48] However, even in these states, the effects of staffing reductions may be mandatory for bargaining if a showing is made that the layoffs substantially impact the workload or safety of the non-laid off employees.[49]

Working Conditions With A Monetary Impact.

Because of their impact on employee compensation, the following working conditions are usually found to be mandatorily negotiable:

- Bedding provided for firefighters working 24-hour shifts.[50]

- Clothing, equipment and tool allowances[51] or reimbursement.[52]
- Defense and indemnification of employees from claims arising out of the job.[53]
- Dress code.[54]
- Health insurance benefits, both for active employees and retirees.[55]
- Jury duty pay.[56]
- Meals and cash allowances for meals.[57]
- Mileage reimbursements for use of an employee's personal vehicle.[58]
- Charges made by the employer for parking in employer lots.[59]
- Pension benefits.[60] In some states, however, pension benefits are "pre-empted" from bargaining by a local pension law.[61]
- Charges made by the employer for recreational facilities such as golf courses.[62]
- Whether take-home vehicles are issued.[63]
- Tuition-reimbursement program.[64]

The negotiability of promotions poses a knotty problem for labor boards. On one hand, promotions have a clear monetary consequence and involve substantial changes in job duties and responsibilities. On the other hand, the right to select who will occupy supervisory positions is often seen as a core entrepreneurial function not subject to bargaining. Add into the mix that civil service promotional systems at times exist as separate from the bargaining environment and it is not difficult to predict that there would be differences in how labor boards would approach promotions.

If there is a predominant trend, it is that *promotion standards* are not mandatory for bargaining while *promotional procedures* are. However, some state labor boards find nothing about promotions negotiable while others find pretty much everything promotion-related to be negotiable. Just about as much uncertainty exists with respect to whether transfers are negotiable.

Working Conditions With An Off-Duty Impact.

Many public employers, and particularly public safety employers, have work rules that either directly control an employee's behavior while off duty, or have a more indirect impact on an employee's off-duty life. The following are examples of mandatorily negotiable working conditions with implications on an employee's off-duty life:

- Anti-nepotism policies that prohibit the employment of spouses.[65]
- Grooming codes.[66]
- Off-duty behavior,[67] including the regulation of off-duty employment.[68]
- Residency requirements.[69]
- Tattoo policies.[70]

Working Conditions Impacting Employee Discipline.

Almost any working condition that either deals with disciplinary procedures or which subjects the employee to the possibility of disciplinary penalties is likely to be mandatory for bargaining. Examples of mandatorily-negotiable disciplinary issues include the following:

- "Bills of rights" establishing disciplinary procedures.[71]
- Changes in disciplinary work rules.[72]
- Institution of civilian review board.[73]
- Discipline, and whether it is subject to binding arbitration.[74]
- "Just cause" as the standard of discipline.[75]
- Last-chance agreements.[76]
- Physical fitness standards.[77]
- Random drug testing program.[78]

Working Conditions With Implications On Job Security.

The job security of the bargaining unit as a whole is almost always considered to be mandatory for bargaining. Among the job security issues found to be mandatory for bargaining are:

- The effects of closing a department.[79]
- Whether layoffs are seniority-based and other layoff and recall procedures.[80]
- Subcontracting, or the use of non-bargaining unit personnel to perform work that has been, or logically should be, performed by bargaining unit members.[81]

Working Conditions Involving Union Activities.

Though some states vary in terms of the negotiability of the employer's facilitation of union activities, the usual rules are that the following are mandatory subjects of bargaining:

- A union's use of the employer's bulletin boards.[82]
- Dues check-off clauses.[83]
- Grievance procedures.[84]
- The union's use of inter-office mail systems.[85]
- Paid release time for general union activities.[86]

- Paid release time for negotiations, both for actual bargaining meetings and for preparation for bargaining.[87]
- Use of offices or rooms by the union in the employer's facilities.[88]

Management Rights Clauses.

There is disagreement among state labor boards as to whether management rights clauses are negotiable. The issue is a key one. As described in the next chapter, the core function of a management rights clause is to allow an employer to make changes in past practices concerning mandatory subjects of bargaining without first bargaining with the union.

Some labor boards find that management rights clauses are mandatory for bargaining, and thus can be the subject of interest arbitration or whatever impasse resolution mechanism exists. However, most state labor boards (and the NLRB) disagree, and conclude that management rights clauses are not mandatory for bargaining.[89] As phrased by the NLRB, the problem is that "to the extent that a management rights clause authorizes unilateral action to change matters that are mandatory subjects of bargaining, it entails a union's waiver of its statutory right to bargain over those matters."[90] Under basic contract law principles, waivers have to be voluntary to be enforceable.[91] Put differently, there can be no such thing as an involuntary waiver of the right to bargain. Washington's Public Employment Relations Commission framed the issue in the following terms:

> The issue in this case is not whether or not an employer had, or has, a management right to make a specific decision or the right to a specific unilateral change via a claimed union contractual waiver. The issue is whether these items are mandatory or permissive subjects which may or may not be submitted to arbitration. The items enumerated in Article 20 are not employer proposals to change or set specific terms or conditions of employment. Rather they are a proposed, non-exhaustive list of subjects over which the employer asserts it has a legal right to during the term of the contract. These proposed assertions are, and can only be, either rights resulting from legally based management rights or rights resulting from proposed, or previously bargained for, contractual waivers.[92]

NOTES

[1] *City of New York*, 9 PERB ¶ 4504 (N.Y. PERB 1976).

[2] *City of Richmond*, 33 PERC ¶ 58 (Cal. App. 2009).

[3] R.C.W. 41.56.030 (4)(emphasis supplied).

[4] *See Local 1277, Metropolitan Coufncil No. 23, AFSCME, AFL-CIO v. City of Center Line*, 327 N.W.2d 822 (Mich. 1982).

[5] Section 288.150, Nevada Revised St¶atutes.

[6] *Pinellas County PBA v. City of St. Petersburg*, 3 FPER 205 (Fla. PERC 1977).

[7] *City of Tarpon Springs*, 16 NPER FL-25162 (Fla. PERC 1994).

[8] *City of Tarpon Springs*, 16 NPER FL-25162 (Fla. PERC 1994).

[9] *Chicago Transit Authority*, 2003 WL 26067300 (Ill. LLB 2003); *Matter of Borough of Little Ferry*, PEB ¶ 45,301 (N.J.)(CCH, 1988); *City of Newburgh*, 19 NPER NY-14635 (N.Y. PERB Director 1996); *Triborough Bridge and Tunnel Authority*, 16 NPER NY-14595 (N.Y. PERB ALJ 1994); *City of Philadelphia*, 18 NPER PA-27133 (Pa. LRB Hearing Examiner 1996).

[10] *Township of Cherry Hill*, 19 NPER NJ-27199 (N.J. PERC 1996); *City of Jersey City*, 17 NPER NJ-26105 (N.J. PERC 1995).

[11] *City of Troy*, 28 PERB ¶ 4657(N.Y. PERB ALJ 1995).

[12] *Washoe County School District*, 2006 WL 7137902 (Nev. LGEMRB 2006).

[13] *Deptford Bd. of Ed.*, PERC No. 81-78, 7 NJPER 35 (¶ 12015 1980), aff'd NJPER Supp. 2d 118 (¶ 98 App. Div. 1982).

[14] *Seminole County Professional Fire Fighters Association, Local 3254*, 19 FPER ¶ 24062 (Fla. PERC 1993).

[15] *Needles Unified School District*, 1999 WL 35113972 (Cal. PERB ALJ 1999).

[16] *American Federation of State, County and Mun. Employees, AFL-CIO, Local 2572 v. Borough of Schuylkill Haven*, 504 A.2d 395 (1985).

[17] *City of Cortland*, 29 PERB ¶ 4534 (N.Y. PERB Dir. 1996).

[18] *City of Bellevue and Local 1604, IAFF*, Decision 2788 (Wash. PERC 1987).

[19] *Fire Rescue Professionals of Alachua County*, 28 FPER ¶ 33, 158 (Fla. PERC 2002); *Brookline Police Association*, PEB ¶ 45,749 (Mass. LRC)(CCH, 1989); *Albany Police Officers Union Local 2841, AFSCME Council 82 and City of Albany*, U-27333 (N.Y. PERB 2008); *City of Pasco, Washington*, Decision #9181-A (Wash. PECB 2008).

[20] *Borough of Union Beach*, 14 NPER NJ-23160 (N.J. PERC 1992).

[21] *County of Elizabeth*, 26 NJPER P 13007 (N.J. PERC 1999); *City of Nassau*, 35 NYPER ¶ 4544 (N.Y. PERB ALJ 2002); *City of Hazleton*, 17 NPER 26018 (Pa. LRB ALJ 1994).

[22] *Bensalem Township Police Benevolent Association*, 36 PERC ¶19 (Pa. LRB ALJ 2005).

[23] *Association of Oregon Corrections Employees*, Case No. UP-33-3 (Or. ERB 2005).

[24] *New Hampshire Department of Safety*, 921 A.2d 924 (N.H. 2007); *City of Onondaga*, 18 NPER NY-17010 (N.Y. S.C. 1996); *City of Orange Township*, 27 NJPER ¶ 32046 (N.J. PERC 2001); *Cleona Borough*, 19 NPER PA-27239 (Pa. LRB ALJ 1996); *City of Pasco*, Decision 9337 (Wash. PERC 2006).

[25] *City of Augusta*, Case No. 11-03SQ (Me. LRB 2011).

[26] *County of Mercer*, Case No. SN-2006-037 (N.J. PERC 2006).

[27] *City of Torrington*, 17 NPER CT-26033 (Conn. SBLR 1995); *Borough of Lodi*, 32

NJPER 33 (N.J. PERC 2006); *City of Newburgh*, 19 NPER NY-14635 (N.Y. PERB Director 1996); *City of Philadelphia*, 18 NPER PA-27007 (Pa. LRB 1995).

[28] *City of St. Petersburg*, 5 FPER ¶ 1038 (Fla. PERC 1979).

[29] *Borough of Taylor*, 14 NPER PA-23067 (Pa. LRB Hearing Examiner 1992).

[30] *Village of Arlington Heights*, 13 PERI ¶ 2026 (Ill. SLRB General Counsel, 1997).

[31] *Los Angeles County Employees Ass'n, Local 660 v. County of Los Angeles*, 108 Cal. Rptr. 625 (Cal. Ct. App. 1973).

[32] *First National Maintenance Corp. v. N.L.R.B.*, 452 U.S. 666 (1981).

[33] See *Springfield Education Assn. v. Springfield School District*, 7 PECBR 6357 (Or. ERB 1984).

[34] *City of New Haven*, 16 NPER CT-25020 (Conn. SBLR 1993).

[35] *City of Iowa City v. Iowa*, PEB ¶ 34,591 (Iowa)(CCH, 1985).

[36] *State of Iowa*, Case No. 6301 (Iowa PERB 2001).

[37] *California Correctional Peace Officers Association v. State of California*, 23 PERC ¶ 30069 (Cal. PERB ALJ 1999).

[38] *West St. Paul v. Law Enforcement Labor Services*, 30 GERR. 343 (Minn. 1992).

[39] *City of Newark*, Case No. SN-2006-026 (N.J. PERC 2006); *City of New Rochelle*, 11 PERB ¶ 7002 (N.Y. PERB 1978).

[40] *City of Torrance*, PERB Decision No. 2004-M (Cal. PERB 2009); *City of Stamford*, 14 NPER CT-23050 (Conn. SBLR 1992); *City of Tampa*, PEB ¶ 45,436 (Florida)(CCH 1988); *Borough of River Edge*, 13 NPER NJ-22001 (N.J. PERC 1990); *City of Nassau*, 35 NYPER ¶ 4556 (N.Y. PERB ALJ 2002); *City of Portland*, 13 NPER OR-21046 (Or. ERB 1990); *Borough of Taylor*, 14 NPER PA-23067 (Pa. LRB Hearing Examiner 1992).

[41] *Town of Orangetown*, 27 PERB ¶ 4532 (N.Y. PERB 1994).

[42] *Hillsborough Classroom Teachers Association, Inc. v. School Board of Hillsborough County*, 423 So.2d 969 (Fla. 1st DCA 1982).

[43] *City of Jackson*, 11 MPER ¶ 29029 (Mich. App. 1998)(firefighters per shift permissive for bargaining).

[44] *Fire Fighters Union v. City of Vallejo*, 12 Cal.3d 608 (Cal. 1974); *Carson City Fire Fighters Association*, Case No. A1-045569 (Nev. LGEMRB 1994).

[45] *City of White Plains*, 9 PERB ¶ 3007 (N.Y. PERB 1976).

[46] *Town of Orangetown*, 27 PERB ¶ 4532 (N.Y. PERB 1994).

[47] *Village of Streamwood*, 26 PERI ¶ 122 (Ill. LRB Gen. Counsel 2010).

[48] *City of Newburgh*, 10 PERB ¶ 3001 (N.Y. PERB 1977).

[49] *Ft. Myers Beach Fire Control District*, 23 FPER ¶ 28209 (Fla. PERC 1997).

[50] *City of Reading*, 12 PPER ¶ 12182 (Pa. LRB ALJ 1981).

[51] *Healdsburg Union High School District and Healdsburg Union School District/San Mateo City School District*, (Cal. PERB 1984)(tool allowance); *City of Fort Dodge & Local 6-502, Oil, Chem. & Atomic Workers Int'l Union, AFL-CIO*, No. 970 (Iowa PERB 1977)(clothing allowance); *City of Augusta*, Case No. 11-03SQ (Me. LRB 2011)(clothing allowance).

[52] *Board of Education of Union Free School Dist. No. 3 of Town of Huntington v. Associated Teachers of Huntington*, 282 N.E.2d 109 (N.Y. App. 1972).

[53] *City of Watervliet*, 13 NPER NY-14514 (N.Y. PERB ALJ 1991).

[54] *County of Riverside*, 27 GERR 1245 (Cal. 1989).

[55] *Detroit POA v. City of Detroit*, PEB ¶ 34,500 (Mich.)(CCH, 1985); *Law Enforcement Labor Services v. Mower County*, 29 GERR 622 (Minn. App. 1991); *Borough of Emerson*, 31

NJPER ¶153 (N.J. PERC 2005); *Borough of Woodcliff Lake*, 29 NJPER ¶ 153 (N.J. PERC 2003); *Delaware County*, 16 NPER PA-24174 (Pa. LRB ALJ 1993).

[56] *State of Illinois*, 8 PERI ¶ 2007 (Ill. SLRB 1992).

[57] *City of Cedar Falls & Int'l Ass'n of Firefighters, Local 1366*, No. 1911 (Iowa PERB 1981).

[58] *Chicago Housing Authority*, 7 PERI ¶ 3036 (Ill. LRB 1991).

[59] *Los Angeles Police Prot. League v. Los Angeles*, 212 Cal.Rptr. 251 (A.D. 1985); *City of Jacksonville*, 17 NPER FL-26178 (Fla. PERC 1995).

[60] *Detroit POA v. City of Detroit*, 214 N.W.2d 803 (1974); *City of Flint*, 18 MPER ¶ 15 (Mich. ERC 2005); *City of Erie Police Department*, 18 NPER PA-27056 (Pa. LRB ALJ 1996); *Town of Barrington*, 1993 WL 65458 (R.I. 1993).

[61] *Des Moines Police Bargaining Association v. PERB*, 423 N.W.2d 885 (Iowa App. 1988)(proposal to provide insurance for retirees was illegal subject of bargaining because of specific statutory language); *De Kalb v. IAFF Local 1236*, 538 N.E.2d 867 (Ill. App. 1989)(clause in collective bargaining agreement providing supplemental disability pension benefits for firefighters was void due to public policy reflected in state statute providing for uniform pension benefits); *AFSCME v. Sundquist*, 338 N.W.2d 560 (Minn. 1983)(illegal to agree to pension provisions where a statute expressly excluded pension considerations from the definition of terms and conditions of employment); *State v. State Supervisory Employees Association*, 78 N.J. 54 (1978)(public employers and employee representatives may neither negotiate nor agree upon any proposal which would affect employee pensions, which are pre-empted by state statute); *Streetsboro Education Association*, 626 N.E.2d 110 (Ohio 1994)(state teachers retirement system requirement prevailed over a provision of collective bargaining agreement because of a statutory provision which "unequivocally evinced a willingness to take a subject or part of a subject out of the realm of collective bargaining"); *City of Seattle*, Decision 4688-B (Wash. PERC 1997)(state pension law pre-empts bargaining over pensions).

[62] *City of Sepulpa*, 102 LA 636 (Neas, 1994).

[63] *Teamsters Local No. 48 v. Bucksport School Dept.*, No. 81-18 at 3 (Mass. LRC 1980)(employer "properly concedes" that use of school buses for transportation to work was a mandatory subject of bargaining); *Town of Jay*, No. 80-02 at 4 (Mass. LRC 1979)(take-home police vehicles); *City of Omaha*, 2007 WL 5114425 (Neb. Cir. 2007)(take-home police cars); *City of Portland v. Portland Police Commanding Officers Association*, 12 PECBR 646 (Or. ERB 1991)(proposal requiring the employer to provide take-home vehicles and raid gear for officers involved a mandatory subject of bargaining as it impacted direct or indirect monetary benefits and safety); *City of Kalama*, Decision 6739-A (Wash. PERC 2001).

[64] *City of Newburgh*, 19 NPER NY-14635 (N.Y. PERB Director 1996).

[65] *Hampton Police Association*, Case No. P-0719-20 (N.H. PERB 2006).

[66] *Fraternal Order of Police v. City of Fort Lauderdale*, PEB ¶ 45,389 (Fla.)(CCH 1988).

[67] *Fraternal Order of Police, Lodge #5 v. City of Philadelphia*, 30 PPER ¶ 30185 (Pa. LRB 1999).

[68] *Elizabethtown Borough*, 29 PPER ¶ 29099 (Pa. LRB ALJ 1998).

[69] *City of Hialeah*, 13 NPER FL-21338 (Fla. PERC 1990); *City of Bernard*, 598 N.E.2d 15 (Ohio App. 1991); *Plains Township Police Bargaining Unit v. Plains Township*, 33 PPER ¶ 33019 (Pa. LRB ALJ 2001).

[70] *Fraternal Order of Police and Anne Arundel County*, Case No. 08-51355 (Simmeljkaer, 2008); *FOP Lodge No. 123 and City of Oklahoma City*, No. 06-552-02 (2006); *Laurel Baye Healthcare of Lake Lanier*, 352 NLRB No. 30 (NLRB 2008).

[71] *County of Passaic*, 29 NJPER ¶ 91 (N.J. PERC 2003).

[72] *City of Detroit and Detroit Firefighters Association*, Case No. C00 F-99 (Mich. ERC 2002); *City of Buffalo*, 13 NPER NY-13050 (N.Y. PERB 1990).

[73] *City of Portland*, http://www.state.me.us/mlrb/decisions/ppc/01-IR-01.htm (Me. LRB 2001); *Pontiac Police Officers Association v. City of Pontiac*, 246 N.W.2d 831 (Mich. 1976). But see *Berkeley Police Association v. City of Berkeley*, 76 Cal. App. 3d 931 (1977).

[74] *City of Pasco*, Decision 3368-A (Wash. PERC 1990).

[75] *Asotin County, Washington*, Decision 9549-A (Wash. PERC 2007).

[76] *Washington State Patrol*, 3 (8) Public Safety Labor News 7 (Wash. PERC 1995).

[77] *City of Danbury*, Dec. No. 1907 (Conn. SBLR, June 19, 1980)(employer's unilateral imposition of physical fitness program on firefighters, which required mandatory participation during work hours, is a mandatory subject of bargaining).

[78] *F.O.P. v. City of Miami*, 131 LRRM 3171 (Fla. 1989).

[79] *IUOE, Local 571 v. City of Plattsmouth*, 660 N.W.2d 480 (Neb. 2003).

[80] *City of Pasco*, Decision 3368-A (Wash. PERC 1990).

[81] *California State Employees Association v. Department of Corrections*, 23 PERC ¶ 30105 (Cal. PERB ALJ 1999); *City of Bridgeport and City of New Haven*, 16 NPER CT-24077 (Conn. SBLR 1993); *City of Boston v. Labor Relations Commission*, 787 N.E.2d 1184 (Mass. App. 2003); *Borough of Paterson*, 26 NJPER ¶ 31041 (N.J. PERC 2000); *Belmar Police Ben. Association*, PEB ¶ 45,692 (N.J. PERC)(CCH, 1989); *City of Akron*, 16 OPER P 1489 (Ohio SERB 1999); *City of Allen Town*, 34 PPER ¶ 90 (Pa. LRB 2003).

[82] *Chillicothe City School District Board of Education*, 6 OPER ¶ 6248 (Ohio SERB ALJ 1989).

[83] *City of Saco*, 2011 WL 6965924 (Me. Lab. Rel. Bd. 2011)(lengthy discussion of contrast between federal and state law on dues check-off).

[84] *City of Pasco*, Decision 3368-A (Wash. PERC 1990), aff'd, *City of Pasco v. PERC*, 119 Wn.2d 504 (Wash. 1992).

[85] *Eugene Education Association v. Eugene School District 4J*, Case No. C-279 (Or. ERB 1974)(inter-office mail system).

[86] *City of Albany v. Helsby*, 48 A.D.2d 998 (N.Y. A.D. 1975).

[87] *Yakima County*, Decision 10204-A (Wash. PERC 2011).

[88] *Springfield Education Association v. Springfield School District No. 19*, Case No. C-278 (Or. ERB 1975)(proposals allowing the union to utilize the employer's school rooms for after-hours meetings at no cost).

[89] E.g., *City of Cocoa*, 18 FPER ¶ 23235 (Fla. PERC 1992).

[90] *Holiday Inn of Victorville*, 284 NLRB 916 (NLRB 1987).

[91] See, e.g., Edward Rubin, *Toward a General Theory of Waiver*, 28 UCLA L. Rev. 478 (1980).

[92] *City of Bellevue*, Decision 11435 (Wash. PERC 2012).

CHAPTER 3

WHEN BARGAINING MUST OCCUR

If a topic is mandatory for bargaining, either side has the right to raise it in bargaining for a new contract. The other party must negotiate over the issue, though it need not agree to the proposal made by the other party. If impasse is reached in bargaining, and if binding arbitration is the last step in the bargaining process, then either party has the right to refer the issue to arbitration, and an arbitrator's decision on the issue is enforceable.

There is also another aspect of the duty to bargain, often referred to as the "continuing duty to bargain."[1] A simple phrasing of the "continuing duty to bargain" is that if a topic is mandatory for bargaining, an employer may not make unilateral changes in past practices in the area without first negotiating with the labor organization unless the union has waived the right to bargain over the issue. This naturally gives rise to two questions: What is a past practice, and how is it that a union can waive its rights to bargain over changes in past practices?

The Bottom Line. The continuing duty to bargain prohibits an employer from making a unilateral change in a mandatory subject of bargaining unless the union has waived the right to bargain over the issue.

What Amounts To A Past Practice?

One of the questions that most bedevils labor arbitrators, employers, and labor organizations is whether particular employer conduct amounts to a past practice. But why is past practice so important? A good starting place is with the Supreme Court's decision in one of what are known as the *Steelworker Trilogy* cases. In the case, the Court quoted approvingly from a law review article explaining how the doctrine of past practice was necessary because of the inability of even the best-written collective bargaining agreement to anticipate every eventuality:

> It is not unqualifiedly true that a collective bargaining agreement is simply a document by which the union and employees have imposed upon management limited, express restrictions of its otherwise absolute right to manage the enterprise, so that an employee's claim must fail unless he can point to a specific contract provision upon which the claim is founded. There are too many people, too many problems, too many unforeseeable contingencies to make the words of the contract the exclusive source of rights and duties. One cannot reduce all the rules governing a community like an industrial plant to 15 or even 50 pages. Within the sphere of collective bargaining, the institutional characteristics and the governmental nature of the collective bargaining process demand a common law of the shop which implements and furnishes the context of the agreement. We must assume that intelligent negotiators acknowledged so plain a need unless they stated a contrary rule in plain words.[2]

The default, then, is that the doctrine of past practice is a part of every collective bargaining agreement unless the parties have negotiated a different result "in plain words." Necessarily, this means that the contract will <u>not</u> contain language dealing with the past practice. As described by Washington's Public Employment Relations Commission, the absence of controlling contract language does not diminish in any way the employer's obligation to bargain over mandatorily negotiable past practices:

It is well settled that an employer violates the duty to bargain if it unilaterally implements a change on a mandatory subject of bargaining, without first giving notice to the exclusive bargaining representative of its employees and fulfilling its collective bargaining obligations. While collective bargaining agreements commonly fix some terms for the life of the contract, the duty to bargain continues to exist during the life of a collective bargaining agreement as to any mandatory subjects of bargaining which are not specifically addressed by the contract.[3]

To become a past practice, action or inaction must occur consistently, openly, and over a period of time. The notion of past practice includes that of repeated conduct, an element of expectation that a particular event will be handled the same way in the future. Some oft-quoted phrasings of the definition include:

- A past practice is "a reasonably uniform response to a recurring situation over a substantial period of time, which is recognized by the parties implicitly or explicitly as the proper response."[4]

- A past practice "must be (1) unequivocal; (2) clearly enunciated and acted upon; (3) readily ascertainable over a reasonable period of time as a fixed and established practice accepted by both parties."[5]

- A past practice is defined as "a course of action knowingly followed by the union and the employer over an extended period of time which both parties have come to regard as the accepted practice. A past practice may take precedence over a written policy if the practice is (1) consistent, (2) uniform, and (3) long term."[6]

- "A custom or practice is not something which arises simply because a given course of conduct has been pursued by Management or the employees on one or more occasions. It must be shown to be the accepted course of conduct characteristically repeated in response to the given set of underlying circumstances."[7]

It can be helpful to think of the past practice analysis as looking at a series of continuums:

- The longer the practice has been in place, the more likely it is that a binding past practice will have arisen. If the event is one that occurs frequently – for example, how biweekly payroll is calculated – then a lesser duration may be necessary for the practice to be binding. If the event occurs only infrequently – for example, the calculation of an annual bonus – then it will take much longer for the practice to become binding.

- To the extent that successor contracts have been negotiated since the practice arose, the practice is more likely to be binding. Labor boards and arbitrators presume that parties know of significant past practices, and put a burden on the party wishing to change the practice to do so at the bargaining table.

- If the practice is described in writing, it is more likely to be binding. For example, if the practice is described in an employer's policies, bargaining notes, grievance settlements, or memoranda of agreement, the practice is more apt to be binding.

- Though perfect uniformity is not required, the more uniformly the employer has acted when faced with a similar situation, the more likely it is that a past practice has been created.

- There must be some knowledge that both parties knew of the practice. If the employer's knowledge is at high supervisory levels, the more likely it is that the practice will be binding.

If a past practice has been established, the employer must negotiate with the union before changing the practice unless the union has waived the right to bargain. The two ways a union can waive the right to bargain over changes in past practices are known as waiver by inaction and waiver by contract.

The Bottom Line. A binding past practice must be known to both parties, have lasted a substantial period of time, and must have occurred relatively uniformly.

Waivers By Inaction — How A Union Forfeits Its Right To Bargain Over Changes In Past Practice By Not Acting In A Timely Fashion.

As the NLRB once put it, "once an employer notifies a union of a proposed change in conditions of employment, it is incumbent upon the union to act with due diligence in requesting bargaining."[8] If the union does not act in a timely fashion, it will have waived its bargaining right "by inaction." While labor boards are reluctant to find waivers by inaction,[9] they will do so if a union simply sits on its hands without asserting its bargaining rights while the employer goes through the process of considering and eventually adopting a change in past practice.

The evidence of a waiver by inaction must be strong. As the Florida labor board put it, a waiver will occur only if "consideration of all the circumstances reveals that the only reasonable inference is that the party has abandoned its rights."[10] As the Massachusetts labor board held: "A public employer that asserts the affirmative defense of waiver by inaction must demonstrate by a preponderance of the evidence that an employee organization had (1) actual knowledge or notice of the proposed action; (2) a reasonable opportunity to negotiate about the subject; and (3) unreasonably or inexplicably failed to bargain or request bargaining."[11]

Most labor boards require employers to prove a prerequisite before they can claim a waiver by inaction – that it gave the union notice of its intention to change past practice. Sometimes this requirement for notice is built into a collective bargaining statute.[12] Other times it is simply the product of labor board decisions creating a body of precedent.[13] The purpose behind this notice requirement is the belief that the bargaining process, and not litigation, is the best way to resolve issues about changes in past practice.

An employer's notice of a change in past practice must be given a reasonable amount of time before the change is implemented. This requirement for advance notice is imposed to allow the union to investigate the bargaining issue, decide whether it wishes to assert its bargaining rights, and to formalize any demand to bargain. If a union receives notice of the change contemporaneously with the change itself, there can be no waiver by inaction,[14] and a demand to bargain becomes unnecessary because it would be futile.[15] Put another way, if the employer's decision is presented as a *fait accompli*, then there is no need for a demand to bargain.[16]

California's Public Employment Relations Board put these rules together in a very helpful checklist form:

> Where an employer exercises a management right that has an impact on mandatory subjects of bargaining, the employer has an obligation to engage in "effects bargaining." The employer must thus follow these procedures:
>
> 1. The employer has a duty to provide reasonable notice and an opportunity to bargain before it implements a decision within its managerial prerogative that has foreseeable effects on negotiable terms and conditions of employment.
>
> 2. Once having received such advance notice, the union must demand to bargain the effects or risk waiving its right to do so. The union's demand must identify clearly the matter(s) within the scope of representation on which it proposes to bargain, and clearly indicate the employee organization's desire to bargain over the effects of the decision as opposed to the decision itself.
>
> 3. Having received such advance notice and an opportunity to bargain, a union's failure to demand effects bargaining may waive the right to bargain the reasonably foreseeable effects. Waiver remains, however, an affirmative defense. Where a union alleges that the employer did not provide reasonable notice and an opportunity to bargain prior to the employer's implementation of a change in a non-negotiable policy having a reasonably foreseeable impact on a matter within the scope of representation, a *prima facie* case of failure to bargain in good faith is established. The union need not allege as well that it made a demand to bargain such effects as a condition to seeking PERB enforcement of its right to be free of an employer's failure to provide notice and an opportunity to bargain effects. The employer may raise an affirmative defense of waiver or otherwise challenge the union's claim that the employer did not provide sufficient notice of the change.
>
> 4. Where the employer implements the change without giving the union reasonable notice and an opportunity to bargain over foreseeable effects on matters within the scope of representation, it acts at its own peril. If the employer is ultimately found to have had a duty to bargain over effects and thus to have provided the union reasonable pre-implementation notice and an opportunity to bargain, its implementation without giving such notice and an opportunity to bargain constitutes a refusal to bargain.[17]

There is no "bright-line" test for how much time a union has to assert its bargaining rights. Though a union would be well-advised to send a "demand to bargain" letter within 30 days of learning of an intended change in past practice, some labor boards accept a longer delay. The more difficult it is for the employer to undo the particular change will likely require quicker notice from the union of its intention to assert its bargaining rights.

There has been much litigation over when a union "knows" of a change in past practice. The question is a critical one, since it is the union's knowledge of the change that starts the clock ticking on when it must assert its bargaining rights. The clearest example of union knowledge comes when the employer actually gives written notice to the union of an upcoming change in practice.

What if the employer fails to give the union written notice of its intended change in past practice, and instead individual union members, including members of the union's governing body, only indirectly learn of the change? The law varies tremendously in the area, with some labor boards ascribing the knowledge of individual union members to the union as a whole, and other labor boards insisting that the absence of written prior notice by the employer will excuse all but the most blatant of dilatory conduct by a union in asserting its bargaining rights. What can be said is that, to avoid doubt on the issue, employers would be well advised to always give unions notice of their intent to change past practices, and unions would be well advised to assert their bargaining rights if they get even a hint of the employer's intentions to make a change.

What are the results of a waiver by inaction? The employer will be able to implement the change in past practice free from any challenge by the union. A waiver by inaction does not permanently waive a union's bargaining rights over the area; rather, it waives the union's rights to bargain over the *change*.[18] That means, for example, that a union that fails to assert its bargaining rights over a change in an employer's residency policy will have the right to raise the issue during the next bargaining over the full contract (assuming residency is a mandatory subject of bargaining in the particular jurisdiction). That said, there is little doubt that an implemented change in past practice will be more difficult to alter in negotiations over the next open contract, and that labor organizations get better results bargaining over changes in past practices as they occur.

A union usually asserts its bargaining rights over changes in past practices through sending the employer a document often referred to as a "demand to bargain." What follows is a sample demand to bargain over a change in a grooming code.

> Please be advised that the union has learned that the employer has enacted a new grooming code that prohibits employees from wearing beards. The union believes that a grooming code is a mandatory subject of bargaining, and that the employer is not free to unilaterally implement changes in the past practices in the area. By this letter, the union requests that (1) The employer rescind the change in past practice; and (2) The employer collectively bargain over any changes in its grooming code.
>
> Please get in touch with me at your earliest convenience so that we can set a time and place to begin the bargaining process over this issue.

The Bottom Line. If an employer gives notice of its intent to change past practices, a labor organization must assert its bargaining rights in a timely fashion.

Waivers By Contract And Management Rights Clauses.

The other way a union waives its rights to bargain over changes in past practice is known as "waiver by contract." Waivers by contract occur when the collective bargaining agreement gives the employer the right to make a particular change, even though the change may be a mandatory subject of bargaining. For example, if a contract states, "The employer shall have the right to change residency rules without bargaining with the union," a waiver by contract exists, and the employer will be able to make changes in the area.

With the NLRB in the forefront, labor boards have made clear that to be enforceable, waivers by contract must be "clear and unmistakeable." As the NLRB has put it, "to meet the 'clear and unmistakable' standard, the contract language must be specific, or it must be shown that the matter claimed to have been waived was fully discussed by the parties and that the party alleged to have waived its rights consciously yielded its interest in the matter."[19] State labor boards have not minced their words on the topic:

- "Where an employer raises the affirmative defense of waiver by contact, it bears the burden of demonstrating that the parties consciously considered the situation that has arisen, and that the union knowingly and unmistakably waived its bargaining rights."[20]

- "A waiver of the right to negotiate must be clear, unmistakable and without ambiguity."[21]

- "A waiver by contract will not be lightly inferred. There must be a clear and unmistakable showing that such a waiver occurred through the bargaining process or the specific language of the agreement."[22]

- "Waiver will not be found unless the contract language expressly or by necessary implication confers upon the employer the right to implement the change in the mandatory subject of bargaining without bargaining with the union."[23]

- "Waivers by contract language are typically rejected where they invoke broad statements that fail to address particular aspects of the subject matter encompassed within the purported waiver."[24]

At first blush, one might think that a management rights clause is a waiver by contract of whatever topics are listed in the clause. Most likely, that is not the case. As described above, waivers by contract must be both specific and clearly articulated. By "specific," labor boards mean that the language must be specific to the subject matter that is involved. That means that language that reserves as a management right the ability "to set work schedules" is *not* likely to waive a union's right to bargain over the specific area of the length of work shifts. By "clearly articulated," labor boards insist that the language contain clear evidence of the union's intention to waive its bargaining rights. In language borrowed from general contract law, labor boards often define a waiver as an "intentional relinquishment of a known right with both knowledge of its existence and an intention to relinquish it."

The following is a small sampling of holdings from state labor boards that management rights clauses, unless they are tightly worded, do not waive an employer's obligation to bargain over changes in past practices:

- "A broadly-framed management rights clause is too vague to provide a basis for inferring a clear and unmistakable waiver."[25]

- "PERB has found general management rights clauses, such as the one herein, not to give rise to a waiver. I so find here. As to waiver attaching to the union's bargaining behavior, the atmosphere of collective bargaining, and the facts as presented herein, do not rise to the standard necessary to establish a defense of waiver. A waiver of the right to negotiate must be clear, unmistakable and without ambiguity."[26]

- "The clause states that DOC 'retains all inherent rights of management,' including the right to 'schedule work.' A review of the contract, however, does not convince us that the language is sufficiently 'clear and unmistakable' to constitute a waiver. Article 3 gives DOC the right to schedule work. It is unclear, for example, whether the language applies to scheduling services to the public, or instead to individual employee work hours. The language might also apply to the employer's decision about when during the day to schedule a particular task, rather than to the hours a particular employee works. One point is clear: the provision does not expressly give DOC the right to unilaterally change the start/stop times and days off of employees. Such ambiguity and lack of specificity preclude us from finding a clear and unmistakable waiver of bargaining over these subjects."[27]

- "The City contends that the language in the management rights clause stating that it has the right to relieve employees from duty because of lack of work, lack of funds or causes beyond the City's control clearly, unequivocally and specifically permits the City to implement the half-day furloughs. Upon review of the disputed language, I construe the phrase 'relieve from duty' to possibly have more than one meaning and, thus, to be ambiguous. The phrase 'relieve from duty' could refer to an involuntary layoff, which would mean the separation of unit members from their employment and the removal of any possibility that those employees could perform their duties. The phrase could also refer to furloughs of various lengths and frequencies. Unlike involuntary layoffs, the furloughs ordered here do not separate unit members from their employment, but instead unit members perform the same duties for fewer hours and lower pay. Involuntary layoffs and half-day furloughs can have significantly different impacts on unit members' terms and conditions of employment."[28]

- "I find most of the provisions are clearly ineffective waivers, including the right to lay off employees, determine the size and composition of the workforce, and determine the kinds of personnel by which government operations are conducted. I find these to be simply the types of broad principles of organizational prerogatives which do not operate as waivers in the context of negotiable unilateral changes."[29]

Employers often argue that waivers by contract exist in the "complete agreement" or "zipper" clauses of collective bargaining agreements. These clauses have a variety of titles, but all essentially say something like: "This Agreement spells out the total agreement in its entirety between the parties, including wages, salaries, pensions and all fringe benefits, and there shall be no other additions or changes during the term of the Contract." Labor boards are no more sanguine about zipper clauses amounting to a waiver than they are about management rights clauses. The NLRB has held that "although the waiver of bargaining rights may be based on either express contract language or by necessary implication, a generally worded bargaining waiver or zipper clause does not provide the clear and unmistakable waiver language needed to waive a union's right to bargain over extra-contractual past practices."[30] New York's Public Employment Relations Board has ruled much the same way:

> Management rights and zipper clauses are frequently cited as the dual bases for a defense of waiver by agreement and are most often rejected. Without supporting evidence in other substantive provisions of the contract, the parties' negotiating history, or past practice, catch-all contract clauses are not sufficient to evidence a clear and unmistakable waiver.[31]

The Continuing Duty To Bargain And Maintenance Of Benefits Clauses.

No discussion of the continuing duty to bargain would be complete without a review of the impact of "maintenance of benefits" clauses. Like zipper clauses, maintenance of benefits clauses are found under a variety of titles in collective bargaining agreements. However titled, a maintenance of benefits clause says something like: "The employer shall maintain all wages, hours and working conditions not referenced in this agreement at no less a level than in existence at the commencement of this agreement."

A maintenance of benefits clause is, from a union's standpoint, potentially the most powerful clause in a collective bargaining agreement. Conversely, from an employer's standpoint, a maintenance of benefits clause is potentially the most restrictive clause in a contract. In the absence of a maintenance of benefits clause, an employer wanting to change past practices in a mandatory subject of bargaining can usually effectuate some sort of change by giving the union notice of its intent to change the practice, and then going through the bargaining process over the change. The bargaining process may produce precisely the change the employer intended, or some variant of the change. With a maintenance of benefits clause, the union can simply stop the process in its tracks by refusing to even consider negotiations over changes in past practices. In the words of former first lady Nancy Reagan, a maintenance of benefits clause gives the union the right to "just say no" to changes in mandatory subjects of bargaining, at least so long as the maintenance of benefits clause remains in effect.

The Bottom Line. The continuing duty to bargain requires an employer to negotiate before making a change in a mandatory subject of bargaining. A maintenance of benefits clause, on the other hand, <u>forbids</u> an employer from making the change unless the union agrees to it.

NOTES

[1] See A. Cox & J Dunlop, *The Duty To Bargain Collectively During The Term Of An Existing Agreement*, 63 Harvard L.R. 1097 (1950).

[2] *United Steelworkers of America v. Warrior & Gulf Nav. Co.*, 363 U.S. 574 (1960), quoting Shulman, *Reason, Contract, and Law in Labor Relations*, 68 Harv.L.Rev. 999, 1004-1005 (1955).

[3] *City of Lynnwood*, 2013 WL 150226 (Wash. PERC 2013).

[4] *District No. 1 Marine Engineers Beneficial Association*, 2000 WL 36094714 (Wash. PERC 2000).

[5] *Madison Teachers, Inc.*, 2006 WL 6544647 (Wis. ERC 2006), quoting F. Elkouri & E. Elkouri, *How Arbitration Works*.

[6] www.documents.dgs.ca.gov%2Fohr%2Fpom%2FLABOR%2520RELATIONS.doc&ei=82YdVZSpBsvfoATItICACw&usg=AFQjCNFsbs6NaOPgJUZmgWOY587UJ-mA7A&sig2=HAAdgXqKscSNTbihtny74A&bvm=bv.89947451,d.cGU

[7] *County of Allegheny v. Allegheny County Prison Employees Independent Union*, 381 A.2d 849 (Pa. 1977).

[8] *Kansas National Education Association*, 275 NLRB 638 [119 LRRM 1213] (1985).

[9] *Sylvan Union Elementary School District*, 1991 WL 11749863 (Cal. PERB ALJ 1991).

[10] *Florida Department of Management Services*, 28 FPER ¶ 33137 (Fla. PERC 2002).

[11] *Town of Douglas*, 2015 WL 936502 (Mass. LRC 2015).

[12] See Section 243.698(2), Oregon Revised Statutes ("The employer shall notify the exclusive representative in writing of anticipated changes that impose a duty to bargain").

[13] *City of Rock Island*, 31 PERI ¶ 32 (Ill. LRB Gen. Counsel 2014).

[14] *County of Cook (Cermak Health Servs.)*, 10 PERI ¶ 3009 (Ill. LLRB 1994).

[15] *Mutual Organization of Supervisors*, 36 PERC ¶ 142 (Cal. PERB ALJ 2012).

[16] *City of Boston*, 2014 WL 4402448 (Mass. LRC 2014).

[17] *County of Santa Clara*, Case No. 2321-M (Cal. PERB 2013).

[18] *WJBK-TV (Storer Communications, Inc.)*, 22 NLRB AMR 32051 (1988); *City of Detroit*, 3 MPER ¶ 21040 (Mich. ERC 1990).

[19] *Allison Corp.*, 330 NLRB No. 190 (2000).

[20] *City of Boston v. Labor Relations Commission*, 48 Mass. App. Ct. 169 (1999); *Massachusetts Board of Regents*, 15 MLC 1265 (1988).

[21] *Civil Service Employees Association, Inc.*, 26 PERB ¶ 4578 (N.Y. PERB ALJ 1993).

[22] *City of Taunton*, 11 MLC 1334 (1985).

[23] *Commonwealth of Massachusetts*, 19 MLC 1454 (1992).

[24] *City of Sonoma Employees Association*, 31 PERC ¶ 13 (Cal. PERB ALJ 2006).

[25] *Town of Hudson*, 25 MLC 143 (1999).

[26] *Civil Service Employees Association, Inc.*, 26 PERB ¶ 4578 (N.Y. PERB ALJ 1993).

[27] *Association of Oregon Corrections Employees*, 2005 WL 6132390 (Or. ERB 2005).

[28] *City of New Bedford*, 2011 WL 6292255 (Mass. LRC 2011).

[29] *City of Sonoma Employees Association*, 31 PERC ¶ 13 (Cal. PERB ALJ 2006).

[30] *American Medical Response*, 38 NLRB AMR 41 (2008).

[31] *County of Putnam*, 18 NYPER ¶ 4565 (1985); *see County of Santa Clara*, 38 PERC ¶ 30 (Cal. PERB 2013)(zipper clause not waiver of right to bargain); *Florida PBA*, 2011 WL 2468075 (Fla. PERC 2011)(same); *City of Wheaton*, 31 PERI ¶ 131(Ill. PERB (2015)(same); *City of St. Bernard v. SERB*, 1994 WL 16841836 (Ohio App. 1994)(same).

CHAPTER 4

LONG-RANGE BARGAINING PREPARATION

Solid preparation is key to successful bargaining. Not only will being fully prepared save time when bargaining actually starts, having a bargaining team that is fully informed on all bargaining issues cannot help but be an advantage.

When should preparation for negotiations start? The simple answer is that preparation for negotiations should never end. From the moment that negotiations for one collective bargaining agreement end, the employer and labor organization should be gathering information that will assist them in the next set of negotiations. Decisions on contract administration and the settlement of grievances should always be made with one eye on how those decisions impact future contract bargaining.

To be sure, there is a time when formal preparations for bargaining should occur. Formal preparations include the selection of the bargaining team, the development of proposals, and initial discussions with the other party as to the bargaining process. The beginning of formal preparations can be triggered by whatever date is specified in the current collective bargaining agreement for the beginning of negotiations or a date specified by the controlling state statute or collective bargaining ordinance for the beginning of negotiations. Absent either of those, a good way to decide when to begin formal preparations for negotiations is to work backwards from the expiration of the contract. An illustration of the "working backwards" approach would look something like this:

June 30	Expiration of contract.
May 1	Beginning of ratification process (ratification for both employer and labor organization normally takes three weeks each, plus time for preparation of the contract).
January 1	First negotiation session (parties have normally taken three months to complete negotiations process; one month added for additional flexibility).
November 1	Selection of bargaining team (bargaining team has traditionally taken 30 days to prepare proposals; additional time added to account for winter holidays).

The Bottom Line. Work backwards from a meaningful date to determine when bargaining should begin.

Continuous Bargaining Preparation And The Negotiations "Binder" — The Single Most Important Tool In Preparing For Bargaining.

There is one document that any party to the collective bargaining process should have – a negotiations "binder." The binder may be a physical binder (or more likely, binders) holding papers. Far better, the binder should be an electronic database. The binder or database should contain all documents that are relevant to the negotiation and administration of the collective bargaining agreement.

Even if the negotiations binder is electronic, it is helpful to think of it as a standard three-ring binder. The binder should have three sections. The first section should contain separate tabs for every article in the collective bargaining agreement. The second section should contain separate tabs for topics that potentially might be added to the collective bargaining. The third section of the binder should contain separate tabs for general areas that are relevant to the collective bargaining process – areas such as the employer's ability to pay, the cost of living, wage increases in other jurisdictions, contract settlements with the various unions with which the employer bargains, general economic conditions, and wages and benefits in comparable jurisdictions.

What goes in the binder? Every time a grievance is filed, a copy of the grievance should be placed in the binder under the tabs of all contract articles listed in the grievance. Every time a grievance is settled, an arbitrator's decision is received, or a memorandum of agreement or understanding is reached, a copy of the document should be placed in the appropriate tabs of the binder. Correspondence about the contract should be placed in the binder, including e-mail, memoranda, and questions from constituents. If an employer's rules impact one or more contract sections, a copy of the rules should be placed into the binder. Notes taken during the collective bargaining process should be broken down by the contract article involved, then placed into the binder.

As cost of living information is received, the consumer price index data should be placed into the binder. Collective bargaining agreements from comparable jurisdictions, newspaper articles about wage settlements, information about the employer's budget, the employer's Consolidated Annual Financial Report (CAFR), discussions of the general economic climate of the area, projections for key economic indicators, and articles about the members of the bargaining unit should all be placed in appropriate sections of the binder.

For example, assume that Article 43 in the collective bargaining agreement contains the contract's callback language. The negotiations binder might contain these things:

- The text of the contract language.

- Bargaining notes on callback overtime, organized by date.

- Prior proposals by both parties for changes in the callback language of the contract.

- Copies of all grievances dealing with Article 43.

- Copies of any memoranda of understanding resolving grievances or potential issues arising under Article 43.

- Arbitration decisions interpreting Article 43.

- The text of contract articles on callback pay from comparator jurisdictions and from contracts covering other unions with which the employer negotiates.

- The employer's non-represented employee policies covering callback pay.

- Newspaper articles about the cost of overtime in the department.

The best form for the negotiations binder is some sort of electronic database. With a database, documents relevant to the bargaining process are scanned and then are assigned "tags" or labels which associate the documents with different topics. For example, a memorandum of agreement resolving a grievance filed by John Smith on Article 43 of the collective bargaining agreement can be assigned the tags "memoranda of agreement," "Article 43," "callback," and "John Smith." If the database is later queried for any of these tags, the memorandum of agreement will be among the documents retrieved.

An electronic database allows for broad queries of the information in the database. Commands can be given, for example, to tell the system to retrieve all documents dealing with callback pay, or the employer's ability to pay, or detailing wage settlements in other jurisdictions over the last two years.

The Bottom Line. The negotiations binder is the single most important document to be maintained by parties in the bargaining process. The binder should be organized on an article-by-article basis, and should contain all historical information about each contract article. Also, an electronic binder is preferable in collective bargaining.

Trying Your Arbitration Case, Even If You Don't Have Arbitration.

States using binding arbitration as the last step in the bargaining process all list criteria upon which an arbitrator's decision must be based. The most important of those criteria are typically the employer's ability to pay, the total compensation paid in comparable jurisdictions, and the cost of living. A key element of pre-bargaining preparation is gathering and evaluating information as to each of the statutory criteria.

Those in binding arbitration states should think of binding arbitration as a quasi-judicial, rational process that is fairly predictable based upon the criteria an arbitrator must take into consideration. Unless you have a decent assessment of what the results will be if there is a need for arbitration, how can you possibly do the best job of formulating proposals and making key decisions as to settlement?

Those in jurisdictions without binding arbitration should think that there is a reason why legislators have chosen the criteria that are used by arbitrators – those are the same factors that would normally be taken into account in setting wages, even in the absence of binding arbitration. Assessing an employer's ability to pay, for example, is critical in knowing the resources potentially available for a wage increase. Assessing the total compensation in comparable jurisdictions tells a bargaining team what the market is for a particular benefit. Knowing the cost of living not only provides information as to prospective changes in the employer's revenues, but also about how inflation has impacted the wages of employees. Looking at the productivity of employees, or whether particular classifications have fallen away from the general patterns for pay for similar work can assess whether particular adjustments are necessary.

Binding arbitration or not, there is a good reason to gather information about all of these issues, and to do so well in advance of the first bargaining session. The employer's budget, total compensation comparisons, the cost of living, and other factors will no doubt play a part in the bargaining process. Why not know that information before writing bargaining proposals?

The Bottom Line. As part of preparations for bargaining, gather and assess information on the employer's ability to pay, the total compensation paid in comparable jurisdictions, the cost of living, and similar areas.

CHAPTER 5

THE BARGAINING TEAM

In selecting a bargaining team, keep in mind what the negotiations process is all about. By definition, negotiations involve discussions aimed at producing a voluntary agreement. At times, the interests of the parties to negotiations may be shared. For example, it may be that both the employer and the labor organization realize that a new shift schedule must be put into place either to meet particular operating needs or for recruitment purposes. At other times, the interests of the parties differ. A labor organization may want a 10% wage increase; the employer may believe that its resources prohibit it from giving any raise at all. Negotiations is the process of finding the middle ground between these positions, a middle ground forged by compromise, persuasion, and the realization that a settlement is usually better than the alternative for both parties.

With that in mind, a bargaining team should be made up of individuals with a wide range of personality traits and backgrounds. Ideally, one would find the following characteristics among bargaining team members:

Bargaining Experience. There are few substitutes for experience with the bargaining process. One group providing training for negotiators described the value of experience in these terms: "People who negotiate a lot tend to be much more skilled at it than people who have not participated in many formal negotiations. Experienced people are more likely to know what to say when, when to make concessions, when not to, what to concede, what not to, and, in general, how to manipulate the situation to their own advantage. For this reason, negotiation tends to favor the experienced party."[1]

Not all members of a bargaining team need to have had experience with the process. What should be avoided, though, is selecting a majority of team members who have never before been through negotiations.

Work Areas. It is helpful to have a variety of work areas represented on the bargaining team. In negotiations for a city-wide "collector" bargaining unit, for example, both the employer and the union would ideally have representatives from the largest departments in the city, where school district negotiations with a professional staff union might include administrative assistants, nurses, counselors, and occupational therapists. In the fire service, representatives of both 40-hour and 56-hour assignments should be included on the bargaining team, where a negotiations team for a police bargaining unit should have both uniformed and plainclothes representatives.

Patience. Bargaining team members need to realize that the process can be frustrating, can move at what seems to be a terribly slow pace, and may not produce immediate results. The members of a bargaining team should be able to adapt to these conditions without losing focus of the eventual goal.

An article about collective bargaining and the National Football League did a good job of stressing the importance of patience in the bargaining process:

> Like quilting, scrimshaw and ice dancing, collective bargaining has severe limitations as a spectator sport. It is too tedious for television and, on most days, more nuanced than newsworthy. It is a complex competition conducted primarily behind closed doors and, often, over a period of many months. Even when the opposing factions are professional football owners and players, labor negotiations are a mating dance as staged by snails.[2]

Personality. There is no one "right" personality for bargaining team members. It is more important to have a diversity of personality types on the team, not only because they would be fairly representative of the constituency, but also to allow some flexibility in the development and implementation of bargaining strategy.

Credibility. There is no substitute for complete honesty on the part of the members of a bargaining team. If there is not full trust when an individual says something, bargaining can either completely break down or can be slowed to a snail's pace. Stocking a bargaining team with individuals whose reputation for honesty is unchallenged not only makes the process more efficient, but can produce better results. As Edward R. Murrow said, "To be persuasive we must be believable; to be believable we must be credible; to be credible we must be truthful. It is as simple as that."

Stamina. A negotiated agreement can occur quickly, but can also take many months, and sometimes years, to produce. Bargaining team members need to be able to bring the same energy to a meeting occurring five months into the process as they do to the first bargaining session.

Authority. There is an understanding, of course, that decisions made at the bargaining table are only tentative, and that any eventual settlement is a recommendation only, subject to ratification by both the employer and the membership of the labor organization. Within that framework that the final product is always subject to ratification, those at the bargaining table need to be able to make day-to-day bargaining decisions without checking with others. If every minor point discussed during the negotiation session has to be immediately reviewed with various layers of command, bargaining will quickly grind to a halt.

Persuasiveness. Some results in bargaining are achieved because both parties realize that the end product is in their mutual interest. Other results are achieved simply because the negotiating team is able to persuade the other team to accept a particular result. Though defining what it is that makes someone persuasive is a difficult task, the following observations are all apt:

> "One of the best ways to persuade others is with your ears – by listening to them." Dean Rusk.

> "If you would persuade, you must appeal to interest rather than intellect." Benjamin Franklin.

> "The secret is to always let the other man have your way." Claiborne Pell.

> "If you're trying to persuade people to do something, or buy something, it seems to me you should use their language." David Ogilvy.

> "If you wish to win a man over to your ideas, first make him your friend." Abraham Lincoln.

Objectivity. Contributing members of a bargaining team need to be able to shelve their emotions and objectively evaluate not only their proposals and those of the other side, but also the reasons for those proposals. Making assessments of potential agreements requires a negotiator to shelve biases and to evaluate the situation on an impersonal basis. A group providing training for negotiations described the value of objectivity in the following way:

> Often, in negotiations, people get bogged down in positional bargaining, butting heads and wills in a way that frays nerves, destroys relationships and may not ultimately get anyone what they truly want. One way around the perils of positional bargaining (and there are a variety of ways) is to turn the discussion into a rational one. Switch the focus from a battle of wills into a

search for the appropriate external fair standards or benchmarks, often called objective criteria.[3]

Timing and Tact. "To everything there is a season," Pete Seeger counseled us, channeling Ecclesiastes. That is very much the case in bargaining. Simply because something is true does not mean it has to be said, and just because something must be said implies nothing about when it is best to weigh in with the observation. Individuals with senses of timing and tact will be more effective bargaining team members.

Self Confidence. One might think that only those with a healthy amount of self confidence would even consider serving on a bargaining team, but that is not always the case. Needless to say, bargaining team members must not only possess but be able to convey a strong sense of confidence in their convictions.

Flexibility. A rigid adherence to a firm belief structure may avail in some endeavors, but rarely in bargaining. The ability to shuck, at least temporarily, a pre-conceived way of looking at a problem and to consider alternatives is a valuable trait for bargaining team members.

Creativity. A seemingly intractable problem can be solved by a new approach brought to the table by even the most inexperienced bargaining team member. Members of a bargaining team should be encouraged to not be hidebound to what has occurred before, and be willing to explore new possibilities.

Race/Gender. Though no bargaining team member should be selected solely for this reason, it is important that team members be fairly representative of their constituencies from the perspective of race and gender.

Spreadsheet Ability, Internet Savvy and General Computer Knowledge. The adage that "knowledge is power" definitely applies to the collective bargaining process. When one party submits a set of numbers to the other, the bargaining team needs to have the skills to try to check the calculations that produced the information. This requires the ability to do the math on short notice – usually with a spreadsheet – and an ability to understand and replicate the formulas used by the other side. In addition, since so much information relevant to the bargaining process can be found on-line, a bargaining team member with good Internet skills would be an asset to the team.

Note-Taking Ability. Note-taking is discussed in depth on pages 101-104 of this book. Suffice it to say that accurate bargaining notes are vitally important. At least one, and ideally more than one, of the members of the bargaining team should be good note-takers.

Availability, Both During Bargaining Sessions and in the Preparation and Ratification Process. Bargaining sessions can occur at odd times of the day, and occasionally at a moment's notice. Preparation for bargaining can consume a significant amount of time, and at the other end of the process, ratification of a tentative agreement can be quite involved. Bargaining team members should have work and personal schedules that have enough flexibility that they can participate in all these activities.

Willingness to Work. Done right, bargaining is work. Doing the research necessary to analyze even one proposal can consume many hours, and working through an entire slate of proposals is a challenging proposition. Bargaining sessions can last all day, and at times go into the evening and night. Bargaining team members have to possess a good work ethic, and need to understand from the outset that their role will likely involve much more than just showing up for bargaining meetings.

Willingness to Be Part of a Team. At times, a bargaining team will have to shelve individual differences and act as a team. That may mean supporting settlement positions with which individual team members might not wholeheartedly agree.

When To Select The Bargaining Team.

A bargaining team should be selected well in advance of the first negotiations session, ideally about six months before the first formal negotiations meeting. It takes time to train the members of the bargaining team, to educate them as to their roles in the collective bargaining process, and to draft proposals.

Training The Bargaining Team.

Formal bargaining training is offered by a variety of management and labor groups, usually more at the local than the national level. Increasingly, training is available in webinar form, making the training much more cost-efficient to provide.

The following organizations are among those that offer broad-based training on public sector collective bargaining.

Group	Orientation	Training Description	Web Address
CALPELRA	Management	Employer group providing training and webinars on bargaining; California-focused.	https://www.calpelra.org/content-display.aspx?id=2009&level=11&sublevel=14
Cornell University, The Worker Institute	Labor and Management	Collective bargaining training workshops and videos; union skills workshop.	https://www.ilr.cornell.edu/worker-institute/education-and-training
Federal Mediation & Conciliation Service	Labor and Management	Training on interest-based bargaining and contract administration.	http://www.fmcs.gov/internet/itemDetail.asp?categoryID=131&itemID=15804
Government Finance Officers Association	Labor and Management	In-person and webinar training on government finance, with courses for beginners through experts.	http://www.gfoa.org/products-and-services/training/cpe-guide
Labor Education and Research Center	Labor	Three-day training program on public employee collective bargaining.	http://laborcenter.evergreen.edu/Collective%20Bargaining%20Training.htm

Group	Orientation	Training Description	Web Address
Labor Relations Information System (LRIS)	Labor and Management	2.5-day seminars on public sector collective bargaining, grievances and arbitration.	www.LRIS.com
Liebert, Cassidy & Whitmore	Management	Training in the negotiations process and trends in bargaining; California-focused.	http://www.lcwlegal.com/
National Conference on Public Employee Retirement Systems	Labor and Management	Training for pension trustees.	http://www.ncpers.org/teds
National Public Employer Labor Relations Association (NPELRA)	Management	Variety of bargaining training and workshops for elected officials and management representatives.	http://www.npelra.org
Rutgers University	Labor and Management	Labor-management training conferences and public sector labor certification program.	http://smlr.rutgers.edu/labor-and-employment-relations/learn
University of California (Berkeley)	Labor	Workshops and publications on bargaining.	http://laborcenter.berkeley.edu/labor-education/
University of Oregon, Labor Education & Research Center	Labor and Management	Seminars and publications on public sector bargaining.	http://lerc.uoregon.edu/lerc-events/

Informal bargaining team training can be as valuable as formal training. A good individual to conduct informal training is the person who acted as the chief spokesperson for the bargaining team in the last bargaining session or who will do so in the upcoming bargaining. A significant block of time — at least a half to a full day — should be set aside for the training. The training should cover everything from the various roles for bargaining team members to note-taking to a review of the laws under which the bargaining is conducted.

In addition, there are many written materials on bargaining that would be helpful for the bargaining team to review. To avoid overloading team members, it is best to focus on one or two publications. Among the best are the following:

Publication	Publisher	Description
Bargaining For Advantage: Negotiating Strategies for Reasonable People, by Richard Shell	Penguin (Non-Classics)	320-page book by the director of the Wharton School of Business, who has taught thousands of professionals about negotiations strategies and pitfalls.
Getting To Yes: Negotiating Agreement Without Giving In, by Roger Fisher, William Ury and Bruce Patton	Penguin (Non-Classics)	200-page book describing a five-step system for how to act during any kind of negotiations.
Interest Arbitration, by Will Aitchison	Labor Relations Information System, www.LRIS.com.	271-page book describing the process of interest arbitration and how arbitrators analyze issues such as comparability, the cost of living, ability to pay, and total compensation.
Labor Relations in the Public Sector, Fifth Edition (Public Administration and Public Policy), by Richard Kearney and Patrice Mareschal	CRC Press	428-page survey of the legal and institutional setting of public sector collective bargaining.
Negotiation: Readings, Exercises, and Cases, 6th Edition, by David Saunders, Bruce Barry & Roy Lewicki	McGraw-Hill Higher Education	720-page textbook on the essentials of negotiation tactics.
Public Workers: Government Employee Unions, the Law, and the State, 1900-1962, by Joseph Slater	Cornell University ILR Press Books	272-page history of public sector collective bargaining.
Winning at Collective Bargaining: Strategies Everyone Can Live With, by William Sharp	Rowman & Littlefield	184-page book on negotiations strategies. Also contains discussion of history of public employee bargaining.

Selecting The Chief Negotiator.

Often, the identity of the chief negotiator is pre-determined. For example, an employer may always use a particular labor relations representative to serve as its lead negotiator; a labor organization may always use its president in a similar capacity. Where there is discretion as to who the negotiator should be, the decision has to be made whether to hire a professional negotiator.

There is no requirement in labor relations that the parties' bargaining representatives be licensed attorneys or have any other license, training or experience. A representative's "authority to bargain" is neither necessarily reduced nor enhanced based on any license, knowledge, experience or training. As Washington's Public Employment Relations Commission commented, "it is up to each party to choose their own representatives based on the level of knowledge (legal or otherwise), experience, and training they feel is sufficient to carry out meaningful bargaining."[4]

A publication from the California Public Employers Labor Relations Association lays out the pros and cons of hiring an outside negotiator. CALPELRA's advice, though aimed at management, makes a number of points equally applicable to unions:

The Pros Of Hiring An Outside Negotiator.

- An outside negotiator can "protect the agency staff relationships during and post negotiations. An outside negotiator can take a hard line at the table and act as an intermediary between human resources and management representatives and unions, thus preserving the ongoing relationship between the human resources agency staff and employees."

- Using an outside negotiator "creates a buffer between the Human Resources Director and other management representatives during difficult negotiations."

- Hiring an outside negotiator "avoids the possibility of a perception of a conflict of interest. A [city council] may see an outside chief negotiator as an unbiased party since s/he would not personally benefit from negotiated salary increases or benefit/retirement enhancements."

- Because bargaining is time-consuming, "an outside negotiator can alleviate the considerable time commitment required from employees of the agency."

The Cons Of Hiring An Outside Negotiator.

- "The primary disadvantage of contracting the agency's chief negotiator is the cost. It is expensive."

- Outside negotiators "often lack the first-hand knowledge of the organization and are not familiar with the operational impact."

- Outside negotiators "can make the bargaining process overly formal and positional."

- Outside negotiators "may not have the best interest of the agency in mind, especially if s/he is anxious to get a deal."[5]

The decision as to whether to retain a professional negotiator is probably more influenced by the size of the employer and the labor organization than any other single factor. Professional negotiators – whether attorneys or not – typically charge on an hourly basis, with rates ranging from $150 to above $500 per hour. Larger organizations with considerable resources are far more able to bear the cost of a professional negotiator than would small organizations.

The economics of modern-day collective bargaining in the public sector often suggest that hiring a professional negotiator makes good financial sense. For example, assume that a bargaining unit is made up of 100 employees, each of whom earn a total compensation of $75,000 annually. A 1.0% difference in total compensation amounts to $75,000 per year. And, of course, that 1.0% difference "rolls up" into all future years' costs. If the use of a professional labor negotiator can produce a 1% marginal difference in the result, and the labor negotiator charges $50,000 for his or her time, the use of the negotiator would be cost-efficient.

If a professional negotiator is retained, care must be taken to research the background and personality of the negotiator to make sure it fits with the organization's objectives. Negotiators who are particularly hard-line may well not fit in a process that has usually seen collaborative bargaining.

Using a symphony orchestra as a metaphor, some professional negotiators prefer to be the *conductor* of negotiations, freely calling upon bargaining team members to offer their perspectives. Other negotiators prefer to be the *soloist*, and insist that most if not all communication across the bargaining table comes through the lead negotiator. Some negotiators are *facilitators*, who act almost as mediators while still advocating for their team's bargaining position. Others are *technicians*, with an almost single-minded focus on the preciseness of contract language and the need to conform to a structured bargaining process. Others are *antagonists*, who believe they are successful by bringing aggressiveness to the bargaining table. Some negative personality traits can also characterize some lead negotiators, including the *unskilled*, the *unprepared*, and the *uncontrolling*.

In choosing a lead negotiator, an organization needs to take into account all of these issues of negotiations style, and select the individual who can best represent it, given all of the factors bearing upon the negotiations process.

The Bottom Line. *The most important characteristic in a lead negotiator is personality. Make sure that the negotiator you select is a good personality fit with the bargaining situation.*

NOTES

[1] Nagaraja Roa M R, *The Art of Negotiating* (2007).

[2] http://www.utsandiego.com/news/2011/feb/10/collective-bargaining-requires-patience-plays-deve/.

[3] http://www.sfhgroup.com/blogs/news_and_articles/2005/09/02/using-objective-criteria-to-negotiate-better-agreements/.

[4] *Kitsap County*, 2014 WL 5149992 (Wash. PERC 2014).

[5] https://www.calpelra.org/pdf/Dino,%20Corazon.pdf.

CHAPTER 6

WRITING BARGAINING PROPOSALS

The main pre-bargaining chore for a bargaining team is writing proposals. As with most of the bargaining process, preparation is the key to successfully completing the task. To write good proposals, a bargaining team must determine what is important to the team's constituents, anticipate what issues the other party may be raising, gather information about bargaining history on all of the topics, gather information from other jurisdictions about the same issues, write proposals, prioritize proposals, and, as discussed in the next chapter, determine the economic impact of the proposals.

Determining What Is Important To Constituents.

A usual first step of bargaining preparation is some sort of constituent survey. Labor organizations will typically circulate surveys to their members, allowing them to weigh in on their bargaining priorities. Employers will typically discuss bargaining issues with high-level supervisors, and may even circulate a survey among supervisors.

There are questions as to the value that constituent surveys actually bring. For example, if a labor organization surveys its members about bargaining, a likely question would focus on the wage adjustment the members feel is appropriate. Bargaining over wages often involves complicated issues such as the cost of living, the proper formulation of total compensation, and an analysis of an employer's budget with a view towards assessing its ability to pay. Rank-and-file union members answering a survey question about wage increases are unlikely to have much, and perhaps not any, of the information bearing on these critical issues. That a member thinks a 2% or a 20% wage increase is just right has some importance to the union, but a union would be foolhardy to base a bottom-line wage position on such views.

The same is true with management-side constituent surveys. The opinions of mid-level supervisors and even department heads on what changes are needed in a contract are helpful, but will rarely have the entire context needed by a bargaining team. And, in fact, it is one of the bargaining team's key roles to provide the broader context needed to develop proposals that reach solutions at the bargaining table.

Providing the opportunity for input in the process is important, and knowing the members' interests in the various areas (whether or not they are educated opinions) is important as well. But, in truth, constituent surveys probably only serve two purposes: (1) Making sure that bargaining issues are not accidentally overlooked; and (2) once the contract is settled, giving the bargaining team something to point to should questions arise about whether the settlement accomplished what the constituents wanted.

There is also a problem with constituent surveys, particularly from the union standpoint. If the results are publicized – and they often are – they may become the measuring stick against which bargaining results will be gauged. Particularly in rapidly changing economic times, constituent surveys can set up unrealistic expectations, and a perfectly good settlement may be viewed as less than adequate because it did not accomplish aims that an inadequately-informed membership may have set nine or twelve months before.

The Bottom Line. Use constituent surveys sparingly, if at all, and be aware that they may set unrealistic expectations.

Brainstorm The Contract.

A helpful starting place in preparing proposals is to "brainstorm the contract." Have the bargaining team sit around the table and go through the contract article by article, section by section, and even line by line. Discuss whether any problems have occurred with the operation of the contract language, particularly if the problems have risen to the level of becoming a grievance or the subject of conversation between both sides. As the discussion progresses, one member of the bargaining team should either be drafting proposals as the process unfolds, or should be making notes of the contract changes that may be contemplated.

The list of bargaining topics that results from the "brainstorm" process is typically a lengthy one, and will need to be pared down for future preparation sessions. Simply because one or more bargaining team member has identified an issue does not mean it should be translated into a proposal. What "brainstorming" produces instead is a start and not the end to the proposal-writing process.

Anticipate The Issues The Other Party May Bring To The Table.

As part of the brainstorming process, it is very helpful to anticipate what issues the other party may bring to the bargaining table. Anticipating the bargaining discussion in advance can allow a bargaining team to examine potential solutions and, if necessary, develop counter-proposals, arguments in opposition, and resource materials relevant to the issue.

Research Bargaining History.

Researching bargaining history involves reading through the notes taken during at least the last bargaining session, and the notes of all prior bargaining sessions for every contract section on which a proposal is made. Reviewing prior bargaining notes can provide all sorts of information, including:

- The proposals made by each side and how those proposals evolved over the course of bargaining.

- The documents produced by each side during the bargaining process.

- Who served on the other party's bargaining team and the roles they played.

- The timing of how negotiations proceeded, including when agreements were reached, and whether they were reached at the bargaining table or as part of a side discussion.

Gather Contract Language From Comparable Jurisdictions.

While bargaining teams customarily gather wage and benefit information from comparable jurisdictions, often overlooked is the need to gather contract language from the comparables. For each issue that is likely to arise in bargaining, it is helpful to study the contract language dealing with the issue in the comparables. Not only will contract language help a bargaining team in writing its own proposal, the language may suggest alternatives as to how an issue should be treated in the bargaining process.

The process of researching contract language from other jurisdictions should not necessarily stop with simply gathering the contract language. If a bargaining team is inclined to use language borrowed from another contract, it can be very helpful to reach out to those in the other jurisdiction to learn how the language has worked in practice. Language pitfalls that may not be immediately apparent can be discovered in those conversations, and proposals amended accordingly.

If the employer is party to multiple collective bargaining agreements, both bargaining teams should analyze how the employer has treated the issue with other labor organizations and with non-represented employees. While not binding, a practice set by the employer with other employee groups may be a pattern that is difficult to break. A simple matrix like this on every open issue can be a very useful tool in bargaining:

Contract	Graveyard Shift Differential	Holidays	Vacation, 10 Years of Service	Employer Insurance Contribution
40-Hour Firefighters	None	96 hours	96 hours	$1,397
General Employees	$0.40 per hour	96 hours	80 hours	$1,397
Non-Represented Employees	$0.40 per hour	96 hours	80 hours	$1,215
Nurses	$1.25 per hour	108 hours	100 hours	$1,397
Police	$0.75 per hour	108 hours	108 hours	$1,425

Write Proposals.

The next step in the process is to draft proposals and circulate the draft among bargaining team members. A meeting should then be scheduled for the purposes of critiquing the draft proposals. In preparing for the meeting, bargaining team members should ask themselves questions such as:

- Is the draft language clear and understandable?
- What contract language have others used to deal with the situation?

- How could the draft language possibly be misinterpreted? How could the language be changed to eliminate the possibility of misinterpretation?

- If I were assigned the task of drafting the proposal, what language would I have chosen?

- Does the language deal with every known problem that could arise in the area?

- What is the worst-case scenario as to how the draft language could be construed? Should the draft language be changed to deal with that scenario?

Contract proposals should be prepared in "legislative style," clearly showing language being deleted and new language that is being added to the existing contract. Using a feature such as Microsoft Word's "Track Changes" can save much time at the bargaining table figuring out what changes a party is proposing to the contract. For example, an employer's proposed changes to a "bulletin board" provision in a contract could be written as follows:

> The City agrees to furnish ~~and maintain~~ separate suitable bulletin boards in convenient places in each work area to be used exclusively by the Association. The Association shall limit its posting of notices and bulletins to such bulletin boards, and such notices and bulletins shall be signed. <u>The contents of postings on bulletin boards shall not be defamatory or discriminatory.</u>

Remember The Basic Rules Of Contract Interpretation.

When writing proposals, keep in mind the basic rules of contract interpretation. Though some of the principles vary a bit from state to state and from arbitrator to arbitrator, this is a useful checklist to refer to when drafting proposals.

Proposals Will Be Construed Against Whoever Wrote Them.

If there were no other reason to be careful about writing contract language, it is the principle that ambiguous contract language will be construed against whoever wrote it.[1] There are several reasons for this rule, including (1) encouraging those who write contracts to be as clear and specific as possible and to think through likely contingencies that might result from the contract language, and (2) discouraging the use of "boilerplate" language drafted without consideration of the bargaining history and past practices of the parties. In some states, the "construed against the drafter" principle has even been written into statutes.[2]

Technical Words Will Be Interpreted In Light Of The Employer's Business.

If a contract uses technical words that are common in the employer's business, then an arbitrator or a court will give the common meaning to the words as used in the industry.[3] For example, the terms "arrest," "less-lethal weapon," "sworn officer," and "chemical agent" appearing in a law enforcement collective bargaining agreement would all be given their usual law enforcement definitions. Similarly, terms such as "active learning," "classroom management," and "lesson plan" appearing in a teacher contract would be given their usual educational definitions.

Specific Contract Language Will Control Over General Language.

If there is specific language in a collective bargaining agreement covering a topic, the specific language will prevail over general language found elsewhere in the contract. Applying this rule, arbitrators have found (for example):

- That specific language covering the frequency of and compensation for faculty and other professional meetings prevailed over general language allowing a school to call any number of meetings with teachers "to accomplish the task at hand."[4]

- That specific drug testing language allowing termination for a first-time offense prevailed over general disciplinary language generally requiring that a five-day suspension precede a discharge.[5]

- That specific language allowing the employer to require employees to serve on standby status controlled over general language making overtime voluntary.[6]

- That specific language prohibiting layoffs except in limited circumstances prevailed over general language in a management rights clause giving a city broad powers in the case of an emergency.[7]

The Agreement Will Be Interpreted As A Whole.

Collective bargaining agreements are read as a whole, with the intent to give effect to all clauses in a contract.[8] The idea is to determine from the contract as a whole the true intent of the parties and to interpret the meaning of a questioned contract provision in relation to all other provisions.[9] Under this rule, each contract clause helps interpret the others,[10] and if one reading of a contract clause will avoid a contradiction with other language, an arbitrator will settle on that reading.

The *Expressio Unius Est Exclusio Alterius* Rule.

The principle of contract interpretation known as *expressio unius est exclusio alterius* proves the adage that if you use Latin to capture a simple principle, it will sound more complicated. *Expressio unius est exclusio alterius* means that "the mention of one thing implies the exclusion of another."[11] Assume that the education incentive clause in a teacher's contract reads as follows:

> To further professional development of teachers, a 5.0% incentive shall be paid to each employee who attains a Master's Degree. This incentive shall not be paid for degrees in the following majors: Civil Engineering, Family/Consumer Science, and Organic/Urban Farming.

The listing of the three exceptions will likely be construed as meaning the parties did not intend any other exceptions to apply. So, if an employer denies a request for incentive pay for a degree the employer considers not in keeping with the theme of the education incentive – for example, a degree in Interior Design – an arbitrator would likely overturn the denial by applying the *expressio unius est exclusio alterius* rule, essentially telling the employer "if you wanted any other exceptions, you should have bargained for them."

Contract Language Will Be Interpreted Using The Ordinary Meaning Of Words.

Of all of the rules of contract interpretation used in arbitration, the "plain meaning" rule is perhaps the most controversial. With roots in centuries-old British jurisprudence, the "plain meaning" rule is that words used in a contract clause should be interpreted in their "ordinary" sense unless doing so would produce an absurd or unjust result.[12] Under the rule, if an arbitrator decides that words have a "plain meaning," the arbitrator's job is done and no evidence of past practice or bargaining intent should be considered.

The "plain meaning" rule has been repeatedly criticized by commentators[13] and courts,[14] and the Uniform Commercial Code rejects it.[15] However, the rule lives on in arbitration, though often one finds an arbitrator reciting the rule and then proceeding to ignore it by considering past practice or bargaining history. The continued viability of the "plain meaning" rule, if only a limping viability, means that those drafting contract language should make sure that the dictionary definitions of the operative words in a contract clause match the bargaining intent.

Lawyers And Drafting Contract Language.

As discussed elsewhere in this book, it is not necessary to involve a lawyer in all aspects of the bargaining process. That said, lawyers can be helpful in drafting proposals. The cost of having a lawyer spend an hour or three reviewing proposals and preparing the language, or even suggesting changes, can easily be recovered by avoiding even a single grievance about the intent of the contract language.

The Bottom Line. After you initially draft a proposal, challenge every word you have written. Try to make the language as clear as possible, avoiding ambiguous words, and craft the language to avoid problems in the future.

Prioritize Proposals.

Once proposals have been written, it is time to prioritize them. Prioritization on the employer side of the table is generally a more top-down process. For example, a city administrator and HR manager can collaborate to set priorities, assigning proposals to general categories such as "Need To Have," "Want To Have," and "Discretionary."

Unions tend to follow a more egalitarian approach, with the opinions of all members of a bargaining team having roughly equal weight. This is not to say that union bargaining teams function as a pure democracy; in actuality, the views of the union president and/or business agent generally lead the way. However, most unions do ask all bargaining team members to fully participate in setting bargaining priorities. A usual method is to assign a value between 1 and 10 to each proposal, and then total the results. The result might look something like this, with the lowest total being the highest priority:

Issue	Alan	Rob	Everett	Derek	Total
Wage Increase	1	1	2	3	7
Health Insurance, Maintain Benefits	2	3	1	2	8
Disciplinary Procedures	10	5	9	1	25
Callback Pay	8	7	5	5	25
Clothing Allowance Increase	7	10	7	4	28
Mileage Rate	6	8	8	6	28
Additional Holiday	9	6	7	8	30
Funeral Leave	5	9	10	10	34

Little in the bargaining process is immutable, and so it is with priorities. As the negotiations progress, priorities do change and reassessments of the total package will occur. Bargaining teams should expect this evolution and not be tied unnecessarily rigidly to priorities set before the first bargaining session was held.

How Many Proposals Should Be Made?

Ideally, one would come to the bargaining table with only those proposals that mattered. Reality often intrudes upon that ideal. One may be dealing with an opposing bargaining team that will bring to the table dozens of proposals, many of which would, at best, fall in the low priority category. From a strategic standpoint, it would be folly to bring to the table eight proposals anticipating that the other party would be presenting eighty.

The easiest way to tease out the issue is to ask the other party about its intentions. If the answer is non-committal, then a good approach would be to bring to the table a limited set of proposals, but be prepared to submit additional proposals if the other party makes dozens of proposals.

Is There An Obligation That Proposals Be Reasonable?

There is no easy answer to the question of whether a party should formulate reasonable proposals calculated to reach an early settlement, or instead should have proposals that "shoot for the moon." For example, if a union is willing to settle for a 3.0% raise, what should its opening proposal be: 3.0%, 5.0%, or 10.0% or higher? If an employer wants some modest changes in overtime practices, should it begin by proposing that the employer move to the Fair Labor Standards Act (FLSA) standards for the accrual of overtime?

The answer to this question depends upon a variety of things. Most importantly, what does the bargaining team expect from the other party? If the other party has a practice of opening with proposals that would enact sweeping changes in the contract, it might be wise to open with proposals of the same ilk. On the other hand, if the other party finds reasonableness a more readily acquired trait, then proposals should be more realistic.

Other facts bear upon the structure of a party's opening proposals. A union, for example, may have membership expectations that proposals will begin at a particular level. An employer may have to open with certain proposals because of pre-adopted policies, or because negotiations with other unions suggest or demand such an approach. The personality of the negotiators on the other side can impact one's opening proposals. Negotiators who prefer broad compromises and "wheeling and dealing" may well find more room for movement with sweeping opening proposals.

In any case, remember the power of compromise. Just as it's rarely a good idea to walk into an automobile showroom and offer to pay the sticker price for a car, so it is important to leave bargaining room on many, if not all, of your proposals. Bargaining is a process of compromise, and contract settlements rarely alight upon the language or the wage and benefit levels first proposed by either side. Be aware that the process of compromise can be frustrating, particularly to first-time participants in bargaining. Compromise, though, is almost constitutionally necessary in negotiations – we simply feel better about a deal if it is produced after the other side has whittled down its position.

Pre-Bargaining Discussions With The Other Party.

There is great value in meeting with the other party prior to the formal commencement of negotiations. Typically, such a meeting works best if it involves a small group, perhaps the lead negotiators for each side plus an additional person. The pre-bargaining meeting should be off the record, with each side promising the other that statements made in the meeting will never be used in the future.

During the pre-bargaining meeting, a frank discussion can be held on the following:

- Is there a chance for a quick settlement, and if so, on what terms?
- How many proposals will the parties be making?
- How large will the bargaining teams be?
- What will the bargaining calendar look like?
- The politics attendant to the bargaining process.

NOTES

[1] *Palm Beach County Police Benevolent Association*, 38 FPER ¶ 171 (Fla. PERC 2011); *University of Alaska*, 2004 WL 6016196 (Landau, 2004); *Independent School District 2397*, 1997 WL 34824911 (Roszak, 2004); *Public Employees of Brewster*, 29 LAIS 3150 (Wilkinson, 2001).

[2] *E.g.*, California Civil Code, Section 1654.

[3] *Flaherty v. Pittsburgh School District*, 660 A.2d 218 (Pa. Cmwlth. 1995); *San Marcos Unified School District*, 25 PERC ¶ 32116 (Cal. PERB ALJ 2001).

[4] *Long Beach Island Board of Education*, 1978 WL 428038 (Parker, 1978).

[5] *City of Lakeville*, 2010 WL 6779417 (Johnston, 2010).

[6] *City of Duluth*, 1997 WL 34824851 (Gallagher, 1997).

[7] *Borough of Shenandoah*, 1988 WL 1591778 (Wolf, 1988).

[8] *City of Riverside*, 33 PERC ¶ 97 (Cal. PERB 2009).

[9] *Ohio State Troopers Association*, 2002 WL 34677192 (Brundige, 2002).

[10] *Benecia Teachers Association*, 2006 WL 6826815 (Riker, 2006).

[11] *New York City Board of Education*, 1984 WL 972174 (Bergman, 1984).

[12] *San Francisco Library Commission*, 23 PERC ¶ 30002 (Cal. App. 1998).

[13] C. Snow, *Contract Interpretation: The Plain Meaning Rule In Arbitration*, 55 Fordham L.R. 681 (1987).

[14] *Pacific Gas & Electric Co. v. G. W. Thomas Drayage & Rigging Co.*, 442 P.2d 641 (1968).

[15] Uniform Commercial Code, Section 2-202.

CHAPTER 7

COSTING PROPOSALS

Good faith bargaining requires answering the other side's questions about the costs or savings produced by a proposal. That means that sooner or later, each bargaining team will have to calculate those amounts. It is best to do so before bargaining starts, as knowing the economic impact of a proposal may cause a bargaining team to press for the proposal more ardently, abandon it, or modify it.

Depending upon the proposal, calculating costs may be a simple mathematic calculation or it may involve assumptions and complicated formulas. For example, calculating the value of an additional vacation day is straightforward math. However, the value of an additional sick leave day is open to debate, as sick leave is a conditional benefit that may or may not be actually used by employees. Similarly, costing a physical fitness incentive will necessarily involve assumptions as to how many employees will qualify at each level of the plan.

The Most Accurate Way To Cost Proposals.

The best way to evaluate the economic impact of proposals is through *specific costing*. With specific costing, an array of the wages and benefits paid each bargaining unit member is created. Employers are already in possession of the information through electronic payroll systems; unions are able to obtain the information from employers as part of the obligation of each side to share information relevant to the bargaining process.

Usually, specific costing is handled through a spreadsheet, though databases are also well-suited for the task. The data array should contain every component of total compensation, including at least the following:

- Equipment and clothing allowances
- Health insurance premium payments
- Holiday pay
- Longevity, education, certification and other incentive pay
- Overtime
- Retirement contributions
- Shift differential
- Sick leave accrual and use
- Social Security (if applicable) and Medicare
- Specialty, hazardous duty, and other assignment pay
- Unemployment and workers' compensation insurance
- Vacation accrual
- Wages
- Other economic benefits paid by the employer that might be an issue in bargaining, such as mileage allowances, tuition reimbursement, and sick leave conversion on retirement.

An extremely simplified form of a costing spreadsheet measuring changes in annual costs would look something like this:

A	B	C	D	E	F	G	H	I
1	Employee	Wages	Overtime	Pension	Insurance	Education Pay	Longevity	Total
2								
3	Adams, Cynthia	$48,348	$2,417	$6,769	$15,360	$3,868	$4,835	$81,597
4	Drake, John	$50,868	$0	$7,122	$15,360	$2,035	$0	$75,384
5	Jefferson, Francis	$48,588	$5,831	$6,802	$15,360	$0	$2,915	$79,496
6	Wilson, Thomas	$49,584	$8,925	$6,942	$15,360	$3,967	$1,983	$86,761
7								
8	Total for Bargaining Unit	$197,388	$17,173	$27,634	$61,440	$9,869	$9,733	$323,238
9	Assumption As To Wage Increase	2.50%						
10	Assumption as to Insurance Increase	$1,068						
11								
12	Costs for Bargaining Unit After Increases	$202,323	$17,602	$28,325	$65,712	$10,116	$9,733	$333,812
13	Increased Costs	$4,935	$429	$691	$4,272	$247	$0	$10,574

Two comments about the spreadsheet are in order. Most of the previous year's sums in Row 8 increase in Row 12, while the value for longevity in Cell H13 does not. This was done to illustrate the difference between salary-dependent and salary-independent costs. In the example, overtime, pensions, and education pay are all tied to salary in some fashion (overtime is time and one-half the hourly wage, and pensions and education are a percentage of salary). Longevity, on the other hand, is a fixed dollar amount that will not change with an across-the-board wage adjustment.

Also, the formulas in the spreadsheet are fairly straightforward. Column I's formula is the sum of Columns C through H, or in spreadsheet parlance for Row 3, =SUM(C3:H3). Row 8's formulas are also a sum, in this case for Rows 3-6. The values for increased costs in Cells C13, D13, E13 and G13 increase the previous year's totals by the assumption as to the wage increase. The formula for Cell C13 can thus be written =C8*C9. The increased costs for insurance in Cell F13 simply multiplies the number of bargaining unit members by the per-person increased cost in Cell C10, or =C10*COUNT(C3:C6).

From this basic spreadsheet, the costs for the entire bargaining unit of different wage and benefit adjustments can be calculated. Most entries are amenable to simple formulas like those described in the previous paragraph. However, some increased costs will likely have to be calculated using somewhat different formulas. The following list illustrates some of the more common variances from the simple costing formulas:

- **Adjustments in Leave Accruals.** A proposal may call for an increased vacation day. The easiest way to calculate time-dependent proposals of this sort focuses on calculating the value of a day. The usual formula is to divide the employee's salary by the number of work hours per year. For example, an employee working a 40-hour week will, on the average, work 2,086 hours per year (2,087 if leap years are factored in). The math on calculating the value of an additional vacation day would look like this:

Annual Salary	$50,218
Hourly Salary	$50,218 ÷ 2,086, or $24.07
Work Hours per Day	8.0
Value of Vacation Day	8.0 x $24.07, or $192.59

  The value of a vacation day for an eight-hour employee, which equates to 0.38% of salary, might change depending upon the length of the work shift. Public sector employees work a variety of different shifts, with eight, ten, twelve and 24-hour shifts being the most common. If adjustments to leave benefits are expressed in days as opposed to hours, then the value of (for example) an additional vacation day will be more for an employee working a 10-hour shift than one working an eight-hour shift.

- **Sick Leave and Other Conditional Time Off.** Sick leave, bereavement leave, and some other forms of leave are conditional in that an employee has to meet some conditions to use the leave (*e.g.*, being sick, having a member of the immediate family who has died, etc.). Changes in conditional time off do not have the same 1:1 value as vacation time, since not all employees will be eligible to use the leave each year. Instead, costing calculations might look like this:

Cost of one eight-hour day	0.38% of salary
Current annual sick leave accrual	12 days
Average annual sick leave use	4.3 days
Percent of annual sick leave used	4.3 ÷ 12, or 35.8%
Cost of one additional sick leave day	35.8% x 0.38%, or 0.13%

- **Benefits Requiring Assumptions.** Some proposals call for costing assumptions that will produce only an estimate of the costs the employer will actually incur. For example, an educational incentive plan that rewards different levels of education with premium pay requires assumptions as to how many employees will qualify at each level. The best approach is to try to reach an agreement with the other party to bargaining as to how many employees will qualify at what levels. Absent an agreement – or at least a rough consensus – costing estimates will necessarily be imprecise.

Most public employers assess costs over a five-year period of time, building in assumptions as to the rate of inflation and other variables. A five-year costing method not only shows the long-term value of contract changes, but also allows for more predictability and budget planning.

As the bargaining process proceeds, each side should ask the other to produce its costing figures on the proposals that remain on the table. Since the obligation to collectively bargain in good faith includes within it the obligation to exchange information relevant to the bargaining process, neither party is allowed to withhold from the other its costing estimates. A good practice is to exchange not just the "bottom line" numbers, but also to provide the other party with the spreadsheets or other computer programs used to calculate costs so that costing methodologies can be evaluated and, if appropriate, challenged.

Estimating Costs.

If either the time or the resources are not available to more precisely calculate the costs of proposals, estimating costs will have to do. Cost estimates usually start with calculating the total cost of the employer's payroll, from which the value of a 1.0% wage increase can be measured. If the employer's total payroll costs include overtime, then the 1.0% estimate will be roughly accurate. From the 1.0% estimate, proposals calling for adjustments to other compensation and leave benefits can then be calculated.

CHAPTER 8

GROUND RULES FOR BARGAINING

Usually the first issue discussed in bargaining is the question of what ground rules will control the bargaining. Ground rules are a set of agreed-upon rules that largely deal with the mechanics of how bargaining will occur. The purpose of ground rules is to smooth the process of negotiating, thereby improving the chances of the parties ultimately reaching an agreement.[1] Ground rules set such things as the time, place, and length of bargaining sessions, and generally establish the procedures that will be followed in negotiations.

Though there are some exceptions,[2] most states hold that ground rules themselves are not mandatory for bargaining.[3] That means that neither party can insist on a ground rule to the point of impasse, nor can a party refuse to bargain unless the other side agrees to a particular ground rule. If a party violates these principles and insists upon a particular ground rule, it will commit an unfair labor practice.

There is often an inverse correlation between the length of ground rules and the soundness of the relationship between the parties. The more trust and a cooperative working relationship, the shorter the ground rules will need to be. The greater distrust and the greater degree of problems in the past and ground rules can swell to novel length.

Ground rules can address some or all of the following topics.

Bargaining Sessions.

Place of Bargaining Sessions. Ground rules typically set the location of bargaining meetings. With larger employers, the parties may agree to bargain at a neutral site, or to alternate bargaining sessions between the employer's and union's locations. With smaller employers, bargaining is usually held at the employer's facilities. Bargaining requires at least two rooms, a room in which bargaining is held and an additional room so that caucuses can be held. As bargaining progresses, it may even be advisable to have a third room available for meetings between the chief negotiators for each team.

Frequency of Sessions. Bargaining sessions should be held frequently enough such that momentum in the bargaining process is not lost, but not so frequently that team members cannot attend to normal jobs or check with others on the viability of proposed contract resolutions. Having one or two full or part-day bargaining sessions a week is often a reasonable frequency.

Length of Sessions. There is no clear answer as to whether it is better to have half-day or full-day bargaining sessions. Half-day sessions can seem too short, where the first few hours of whole-day sessions can occasionally be unproductive. On balance, whole-day sessions are likely more useful because they allow more detailed discussions of complicated issues.

Schedule for Meetings. Ground rules often set the schedule for meetings. The schedule can be generic and repeating (*e.g.*, every other Thursday) or it can contain specific dates for bargaining. If there have been problems with meeting cancellations in the past, ground rules can specify a minimum notice period for cancellation of a bargaining session.

Bargaining Equipment. Once, the only bargaining "equipment" needed was a paper and pen. Now, it is almost unthinkable for bargaining sessions to occur without immediate access to the Internet and the availability of a printer. Having a projector handy so that possible contract language or economic calculations can be jointly reviewed has also become an important aspect of the bargaining environment.

Proposals.

Written Proposals. An important ground rule is that proposals be in writing and initialed by the chief spokesperson for a party. Beyond the obvious reason of formality, there is an additional, more subtle reason why proposals should be in writing and initialed – how the principle of "regressive bargaining" applies when a number of proposals are made as part of a package.

"Regressive bargaining" is the unfair labor practice that occurs when a party makes a bargaining proposal *more* favorable to it than its previous proposal. Put more broadly, regressive bargaining is conduct that is designed or can be reasonably expected to move the negotiations backwards.[4] Regressive bargaining amounts to a breach of the obligation to bargain in good faith.[5]

For example, it would be regressive bargaining for a union to propose a 3.0% pay raise for the first two months of bargaining, and then to change its proposal to a 4.0% raise. However, it is common in package proposals for parties to compromise on some issues in order to make achievements in other areas. If package proposals fail, each party needs to be able to "snap back" to their pre-package positions without fear of facing a regressive bargaining charge. An easy way to accomplish this is for the parties to <u>not</u> initial a package proposal or to characterize it as a "what-if" concept rather than as a formal proposal, meaning that under the ground rules, the package proposal could not later trigger regressive bargaining if elements of the the package were withdrawn.

Cutoff Date For New Proposals. Highly recommended for ground rules is setting a cutoff date after which neither side can submit new proposals. Having a cutoff date brings finality to the opening stages of bargaining and eliminates the possibility of a "late hit" that can disrupt the bargaining process. A good cutoff is the third or fourth bargaining session, by which time both parties should have little need for new proposals.

Negotiators.

Number of Negotiators. Ground rules can describe the rough makeup of each side's bargaining team, including the number of negotiators. Ground rules of this sort usually build in flexibility for changes in the size of a bargaining team if needed because of bargaining complexities.

Spokespersons. Ground rules often specify who the chief negotiator or spokesperson is for each side, and make clear that all proposals must be submitted by the spokesperson.

Paid Status of Negotiators. Though the matter is usually controlled by the underlying collective bargaining agreement, ground rules often describe whether union negotiators are to be granted paid release time for the purpose of attending and/or preparing for bargaining sessions. Ground rules can also describe whether and how the work shifts of bargaining team members are to be adjusted to facilitate attendance at bargaining.

Observers. Ground rules often allow designated "observers" to attend bargaining sessions. For example, observers can be members of a union's executive board or general membership who have not been chosen for the bargaining team. From the employer's standpoint, an observer might be additional labor relations personnel who are there to either assist the bargaining team or to gain training in how to negotiate. Where ground rules permit the presence of observers, they almost always indicate that observers are not allowed to speak during the bargaining sessions.

Bargaining Sessions.

Are Meetings Open Or Closed? Typically, ground rules specify that members of the public will not be allowed to attend bargaining sessions unless both parties agree. This can be impacted, of course, by "public meeting" or "sunshine" laws, which may require that bargaining be held in open sessions. Most states either designate bargaining sessions as "closed" meetings not open to the public or allow either party to insist that sessions be closed. A few states call for open bargaining sessions.

Where bargaining is open to the public, a delicate problem is presented for negotiators. It is normally unthinkable to negotiate a contract in the presence of third parties. We do not negotiate treaties, corporate mergers, or private-sector labor agreements in the public, nor do we negotiate home purchases, automobile sales, or other personal contracts with members of the public looking on. Bargaining involves discussions of possible settlements, talk of potential concessions, the packaging and unpackaging of proposals, and statements that range from the humorous to the dithering to the hard-nosed.

The presence of the public and the press means that anything that occurs in bargaining may be instantaneously communicated on a wide scale, whether by live-blogging, social media, or other means. That communication inevitably reaches the constituencies of both bargaining teams – the employer's governing body and executive staff and the union's membership. The communication may or may not be accurate (depending on the accuracy of the reporter), but it will surely be shorn of its context. More than occasionally, bargaining occurring in the public has been derailed by premature or inaccurate publication of bargaining discussions.

What often occurs where there is public bargaining is that the real negotiations happen in sidebar conversations between the lead negotiators. These conversations are usually not categorized as "public meetings" and so may occur in private.

Press Releases And Communications With The Public. Ground rules commonly specify whether and when communications to the media and public will be permitted. Because negotiators realize that the only thing usually accomplished with press releases is posturing and not bargaining, the usual rule is that media and public communications are off limits until impasse is declared or unless the lifting of the restriction is mutually agreed.

Caucuses. A caucus is a short recess in a bargaining session to allow one or both bargaining teams to privately confer. Though many ground rules try to set the length and frequency of caucuses, ground rules of this type are usually only observed in the breach. If there is a perceived need for a caucuses ground rule at all, the better approach would be to require each party to notify the other of the anticipated length of a caucus and to let the other party know if those time estimates change.

Bargaining Notes. Usually, each party is responsible for keeping its own notes of bargaining sessions. Occasionally, ground rules will provide either that notes be taken by a mutually-agreed-upon third party, or that both parties' notes from the previous session will be exchanged with the other at the start of the next session. Having an agreed-upon set of bargaining notes provides a good foundation from which to analyze disagreements that may occur years later as to what contract language means.

Recording Bargaining Sessions. Ground rules can describe whether any type of audio or video recording will be allowed in bargaining sessions. Usually, bargaining sessions are not recorded, with negotiators believing that recording impairs the free exchange of ideas critical to the bargaining process. The NLRB feels strongly enough about recording bargaining sessions that it has held that the insistence upon recording is in itself an unfair labor practice. The core NLRB decision, issued more than 60 years ago, involved the use of a stenographer:

> The presence of a stenographer at such negotiations is not conducive to the friendly atmosphere so necessary for the successful termination of negotiations, and it is a practice condemned by experienced persons in the industrial relations field. Indeed the business world itself frowns upon the practice in any delicate negotiations where it is so necessary for the parties to express themselves freely. The insistence by the respondent in this case upon the presence of a stenographer at the bargaining meeting is, in our opinion, further evidence of its bad faith.[6]

The NLRB has since held that insistence on "the use of a device" to record bargaining sessions is also an unfair labor practice.[7] Several state labor boards have ruled the same way.[8] Of course, if a state's public meetings law makes bargaining sessions open to the public, the usual ban on recording bargaining would not apply.[9] Where recording is allowed, ground rules should describe the ownership of the recordings, and whether the recordings must be shared with the other party.

Cell Phones And Other Handheld Devices. Ground rules are only starting to address the topic of cell phones and other handheld devices in bargaining sessions. For several reasons, a good practice is to leave cell phones in the pockets and purses of members of the bargaining team. To begin with, cell phones are distracting. Also, the use of cell phones for texting, emailing, or other purposes while bargaining is occurring conveys a message of at least disinterest to the other bargaining team, and can be construed as a message that what is being said at the bargaining table is a lesser priority than whatever is going on with the cell phone. Finally, it is worth bearing in mind that in addition to being data and voice transmission devices, cell phones are recording devices.

Reaching Agreement.

Tentative Agreements. Chapter 10 will describe what tentative agreements are and the purposes they serve. For purposes of ground rules, it is important to describe what level of formality is required for tentative agreements. Usually, ground rules require that tentative agreements be in writing and initialed and dated by the chief spokespersons.

Recommendation. The duty of bargaining teams to recommend proposals will also be described in Chapter 10. Suffice it to say that ground rules routinely state that both parties have an obligation to support and recommend tentative agreements to their constituents.

Miscellaneous Ground Rules. Other topics that ground rules can address are varied, and include issues such as the number of copies of written materials that must be furnished to each side, providing proposals in electronic form, and how an eventual contract will be physically prepared.

It is wise not to get too caught up in debates over particular ground rules. Remember that the real purpose of bargaining is to reach an agreement on the underlying contract, not to construct the best possible ground rules. Even if no ground rules at all are adopted, the obligation to bargain in good faith furnishes a reasonableness standard against which bargaining conduct can be measured.

Breaches of Ground Rules.

If the parties agree to ground rules, the ground rules become an independently enforceable contract.[10] The usual rule is that breaches of ground rules either amount to or are strong evidence of the unfair labor practice of bad faith bargaining.[11] That said, it is rare to find a remedy ordered by a labor board in a ground rules case that goes much beyond a requirement to comply with the ground rules and to post or circulate a notice to employees of the violation.[12]

NOTES

[1] *City of Augusta*, 2011 WL 6965927 (Me. LRB 2011); *see Town of New Milford*, 2001 WL 35807643 (Conn. Dept. Labor 2001)(purpose of ground rules is to facilitate bargaining).

[2] *City of San Jose*, 38 PERC ¶ 94 (Cal. PERB 2013); *Bristol Board of Education*, 2014 WL 7967522 (Conn. Dept. Lab. 2014).

[3] *E.g., City of Leesburg*, 36 FPER ¶ 304 (Fla. PERC 2010); *City of Mattoon*, 13 PERI ¶ 2016 (Ill. SLRB 1997); *Town of Orono*, 2011 WL 6965934 (Me. LRB 2011); *Department of Maryland State Police*, 2007 WL 5463355 (Md. SLRB 2007); *Taylor School District*, 1976 MERC Lab Op 1006 (Mich. ERC 1976); *City of Reno*, 1991 WL 11746841 (Nev. LGEMRB 1991); *OPEU v. State of Oregon Executive Director*, UP-71-93, 14 PECBR 14/767 (1993); *Fish and Wildlife Officers Guild*, 2012 WL 6660798 (Wash. PERC 2012).

[4] *Fall River School Committee*, Case No. MUP-12-1508 (Mass. LRC 2014).

[5] *City of Wenatchee*, Decision 8028 – PECB (Wash. PERC 2003).

[6] *Reed & Prince Mfg. Co.*, 96 NLRB 850, 28 LRRM 1608 (1951), *enf'd on other grounds*, 205 F.2d 131, (Cal. 1 1953).

[7] *Bartlett-Collins, Co.*, 237 NLRB 770 (1978), *enf'd*, 639 F2d 652 (10th Cir.), *cert denied*, 452 U.S. 961 (1981).

[8] *City of Reno*, 1991 WL 11746841 (Nev. LGEMRB 1991); *Miami County Sheriff*, 5 OPER ¶ 5104 (Ohio SERB ALJ 1987); *Washington County*, 2014 WL 3339216 (Or. ERB 2014).

[9] *Orange County*, 9 FPER ¶ 14372 (Fla. PERC 1983).

[10] *Oregon AFSCME, Council 75*, 2012 WL 3200648 (Or. ERB 2012).

[11] *City of Augusta*, 2011 WL 6965927 (Me. LRB 2011).

[12] *Town of Plymouth*, 2013 WL 4027289 (Mass. LRC 2013).

CHAPTER 9

SHARING BARGAINING INFORMATION

The duty to collectively bargain in good faith includes not only the obligation to engage in good faith communications – both written and oral – but also the obligation to exchange information relevant to the bargaining process.[1] In some states the duty to exchange information is built into collective bargaining statutes themselves,[2] while in other states it is the product of decisions by labor boards. The duty applies both to information about day-to-day contract administration such as grievance processing, but also to information about the bargaining process itself. As put by Oregon's Employment Relations Board:

> The duty to supply information is part of the duty to bargain in good faith and applies to both employers and labor organizations. In contract administration, the duty arises so long as the information sought is of probable or potential relevance to a grievance or other contractual matter. In contract negotiations, the duty arises so long as the information sought is reasonably necessary to allow meaningful bargaining on a contract proposal.[3]

On several occasions, the United States Supreme Court has endorsed the notion that the duty to bargain in good faith includes the obligation to share bargaining information. Perhaps most notably, in *NLRB v. Truitt Mfg. Co.*, the Court held:

> Good-faith bargaining necessarily requires that claims made by either bargainer should be honest claims. This is true about an asserted inability to pay an increase in wages. If such an argument is important enough to present in the give and take of bargaining, it is important enough to require some sort of proof of its accuracy.[4]

The duty to exchange information pertains not just to mandatory subjects of bargaining, but also to non-mandatory subjects that might have some mandatorily negotiable impacts. So, for example, even though class size might not be mandatorily negotiable for a teachers' union, information about class sizes would have to be exchanged "so that effective and intelligent discussions can proceed on the mandatory subjects upon which they impact."[5]

Labor boards assess a variety of factors in determining the extent of the duty to provide relevant bargaining information. Most important among those factors are the following:

(1) **The reason given for the request.** Usually, labor boards require that a party state the reasons why information is being requested.[6] The more specific the reason, the more likely it is that the information must be produced. For example, a request that an employer "provide its current budget so that the union can assess the employer's ability to pay" is more likely to be upheld than a request that the employer simply "provide its current budget."

(2) **The relevance of a potential subject for bargaining.** A party requesting bargaining information must establish the relevance of the requested information. Although "the burden is not exceptionally heavy," there must be some proffer as to relevance.[7] There is a presumption of relevance for information which relates to the employer/bargaining unit employee relationship, and specifically relating to wages, benefits, hours, and other working conditions.[8]

(3) **The ease or difficulty with which the data can be produced.** Where the material is already electronically compiled or is printed, the information must be quickly produced. Where the information must be gathered or be electronically exported into a usable form, a lengthier time frame exists for the production of the material. The workload priorities of the responding party and the amount of data requested are relevant considerations.

Neither party is obligated to create information in response to a bargaining request. Instead, the obligation to share information only applies to data that is within the other party's possession or can be obtained from a third party with a reasonable effort.[9] This means, for example, that an employer is not required to create a financial report it has not previously generated.[10]

(4) **Whether the requested information is confidential.** There is no obligation to produce information that is confidential under the law. For example, a party need not produce drafts of proposals, or minutes or notes of bargaining team meetings. A party may only refuse to provide *bona fide* confidential information after it has made a good faith effort to provide the information in an alternate form that avoids disclosure of the confidential portion.[11] One labor board has noted that "the defense of confidentiality is very narrowly construed and rarely granted."[12]

Simply because information is exempt from disclosure under a public records law does not mean it need not be produced if a proper request is made in the bargaining process. The usual rule is that the obligation to collectively bargain in good faith, which carries with it the obligation to disclose relevant bargaining information, supersedes any provisions of a public records law (assuming an agreement is reached by both sides to protect the confidentiality of the information).

(5) **Whether the information is freely available elsewhere.** Most labor boards will not require a party to produce information if the information is freely available elsewhere[13] or is already in the possession of the requesting party.[14] For example, if an employer's budget is on the Internet, a labor board will likely look askance at a union's demand that the employer produce a hard copy of the document.[15] However, even if both parties have the same access to the information, the party receiving the request is not free to simply ignore the request, but instead must notify the requesting party where the information can be obtained.[16]

Categories Of Information Considered Relevant To The Bargaining Process.

The obligation to exchange information requires sharing data about the following categories of information.

Wage and Benefit Comparisons.

- The comparable jurisdictions used by each party in negotiations.[17]
- How each party calculates total compensation, and the way in which salary formulas were calculated.[18]
- The approach taken by each party in calculating changes in the cost of living, and how each evaluates the employer's ability to pay.[19]
- A consultant's report on the grouping of employees for purposes of wage categories.[20]

- The salaries, promotions, and bonuses of management employees.[21]

Health Insurance Information.

- Reports and analyses received from an employer's health insurance consultant.[22]
- Health insurance utilization data and rate calculations,[23] though health care utilization information that identifies employees may be protected from disclosure under the Health Insurance Portability and Accountability Act (HIPAA).
- How the employer's insurance company has calculated prescription drug co-payments.[24]

Budgetary Information.

- Budgetary information, including current and past budgets, and the employer's Comprehensive Annual Financial Report.[25]
- Bond prospectuses or disclosure reports to bond rating agencies.[26]
- The employer's budget as reported on a standardized state form.[27]

Vacation, Sick Leave, Holidays, and Other Leave.

- Records of how an employer has administered a return-to-work program as part of its workers' compensation system.[28]
- Applications for paid leave made by bargaining unit members.[29]
- The names of employees with high vacation leave balances.[30]
- Records of alleged sick leave abuse on the part of bargaining unit members.[31]
- Records of use of unpaid sick leave.[32]

Contract Administration.

- A list of employees slated for layoff.[33]
- Information about an employer's intention to subcontract certain bargaining unit positions.[34]
- How the employer has enforced contract clauses such as an employer's residency and drug testing requirements.[35]

- A justification of how an employer has made assignment decisions.[36]
- The costs of enforcement of rules pertaining to residency and drug testing.[37]

Work Schedule Information.

- Information about the specific work schedules that would result for employees should a new schedule "chart" be bargained.[38]
- Studies regarding the efficacy of a 4/10 shift.[39]

Promotional Information.

- A third-party consultant's report on how the employer's promotional system had been functioning.[40]
- The method of composition of a promotional eligibility list.[41]
- The academic credentials of individuals who have been promoted.[42]

Disciplinary Information.

- Information about prior disciplinary cases, including the recommendations of line supervisors for discipline in a particular case.[43]
- Information about an investigation leading up to a reprimand, even though the underlying contract itself did not allow the filing of grievances challenging reprimands.[44]
- Witness statements and police reports of a disciplinary incident.[45]
- Records of a meeting with a probationary employee.[46]
- A report of a fitness-for-duty evaluation of a bargaining unit member who was being considered for discipline.[47]

Retirement Information.

- Actuarial evaluations of the cost of an employer's other post-employment benefits, including post-retirement health insurance.[48]

Other Information.

- An internal performance audit of the functioning of an agency.[49]

- Job descriptions.[50]
- Recruitment, retention, and hiring information.
- A list of part-time and temporary employees.[51]

In most states, where the responding party incurs expenses in providing the information, it may ask for reimbursement of such reasonable costs after informing the requesting party of its intention to do so. If payment is refused, the party may decline to provide the data. However, the rates of charges for the information may be a mandatory subject of bargaining.[52]

In some cases, a responding party may simply make the raw data available to the requesting party and allow the requesting party to compile the information itself. In cases where the requested information is more easily available from another source, a party might respond by identifying the other source.[53]

Typically, an employer will be in possession of more bargaining information than will a labor organization. Even so, the duty to exchange information is reciprocal, and if bargaining information is in the possession of a labor organization, it must produce the information upon request of the employer.[54]

What Should Happen When An Information Request Is Received.

The obligation to disclose information is triggered by a request; absent a request, there generally is no obligation to self-disclose bargaining information.[55] Upon receiving a relevant information request, the receiving party must either provide the requested information or notify the other party if it does not believe the information requested is relevant to collective bargaining activities. If a receiving party believes a requested item is irrelevant or unclear, it is obligated to notify the other party in a timely manner.[56] If a party views an information request as too burdensome, it must assert its concerns and both parties must bargain in good faith to ameliorate them.[57] What a party may not do is simply ignore the request because it considers it too onerous.[58]

The information provided has to be accurate, at least insofar as the party providing the information knows.[59] Labor boards do not look kindly on pure "data dumps" containing a massive amount of information only some of which may be relevant, and do require that information be produced "in a form useful for bargaining."[60] The format does not need to be exactly that desired by the requesting party; the bigger question is whether the information produced is responsive to the request and is in some usable form.[61] Labor boards seem to particularly frown on half-hearted efforts to comply with information requests.[62]

If the party receiving the information is dissatisfied with what it believes to be a partial response, it must communicate its dissatisfaction or reassert or clarify its request.[63] Bargaining information must be produced in a timely fashion, and an unreasonable delay in providing relevant information is an unfair labor practice.[64] If the representative assigned to respond to the request is not available to gather the information for a period of time such that it would make the request untimely, another person should be assigned even if it will be more difficult for that person to gather and process the information.[65]

The last few years have seen a significant reduction in the types of information requests made by labor organizations. Public sector employers now make so much information available to the general public through web pages that it is unnecessary for unions to request the information through the bargaining process. For example, where once the production of an employer's Comprehensive Annual Financial Report (CAFR) might have resulted in debates about whether a union should reimburse the employer for the cost of the production of the CAFR, in most cases today a union can simply download the CAFR from the employer's web page.

The web page for the City of Long Beach, California, is fairly typical in the amount of information it makes available on-line. Some easy digging on the City's web page produces the following information:

- All of the current and recently-expired labor contracts to which the City is a party.

- The contact information for each of the labor organizations with which the City contracts.

- The City's financial policies, including the City's fund balance policy.

- Performance audits on various City functions and departments conducted by the City Auditor.

- More than ten years of the City's CAFRs.

- A map of the City, showing the portions of the City served by each City Council member.

- The City's annual budgets for the current and past ten years, including a budget calendar, mayoral proposed budgets, and the "Community Budget Book."

- Budgets for each of the City's departments.

- Summaries of the City's various funds, including the general fund and restricted-purpose funds.

- The City's Financial Strategic Plan.

- The City's Capital Improvement Program.

- Reports made by various presenters to the City's budget workshops.

- All job descriptions as well as salary schedules.

- Lengthy explanations of the City's various retirement plans.

- The structure of the City's medical plans.

NOTES

[1] *Seattle School District*, Decision 12174 – PECB (Wash. PERC ALJ 2014).

[2] Section 447.203(17), Florida Statutes (2015).

[3] *Washington County School District v. Beaverton Education Association*, Case No. C-169-79, 5 PECBR 4398 (1981).

[4] *NLRB v. Truitt Mfg. Co.*, 351 U.S. 149 (1956).

[5] *City of New York*, 9 PERB ¶ 4502 (N.Y. PERB ALJ 1976).

[6] *Marcellus Faculty Association*, 48 PERB ¶ 4506 (N.Y. PERB ALJ 2015).

[7] *Delaware Transit Corporation*, 2014 WL 1364593 (Del. PERB 2014).

[8] *Diamond State Port Corporation*, 2015 WL 1003777 (Del. PERB 2015); *Milwaukee School Board*, No. 27807-A (Wis. ERC ALJ, 1/94); Aff'd by Op of Law, No. 27807-B (Wis. ERC 2/94).

[9] *Klamath Falls City Schools*, Case No. UP-27-07 (Or. ERB 2009).

[10] *Island County*, Decision 11946-A – PECB (Wash. PERC 2013).

[11] *California Nurses Association*, 32 PERC ¶ 71 (Cal. PERB ALJ 2008).

[12] *City of Detroit*, 16 NPER MI-25066 (Mich. ERC 1994).

[13] *Marcellus Faculty Association*, 48 PERB ¶ 4506 (N.Y. PERB ALJ 2015).

[14] *Frazer Board of Trustees*, 2007 WL 5063232 (Mont. LSB 2007).

[15] *Public Employees Union*, 40 Florida Pub. Employee Rep. ¶ 29 (Fla. PERC 2013).

[16] *County of San Joaquin*, 39 PERC ¶ 84 (Cal. PERB 2014).

[17] *County of Los Angeles v. Los Angeles County Employee Relations Commission*, 35 PERC ¶ 55 (Cal. App. 2011); *City of Bellevue and IAFF, Local 1604*, 831 P.2d 738 (Wash. 1992).

[18] *Bakersfield City School District*, 12 PERC ¶ 19155 (Cal. PERB ALJ 1988).

[19] *City of Seattle*, 1994 WL 899471 (Wash. PERC 1994).

[20] *Trempealeau County*, Decision No. 29598-B (Wis. ERC 2000).

[21] *Regents of the University of California*, 37 PERC ¶ 30 (Cal. PERB ALJ 2012).

[22] *City of Malden*, 2015 WL 456443 (Mass. LRC 2015).

[23] *Klamath Falls City Schools*, Case No. UP-27-07 (Or. ERB 2009).

[24] *Tri-County Metropolitan Transit District*, Case No. UP-56-09 (Or. ERB 2012).

[25] *Boston School Committee*, 2010 WL 5136826 (Mass. LRC 2010).

[26] *City of Malden*, 2015 WL 456443 (Mass. LRC 2015).

[27] *Campbell Education Association*, 27 PERC ¶ 139 (Cal. PERB ALJ 2003).

[28] *Seattle School District*, Decision 12174 – PECB (Wash. PERC ALJ 2014).

[29] *Chula Vista City School District*, PERB Decision No. 834 (1990).

[30] *Montebello Unified School District*, 39 PERC ¶ 51 (Cal. PERB ALJ 2014).

[31] *Deschutes County 911 Service District*, Case No. UP-32-04 (Or. ERB 2006).

[32] *City of Burbank*, 33 PERC ¶ 11 (Cal. PERB 2008).

[33] *Berkeley Unified School District*, 36 PERC ¶ 95 (Cal. PERB ALJ 2011).

[34] *Green Bay Professional Police Association*, Decision No. 32107-C (Wis. ERC 2010).

[35] *City of Detroit*, 16 NPER MI-25066 (Mich. ERC 1994).

[36] *State of California*, 18 NPER CA-26117 (Cal. PERB ALJ 1995).

[37] *City of Detroit*, 7 MPER ¶ 25066 (Mich. ERC 1994).

[38] *City of New York*, 9 PERB ¶ 4502 (N.Y. PERB ALJ 1976).

[39] *Association of Oregon Corrections Employees*, Case No. UP-39-03 (Or. ERB 2004).

[40] *City of Boston*, 2014 WL 6808615 (Mass. LRC 2014).

[41] *City of Chicago*, 12 PERI ¶ 3015 (Ill. LLB 1996).

[42] *City of Detroit*, 6 MPER ¶ 24028 (Mich. ERC 1993).

[43] *Washington State Patrol Troopers Association v. State of Washington*, Decision 4710 (Wash. PERC ALJ 1994).

[44] *Madison Federation of Teachers*, 26 PERI ¶ 94 (Ill. LRB 2010).

[45] *University of Wisconsin*, Decision No. 32239-B (Wis. ERC 2009).

[46] *Town of Athol*, 2014 WL 7477849 (Mass. LRC 2014).

[47] *Eugene Police Employees Association v. City of Eugene*, Case No. UP-43-97, 17 PECBR 634 (1998).

[48] *City of Malden*, 2015 WL 456443 (Mass. LRC 2015).

[49] *Illinois Fraternal Order of Police*, 28 PERI ¶ 145 (Ill. LRB 2012).

[50] *Town of Cicero*, 28 PERI ¶ 112 (Ill. LRB 2012).

[51] *City of Wilmington*, 2010 WL 8424716 (Del. PERB 2010).

[52] *City of Portland*, Case No. UP-46-08 (Or. ERB 2011).

[53] *Oregon School Emp. Assoc. v. Colton School Dist.*, 6 PECBR 5027 (1982).

[54] *City of Wilmington*, 2011 WL 7395253 (Del. PERB 2011).

[55] *State of Wisconsin*, Decision No. 31271-A (Wis. ERC 2006).

[56] *Island County*, Decision 11946 – PECB (Wash. PERC ALJ 2013).

[57] *Nanuet Union Free School District*, 45 PERB ¶ 3007 (N.Y. PERB 2012).

[58] *County of San Joaquin*, 39 PERC ¶ 84 (Cal. PERB 2014).

[59] *City of San Jose*, 39 PERC ¶ 60 (Cal. PERB ALJ 2014).

[60] *State of California (Department of Corrections)*, PERB Decision No. 1388-S (Cal. PERB 2000).

[61] *City of Portland*, 2012 WL 12089266 (Me. LRB 2012).

[62] *Island County*, Decision 11946 – PECB (Wash. PERC ALJ 2013).

[63] *Los Angeles Superior Court*, PERB Decision No. 2112-I (2010).

[64] *Seattle School District*, Decision 12174 – PECB (Wash. PERC ALJ 2014).

[65] *Skagit Public Hospital District 1*, Decision 11949 (PECB 2013)(family emergency of representative not a defense);*University of Washington*, Decision 10226 (PSRA, 2008)(employer representative's unavailability not a defense).

CHAPTER 10

THE BARGAINING PROCESS

A description of the bargaining process reads much like the questions journalists are supposed to pose. Who, what, when, where, and how? The "who" is the easiest of the questions – it will be the two negotiating teams that will be doing the bargaining. The remainder of the questions sometimes involve more complicated issues.

When to start negotiations. Chapter 4 discusses setting a bargaining calendar, and working backwards from a significant date such as the adoption of the employer's budget. The whole idea is that the bargaining process should dictate the composition of the budget, and not *vice versa*. If that's not the case, and if a mid-year budget adjustment is necessary to accommodate a bargaining settlement, significant disruption can occur.

Where to hold negotiations. Three things are important in selecting negotiations sites: Comfort, communications, and security. Don't overlook *comfort* factors such as separate caucus rooms, an adequately-sized bargaining table, free parking, the availability of beverages and snacks, decent chairs and lighting, and proximity to restaurants where a relatively private lunch meeting can be held. *Communications* should be a given in today's age. It's hard to imagine bargaining without Wi-Fi, access to a printer/scanner and a private place to hold speakerphone conversations.

The *security* of the bargaining site is also important. Ideally, bargaining should be held in a room where there is limited or no public access. The telephone and Internet access used by negotiators should also be secure.

How often to have negotiations sessions. Having too many bargaining sessions seems to impede progress, removing some of the sense that things need to be accomplished at any one bargaining session. On the other hand, having too few bargaining session disrupts continuity, and breeds too many bargaining sessions that start off with the equivalent of "Now where were we?" Having bargaining sessions once a week at the outset of the bargaining, and twice a week as the parties approach settlement, is usually the best frequency.

The length of each individual negotiations session. While no doubt things can be accomplished in half-day bargaining sessions, full-day sessions are preferable. The longer time spent in each day's session allows for fuller discussion of the issues, makes for easier scheduling of resource individuals to attend a portion of a session, and seems to make the process of reaching agreement easier by allowing each bargaining team the opportunity to thoroughly hash out issues during caucuses.

Caucuses – what is reasonable? "Caucuses" is the term used to describe breakout meetings of each bargaining team during the course of a bargaining session. Caucuses can be called for any of a variety of reasons. The usual causes are:

- The need to internally discuss a proposal received from the other party.
- The need to discuss possible options in constructing a proposal.
- The need to rein in a bargaining team member who is being incautious in what s/he is saying.

Ground rules often set limits on caucuses, usually in the form of the maximum time for individual caucuses. In practice, though, ground rules such as these are almost universally ignored. Bargaining teams tend to take as long in a caucus as they feel is necessary, and there is little that a frustrated opposing party can do about that fact other than to grumble.

The real problem with lengthy caucuses occurs when it becomes clear that one party is not adequately preparing between bargaining sessions but rather is using caucuses to do preparation work that should have occurred between bargaining sessions. When this occurs, it is usually appropriate for the two chief negotiators to have a private, heart-to-heart discussion about the pace of bargaining. If that fails, a last resort is for the bargaining team that is sitting idly while the other team is in interminable caucuses to simply tell the other team the equivalent of "we're leaving, come back when you're ready to bargain."

Sidebar meetings and discussions. An almost inevitable feature of the bargaining process – though one that often troubles some bargaining team members – are "sidebar" meetings. A sidebar meeting occurs when some subset of the bargaining teams privately meet to discuss possible resolutions of disputed bargaining issues. Sometimes a sidebar meeting involves only the lead negotiators for each side. More often, sidebar meetings include the lead negotiator and one additional individual from each side.

The reason sidebar meetings are almost inevitable is that bargaining tends to bog down under the weight of multiple personalities expressing different points of view. A sidebar conversation can allow direct, to-the-point conversations that can help break bargaining logjams. During sidebar conversations, parties can suggest possible resolutions, suggestions that might not as easily be made in normal bargaining.

Their benefits aside, sidebar conversations come with a risk. Those not participating in the sidebar conversations can be suspicious of the conversations, and can wonder why discussions cannot be held in open bargaining. If a bargaining team is internally fractured, sidebar conversations will be more readily distrusted. It is critical that those participating in sidebar conversations make full disclosure to their bargaining teams, both that the conversations will occur and, after they occur, what was discussed during the conversations.

If sidebar meetings are to be held, guidelines such as these are helpful:

- *Two-on-two meetings are better than one-on-one meetings.* To avoid "he said/she said" problems, sidebar conversations should involve more than one representative of each side. Notes need not be taken of the conversation – and rarely are – but in the event of problems, the additional recollections could be helpful.

- *Sidebar meetings should be brief.* If a sidebar meeting lasts longer than 10 or 15 minutes, the bargaining team members who are not participating in the meeting can feel left out of the process, and concern can grow about what is occurring in the sidebar meeting.

- *Discussions in sidebar meetings should be conceptual, not direct.* Those participating in sidebar meetings should be suggesting "what-if" alternatives that are contingent upon the approval of each party's bargaining team. Sidebar meetings should not be the place where ultimate deals are made; they should be a forum for conceptually discussing potential deals.

- *Immediate reports should be made of sidebar conversations.* When sidebar conversations conclude, those participating should immediately report to their bargaining teams, describing the general import of what occurred. Reports of sidebar conversations should cover all the highlights of the conversation. Unless these sorts of reports are made, bargaining teams can quickly grow to distrust sidebar conversations.

- *Sidebar meetings should be kept to a minimum.* The more frequent sidebar meetings, the more likely it is that bargaining teams will begin to feel dispossessed, and will wonder why real bargaining is not occurring during bargaining sessions.

The Bottom Line: While sidebar meetings are inevitable, it is best to keep them to a minimum, make them brief, and use them for conceptual discussions.

The Stages Of Bargaining.

Much has been written about the theory of negotiations. Almost all analysts think of negotiations as a process, though they differ somewhat as to precisely what the process is. It doesn't take too much of a dive into the literature to find terms such as morphological analysis, integrative analysis, strategic analysis, structural analysis and many more used to analyze the negotiations process. The theory can be at times both dizzying and contradictory.

From more of a practical level, most public sector bargaining occurs in fairly predictable stages. Think of the first stage as the "initiation" stage. This is the stage during which the parties prepare their proposals, begin meetings, and set ground rules for formal bargaining sessions.

The second stage – the "getting-to-know-you" stage – may be the most important of any. There's an apt analogy in the advice given to American businesses seeking to do business in China, where the caution is that relationships lead to agreements rather than vice versa.[1] During the getting-to-know-you stage, the parties build a rapport, and begin the process of learning to trust each other. It is helpful during this stage to try to reach tentative agreements on non-controversial issues, not just to clear the table for more important discussions, but also to show that you are able to reach agreements. This is also the stage where members of the bargaining team are hopefully building friendly or at least professional relationships with individual members of the other bargaining team.

The getting-to-know-you stage is not always sweetness and light. The early stages of the bargaining process can be punctuated by bluster, posturing, and displays of emotion. What is important is that when these things occur, they are not by happenstance, but are rather planned with an ultimate aim in mind.

The third stage of bargaining is the "probing" stage. This is where the parties explore the proposals made by the other, try to figure out the true motivations behind the proposals, and begin to explore the flexibility on key bargaining issues. It is usually during the probing stage that the parties exchange the most information, including comparability, total compensation, and ability to pay information.

The fourth stage of bargaining is the "packaging" stage. This is the stage where the parties begin combining the open issues into more easily consumable packages. Often, but not necessarily, the packages are of related items. For example, one package could contain all contract articles dealing with overtime, or with seniority. Packages usually involve both the withdrawal of proposals and mutual compromise. The first package tentative agreements that are reached tend to involve more non-controversial matters.

The last stage of bargaining is the "settlement" stage. This is the stage where the parties tackle the most difficult issues, usually including wages and health care benefits. It is at this stage where the most compromise occurs, often incrementally, and occasionally painfully incrementally. It is also at this stage where the parties typically get the most creative in their proposed solutions to contract dilemmas.

Tentative Agreements.

A *tentative agreement* is the usual way of removing issues from the bargaining table. Tentative agreements should recite the language used for the new contract language, and should memorialize the fact that some proposals are either being withdrawn or are being retained as open issues for bargaining. The usual formality for tentative agreements is that they are initialed and dated by the chief spokesperson for each bargaining team.

For example, a tentative agreement could look something like this:

Article	Issue	Resolution
II, Section 5	Complete Agreement	Current contract.
V, Section 1(H)	Employee Rights	Current contract.
VI, Section 3	Shop Stewards and Union Officers	Current contract, with these changes: 1. 20 Shop Stewards instead of 15. 2. Delete last sentence in Section 3(A), replacing it with *Union officers and shop stewards shall be allowed a reasonable amount of time off with pay for the purposes of attending the Union's annual in-house shop steward training and, on an annual basis, no more than 10 training classes for the aggregate of all Union officers and shop stewards.*
VI, Section 8	Pay Day	Current contract.
VI, Section 9	Elections	Current contract.
VI, Section 15	Light Duty	Current contract.
IX, Section 2	Position Seniority	Union's proposal, plus additional sentence, *When employees are promoted on the same date, scores on the promotional examination shall be used to determine the individual with the highest seniority.*
XI, Section 3	Military Leave	Employer's proposal.

Article	Issue	Resolution
XX (all)	Injury Leave	Current contract.
XXI	Temporary Duty Assignments	Union's proposal.
New	Administrative Fees	Do not include in contract.

What does a tentative agreement mean? A tentative agreement conditionally removes topics from the bargaining table, resolving them on the basis recited in the tentative agreement. Almost always, the condition placed on the agreement – what makes the agreement tentative – is that the agreement is subject to settlement of the entire collective bargaining agreement. If impasse is reached, the usual rule is that either party can simply rescind any and all tentative agreements, effectively reopening those issues for the impasse resolution process. In practicality, however, it is rare that tentative agreements come undone. Bargaining teams have usually invested enough effort in the compromises reflected in a tentative agreement that they are willing to maintain the tentative agreement even though impasse is reached.

The Need For An Integrated Approach To Negotiations.

It is important to keep in mind that what happens at the bargaining table is only part of negotiations. The ultimate bargaining decisions by both management and labor can be impacted by a variety of factors. Important among these factors are communications with constituents and dealing with the press and public.

Both parties should regularly brief their constituents as to what is occurring at the bargaining table. There's no need for blow-by-blow accounts, but summaries can be given including when bargaining sessions were held or are scheduled and whether progress is being made on key issues. Negotiators have to take care that these communications do not set unrealistic expectations, and are kept general enough so as not to arouse discontent as to the substance of tentative agreements.

Assuming there are no ground rules to the contrary, negotiators should not overlook communicating with the press while the bargaining process is ongoing. Building public and media support for bargaining positions can assist in the settlement process, particularly if one party has staked out extreme positions. Even if communications with the media are on an "off-the-record, not-for-publication" basis, the communications can help build rapport that may be valuable when a settlement is later reached.

However, bargaining ground rules often address the issue of communication with the press, usually prohibiting it. This might not be in the best interests of both parties. One party is likely to be better at press communications than the other, either through experience, relationships, or ability. It is not this party, but rather the one less skilled at press communications, that should be willing to agree to a ground rule prohibiting discussing bargaining with the press.

End Runs. An "end run" is where negotiators for one party directly contact the constituents of the other party. An end run might occur where union negotiators meet directly with one or more members of a city council, or where a mayor sends an e-mail to bargaining unit members either urging them to support a particular position or trying to sow doubts as to the performance or agenda for the union bargaining team.

In some states, end runs are specifically prohibited by statute and are an unfair labor practice. In other states, labor boards have found end runs prohibited by more general bargaining statutes such as a statute deeming it an unfair labor practice for an employer "to refuse to bargain collectively in good faith with the exclusive representative."[2] Even in some states without statutory prohibitions on end runs, labor boards frown on the practice. As Connecticut's Board on Labor Relations commented:

> We also strongly note that a practice of "end-running" one's bargaining opponent has been frequently criticized, because if successful, it tends to encourage parties to look toward the political process rather than the bargaining process as a means of accomplishing changes in conditions of employment. In *State of Connecticut, supra,* we reiterated that criticism and we do so again here. This Board still believes that criticism of such action is well founded, and that changes should be effected through the bargaining process and not the political process as a matter of public policy. That is why we have public employee bargaining statutes. Moreover, if these sorts of end runs become *de rigueur,* the bargaining process will be so severely undermined as to cause irreparable damage to relations between labor and management. As such, we wish to clearly state that this type of activity is not the preferred method of resolving disputes in this jurisdiction even if protected against sanctions from this Board.[3]

The perception is that end runs are more harmful to employers than to unions. In the face of an employer end run, unions tend to turn to internal communications systems to counter an employer's direct communication with a bargaining unit. Employers, on the other hand, face the complicating factor that union end runs are typically directed at elected officials. A glossary of labor terms from the New Jersey School Board Association illustrates this in the very definition it gives of an end run:

> **End-Run Bargaining:** An attempt to gain an advantage in negotiations in which a local union contacts individual board members in an attempt to negotiate away from the table. This political power play is an attempt to create a rift on the board or the negotiations committee to allow the union to achieve gains which it might not otherwise have been able to attain. Unauthorized sidebar negotiations have never helped the negotiations process and have often proven to be disastrous for boards of education.[4]

Whether statutory prohibitions on end runs are constitutional is yet another matter. It is difficult to see, for example, how a ban on end runs could trump the free speech rights of unions to directly petition elected officials to try to sway them on a contract issue.

No matter whether end runs are statutorily allowed or not, negotiators should prepare for them to occur. Management negotiators should caution elected officials about giving in to the temptation to speak with union officials about bargaining issues. Sometimes, these cautions even work. Union negotiators, for their part, should make sure they have adequately communicated with their members so that any end run directed at their members will fall on deaf ears, and should be prepared to respond quickly if an improper communication occurs.

Keeping Records Of Negotiations.

It's hard to overstate the importance of good note taking during bargaining sessions. Years down the road, when an arbitrator is interpreting the language of a contract, bargaining notes may make all the difference between winning or losing a grievance. When arbitrators find contract language ambiguous – and it's not hard to find *some* ambiguity in any contract language – they turn to bargaining history as an "extrinsic aid in contract interpretation," and consider that history on par with such things as past practice.[5]

Yet for some reason, the lesson that bargaining notes should be taken, and taken well, is one that needs to be learned and relearned by negotiators for both employers and unions. Start by making it easy – develop a form that can be placed in the bargaining notebook for every member of the negotiating team. There should be a several copies of the form placed in the tab for each open contract article. There's no magic to such a form; something as simple as this will do.

BARGAINING NOTES

Date:	Bargaining Location:

Article/Section:	
Starting Time:	Discussion:

How many note takers? Ideally, each member of the bargaining team other than the chief spokesperson would be responsible for taking notes. In reality, though, having at least two decent note takers is about as much as can be expected. When there are multiple note takers, substantive differences in the notes should be reconciled before the next bargaining session.

What should be recorded in bargaining notes? To the extent possible, note takers should try to capture the back-and-forth discussion on whatever is being discussed. The most important things to record in bargaining notes are:

- The intent of a provision or of particular words. What is the language intended to accomplish, and how do the words of the proposal capture that intent?

- The reason for the contract change. Why is it that one or both parties are proposing the changed contract language? Are there particular operational difficulties that the language is intended to solve? Have there been disagreements as to how the prior language should be interpreted?

- The bargaining history of the issue. Has the issue come up in bargaining before and, if so, how was it resolved?

Sign-in sheets. Along with bargaining notes, there should be two sign-in sheets circulated at the start of every bargaining session. All those in attendance on both bargaining teams record their names and signatures on the sign-in sheets, which then can be stored with bargaining notes to unravel the occasional mystery of who said what during bargaining sessions.

Putting notes and sign-in sheets in the Negotiations Binder. When negotiations are complete and a new contract has been ratified, negotiations notes and sign-in sheets should be placed in the Negotiations Binder. The sign-in sheets should be collected under a single tab; the negotiations notes should be distributed among the tabs for the articles discussed in each set of notes. If you are maintaining an electronic Negotiations Binder, the notes and sign-in sheets should be coded for retrieval.

Circulation of draft bargaining notes. Between bargaining sessions, the note-takers should circulate their draft notes to all other bargaining team members, who should review them and make suggestions for changes. In particular, the chief spokesperson should carefully review the draft notes to make sure that the notes contain the important points made in the last bargaining session.

Audio recording of negotiations sessions. It's thankfully rare, but occasionally the parties to collective bargaining will agree that bargaining sessions will be audio recorded. Usually, audio recording is the product of profound mutual distrust. There's little good that can come out of recorded bargaining sessions. Either the parties remember that the "tape is running," and their discussions are stilted. Or worse, the parties forget that the session is being recorded, and say things or use particular words that they will come to regret.

"Bargaining Intent" videos. One possible way of memorializing bargaining intent is to have the lead negotiators for each side record a video after the new contract has been ratified. On the video, the negotiators discuss each contract change and what the intent of the change was. With bargaining intent videos, there should be no controversy years down the road as to what each party really intended in adopting or altering contract language.

The Bottom Line. Good negotiations notes can make the difference between winning and losing important grievances.

Bargaining Strategy. A quick search on www.amazon.com suggests thousands of results on the topic of bargaining strategy. As one might expect, the cacophony of advice yields some occasionally disparate suggestions. However, as the following table shows, there are many common themes from the experts, not the least of which is the proposition that negotiation success is traceable to the combination of preparation and open communication.

Tip	Peter Stark, *Negotiating With Confidence*[6]	Marty Latz, *The Five Golden Rules of Negotiation*	Canadian Association of Labour Media, *Bargaining Communications*[7]	Benjamin Franklin, *Five Bargaining Tips*[8]	David Butcher, *Tips for Effective Negotiating*[9]	Miller Canfield, *Collective Bargaining Strategies and Pitfalls*[10]
1	Preparation . . . preparation . . . preparation	Information is power	Start communicating now	Be clear, in your own mind, what you're after	Separate the people from the problem	Be prepared
2	Develop options and alternatives	Maximize your leverage	Have a message	Do your homework	Focus on interests, not positions	Know the other side
3	Have a clear, positive vision of the outcome	Employ fair objective criteria	Tailor your message to the audience	Be persistent. Your first job is to start the other person thinking	Invent options for mutual gain	Have the data to support your positions
4	Hold your counterpart accountable	Design an offer-concession strategy	Don't make it all about you. The best way to get someone's attention quickly is to talk about them	Make friends with the person with which you are bargaining	Insist on using objective criteria	Provide information to the other side
5	Trust your gut	Control the agenda	Keep it simple	Keep your sense of humor		Provide accurate information
6			Contrast and respond			Don't allow the other side to stall
7			Deliver the right message to the right people at the right time			
8			Research			

The Process Of Contract Ratification.

Each party has the duty to recommend that their constituents ratify tentative agreements. To be sure, there are times when one party or the other refuses to recommend a tentative agreement, and instead insists on making no recommendation on the settlement to its constituents. Why the other party would agree to such a process is a bit of a mystery, since "no recommendation" settlements are much more often doomed to failure.

Usually, unions ratify contracts before the proposed settlement is approved by the employer's governing body. There are many reasons for this, but the most important is that the process used by governmental bodies for ratification – scheduling a public meeting, drafting the ratification ordinance, and perhaps multiple hearings on the ordinance – is more cumbersome than that used by unions.

When unions go about the ratification process, they face an immediate conundrum: Who should vote on the contract ratification? Should voting be limited to those who attend a ratification meeting and are actually educated in the details of the settlement, or should the entire membership be allowed to vote? From the standpoint of one who has bargained many labor contracts, attendance at a ratification meeting should be a prerequisite to voting. There is little as disheartening to negotiators as working long and hard on contract bargaining only to hear those opposing the contract make inaccurate statements about what is or isn't in the agreement.

Typically, unions will have their executive boards vote on the proposed contract before membership ratification meetings are held. The recommendation of the Board is then sent to the membership along with the proposed contract.

Unions should hold as many ratification meetings as are necessary to give the membership a reasonable opportunity to attend. For employees working day shifts such as teachers and office workers, that may mean meetings during the workweek but after the workday, during lunch hour, or on weekends. For employees performing shift work such as police officers and firefighters, that may mean meetings at various times during the day, and on different days.

During union ratification meetings, the lead negotiator for the union should review the tentative agreement line-by-line, describing the rationale for each contract change. Ratification meetings work best when negotiators make full disclosure to union members, highlighting the strengths and weaknesses of their arguments. If a state statute calls for binding arbitration, the negotiators should discuss local trends in arbitration, and review how the criteria used in arbitration (*e.g.*, cost of living, ability to pay, comparable jurisdictions) would likely be analyzed by an arbitrator.

From the employer's standpoint, the ratification process usually begins with the preparation of an informational memorandum from the lead negotiator or the head of the employer's labor relations office to the governing body. The memorandum should discuss each of the significant contract changes and should contain an overall summary of why the contract is being recommended for ratification. The summary should discuss how the settlement fits within any pre-determined parameters for total compensation adjustments that may have been established in the past by the governing body.

Most public bodies adopt contract settlements through the passage of an ordinance; others do so through voting on a resolution. Because both of these processes require formal governmental action, state open meetings law almost inevitably decree that the media be allowed to be in attendance during the governmental body's discussion of the settlement. Typically, the governmental body is able to label the meeting an executive session, which allows it to forbid the media from actually reporting on the discussions at the meeting.

Relationship With Other Labor Organizations.

Public sector labor negotiations rarely occur in a labor relations vacuum. Employers usually negotiate with multiple unions. School systems bargain with teacher and classified employee unions. Cities, counties, and states bargain with law enforcement, fire, general employee, and other unions. The wage and benefit structure in those labor relationships can influence bargaining results with other unions.

Parity or "Me-Too" Clauses. The greatest external influence comes when one or more unions have parity or me-too clauses in their collective bargaining agreements. A parity clause ties one or more items in a union's contract to what occurs with one or more labor agreements the employer has with other unions. Here is an example of a wage parity clause:

> If the employer grants any group of bargaining unit or non-bargaining unit employees an annual wage increase in excess of the 3% annual increase provided by this agreement, the increase provided by this agreement shall be amended to conform to that higher percentage increase.[11]

Me-too clauses come with three distinct risks. First, some states find parity clauses unenforceable, believing that they wrongfully impair the bargaining rights of the other unions with which the employer bargains.[12] Second, from the employer's standpoint, me-too clauses can result in litigation unless they are carefully drafted. As one management-side law firm has cautioned:

> Notwithstanding possible assurances from your Union bargaining team that it seeks a "me-too" clause merely as insurance that the employer will play fair, a clause of this kind may present far more trouble that it is worth. You can face costly and time-consuming challenges by the Union when it inevitably seeks to enforce its rights under the clause.[13]

Third, from the union's perspective, agreeing to a me-too clause is likely to engender ill will with other labor organizations. When those organizations bargain and the topic that is the target of the me-too clause is discussed, the employer should be considering the impacts of the me-too clause. That fact inevitably will make a settlement that would trigger the me-too clause more difficult to accomplish.

Hiding Money In Settlements. Another outgrowth of an employer having multiple bargaining relationships is the tendency in the bargaining process to disguise wage increases. Without regard to me-too clauses, most employers have a preference for at least seeming to give the same wage adjustment to all unions with which they bargain. This sort of perceived equality of treatment minimizes complaints from other unions that one particular union was treated more favorably.

This tension occasionally leads to settlements disguising what would otherwise be a wage increase. Public safety contracts are particularly laden with clauses like this. For example, in Portland, Oregon, firefighters who are certified as apparatus operators receive 3.0% premium pay. That sounds like nothing more than a form of premium or specialty pay until one learns that 100% of Portland firefighters are certified as apparatus operators. Seattle's 1.5% patrol officer premium pay and Honolulu's "standard of conduct" premium (because officers are subject to the employer's disciplinary rules 24 hours a day) seem suspiciously like efforts to disguise wage increases.

Joint Negotiations. At times, either an employer or a union may be interested in joint bargaining. Usually, joint bargaining is focused on one or two issues, often health insurance and/or wages. Because different unions typically have a variety of interests, joint bargaining rarely occurs, and the process is rife with the opportunity for one or more unions to withdraw because the bargaining is not going the way they would like.

NOTES

[1] http://www.chinesenegotiation.com/2009/04/negotiating-in-china-getting-to-know-the-real-you/.

[2] *District of Columbia Metropolitan Police Department*, 2014 WL 7793687 (D.C. PERB 2014).

[3] *State of Connecticut*, 2008 WL 4095793 (Conn. Bd. Lab. Rel. 2008).

[4] http://www.njsba.org/press_releases/gloss.pdf.

[5] C. Snow, *Contract Interpretation: The Plain Meaning Rule in Arbitration*, 55 Fordham L. Rev. 681 (1987).

[6] http://www.peterstark.com/negotiating-with-confidence/.

[7] http://calm.ca/blog/jessica-bell/bargaining-communications-eight-tips-effective-message.

[8] http://www.1000advices.com/guru/people_skills_negotiating_tips_bf.html.

[9] http://news.thomasnet.com/imt/2010/04/13/tips-for-effective-negotiating-getting-to-yes-method.

[10] http://www.millercanfield.com/resources-274.html.

[11] http://www.lawmemo.com/arb/award/2005/133.htm.

[12] *Plainedge Fed'n of Teachers*, 31 PERB ¶ 3015 (N.Y. PERB 1998).

[13] http://www.vedderprice.com/docs/pub/8a5a924c-fd78-4472-9b48-2818cc0b9deb_document.pdf.

CHAPTER 11

UNFAIR LABOR PRACTICES DURING BARGAINING

During the bargaining process, there are times when one party engages in conduct that amounts to an unfair labor practice. This chapter describes the most-common mid-bargaining unfair labor practices as well as the remedies typically ordered when an unfair labor practice has occurred.

Unfair labor practices are usually described at least in general terms by the collective bargaining statute or ordinance under which the parties negotiate. Section 4117.11 of the Ohio Revised Code contains a fairly representative list of prohibited practices. The statute starts with how an employer can commit an unfair labor practice:

(A) It is an unfair labor practice for a public employer, its agents, or representatives to:

(1) Interfere with, restrain, or coerce employees in the exercise of the rights guaranteed in Chapter 4117 of the Revised Code or an employee organization in the selection of its representative for the purposes of collective bargaining or the adjustment of grievances;

(2) Initiate, create, dominate, or interfere with the formation or administration of any employee organization, or contribute financial or other support to it; except that a public employer may permit employees to confer with it during working hours without loss of time or pay, permit the exclusive representative to use the facilities of the public employer for membership or other meetings, or permit the exclusive representative to use the internal mail system or other internal communications system;

(3) Discriminate in regard to hire or tenure of employment or any term or condition of employment on the basis of the exercise of rights guaranteed by Chapter 4117 of the Revised Code. Nothing precludes any employer from making and enforcing an agreement pursuant to division (C) of section 4117.09 of the Revised Code;

(4) Discharge or otherwise discriminate against an employee because he has filed charges or given testimony under Chapter 4117 of the Revised Code;

(5) Refuse to bargain collectively with the representative of his employees recognized as the exclusive representative or certified pursuant to Chapter 4117 of the Revised Code;

(6) Establish a pattern or practice of repeated failures to timely process grievances and requests for arbitration of grievances;

(7) Lock out or otherwise prevent employees from performing their regularly assigned duties where an object thereof is to bring pressure on the employees or an employee organization to compromise or capitulate to the employer's terms regarding a labor relations dispute;

(8) Cause or attempt to cause an employee organization, its agents, or representatives to violate division (B) of this section.

The Ohio statute continues with a somewhat analogous list of how a labor organization can commit an unfair labor practice:

(B) It is an unfair labor practice for an employee organization, its agents, or representatives, or public employees to:

(1) Restrain or coerce employees in the exercise of the rights guaranteed in Chapter 4117 of the Revised Code. This division does not impair the right of an employee organization to prescribe its own rules with respect to the acquisition or retention of membership therein, or an employer in the selection of his representative for the purpose of collective bargaining or the adjustment of grievances;

(2) Cause or attempt to cause an employer to violate division (A) of this section;

(3) Refuse to bargain collectively with a public employer if the employee organization is recognized as the exclusive representative or certified as the exclusive representative of public employees in a bargaining unit;

(4) Call, institute, maintain, or conduct a boycott against any public employer, or picket any place of business of a public employer, on account of any jurisdictional work dispute;

(5) Induce or encourage any individual employed by any person to engage in a strike in violation of Chapter 4117 of the Revised Code or refusal to handle goods or perform services; or threaten, coerce, or restrain any person where an object thereof is to force or require any public employee to cease dealing or doing business with any other person, or force or require a public employer to recognize for representation purposes an employee organization not certified by the state employment relations board;

(6) Fail to fairly represent all public employees in a bargaining unit;

(7) Induce or encourage any individual in connection with a labor relations dispute to picket the residence or any place of private employment of any public official or representative of the public employer;

(8) Engage in any picketing, striking, or other concerted refusal to work without giving written notice to the public employer and to the state employment relations board not less than ten days prior to the action. The notice shall state the date and time that the action will commence and, once the notice is given, the parties may extend it by the written agreement of both.

The most common mid-bargaining unfair labor practices involve bad-faith bargaining, regressive bargaining, and unilateral alterations of the *status quo*. Some bargaining unfair labor practices are considered *per se* violations in that no proof is necessary of an intent to violate the law. With a *per se* violation, the only question is whether an event happened, not what the motivation for the event might be.[1] Other bargaining unfair labor practices are judged on a "totality of the circumstances" basis, where a labor board focuses on the subjective intent of the parties.[2] Included in the totality of the circumstances rubric are factors such as the parties' bargaining history, the past practices between them, whether dilatory tactics were used, the contents of proposals, the behavior of the parties' negotiators, the nature and number of agreements made, whether there was a failure to explain a bargaining position.[3]

Bad-Faith Bargaining.

Usually, the terms "good-faith bargaining" and "bad-faith bargaining" are not defined by a collective bargaining statute, and are left up to decisional law for whatever labor board administers the statute. A few states, however, do provide at least the start of a definition of good-faith bargaining. Florida, for example, defines good-faith bargaining as:

> [T]he willingness of both parties to meet at reasonable times and places, as mutually agreed upon, in order to discuss issues which are proper subjects of bargaining, with the intent of reaching a common accord. It shall include an obligation for both parties to participate actively in the negotiations with an open mind and a sincere desire, as well as making a sincere effort, to resolve differences and come to an agreement. In determining whether a party failed to bargain in good faith, the commission shall consider the total conduct of the parties during negotiations as well as the specific incidents of alleged bad faith. Incidents indicative of bad faith shall include, but not be limited to, the following occurrences:
>
> (a) Failure to meet at reasonable times and places with representatives of the other party for the purpose of negotiations.
>
> (b) Placing unreasonable restrictions on the other party as a prerequisite to meeting.
>
> (c) Failure to discuss negotiable issues.
>
> (d) Refusing, upon reasonable written request, to provide public information, excluding work products as defined in § 447.605.
>
> (e) Refusing to negotiate because of an unwanted person on the opposing negotiating team.
>
> (f) Negotiating directly with employees rather than with their certified bargaining agent.
>
> (g) Refusing to reduce a total agreement to writing.[4]

As one labor board put it, good-faith or bad-faith bargaining "is a state of mind."[5] Conduct that might well in one context amount to bad-faith bargaining – for example, repudiating a tentative agreement – may not do so under different circumstances. The underlying notion is that the duty to bargain requires a party to participate in bargaining with the intention of reaching agreement.[6] Good-faith bargaining is judged by considering the bargaining as a whole, evaluating the party's conduct over the entire course of bargaining.[7]

The obligation to bargain in good faith does not require either party to make a concession on any particular issue nor to adopt a particular position.[8] Nor does the obligation usually include the requirement that a proposal be reasonable. As the following passage from a decision by Florida's Public Employment Relations Commission indicates, labor boards are reluctant to review the actual substance of proposals for reasonableness:

> Substantive proposals are rarely, if ever, sufficient to warrant an inference of bad-faith bargaining. If the Commission were to consider as evidence of bad faith every proposal made by one party that the other party believed excessive or unreasonable, collective bargaining in the State of Florida would come to a halt while parties filed bad-faith bargaining charges with the Commission. Thus, the unions' economic proposals that the City believes "preposterous" do not provide evidence of their failure to bargain in good faith.[9]

This is not to say that a labor board will never base an unfair labor practice finding on the substance of a proposal. There are times when a proposal can be so extreme that the proposal, in and of itself, establishes bad-faith bargaining. For example, in a Michigan case a city manager made the following bargaining proposals to an electrician's union: (1) That he be the final arbiter on all grievances; (2) that the union employees be at will and not just cause employees; (3) that the employer reserve the right to replace union employees with part-time non-union employees; and (4) that the employer be able to subcontract all bargaining unit work without restrictions. Michigan's Employment Relations Commission found the proposals to be bad-faith bargaining, concluding that the proposals were "far outside the norm in public sector labor law and [were] intended to avoid reaching a contract. A contract based on such terms would be tantamount to no contract at all…[The city's manager's] demand that he be the final decision maker on all grievances, rather than a neutral arbitrator, is evidence of an unwillingness to bargain in good faith. His general bargaining stance, in essence, was that he have unfettered discretion to make all final decisions regarding any labor disputes."[10]

The following are examples of conduct which might cause a labor board to find that bad-faith bargaining has occurred:

Attitude Entering Negotiations. If a party comes to the bargaining table with a "take-it-or-leave-it" attitude, it is a strong indication of bad-faith bargaining.[11]

Authority of Negotiators. A negotiator's lack of authority which delays and/or thwarts the bargaining process amounts to bad faith bargaining.[12] The matter of negotiator authority is usually a dicey one for labor boards, since final bargaining decisions are made by constituents (a governing body on one hand and the union's membership on the other) rather than negotiators themselves.[13] However, a decision of the Illinois Labor Relations Board illustrates the minimum amount of authority negotiators must possess:

> Good-faith bargaining requires that an individual negotiating on behalf of a principal be vested with authority to participate in effective collective bargaining. Further, the negotiators a party sends to bargaining sessions must generally be able to speak for that party if meaningful bargaining is to take place. [Here,] the Union's attorney stated that the Union would not tentatively agree to "any item" until she could review it. [The attorney] was not present during the parties' first six bargaining sessions, so it generally follows that, at least during those sessions, the Union's representatives could not have tentatively agreed to any of the District's proposals. With very few minor exceptions, that arrangement has evidently borne awkward, inefficient results, including at least

one noteworthy instance in which the Union's bargaining team could not even tentatively agree to one of the Union's own proposals at the bargaining table. In the absence of a compelling explanation, that sort of outcome can be taken as an indication of a lack of proper intent and good faith in collective bargaining. A negotiating party must treat bargaining sessions as something more than an exchange of ideas.[14]

Conditions. A party that imposes pre-conditions on its willingness either to negotiate or reach agreement may well be bargaining in bad faith. Impermissible conditions include:

- Conditioning agreement on economic matters upon prior agreement on non-economic subjects.[15]

- Conditioning a willingness to bargain on the other party's agreement to a non-mandatory topic such as the composition of the other party's bargaining team.[16]

- Conditioning a willingness to agree to a settlement until another employer reaches a settlement of its own bargaining.[17]

Delay. Delaying tactics, recalcitrance in the scheduling of meetings, canceling meetings, or failing to prepare for meetings all are suggestive of bad-faith bargaining.[18]

Ground Rules. Ground rules themselves are typically not mandatory subjects of bargaining.[19] Hence, insistence on ground rules before negotiating substantive issues suggests bad-faith bargaining.[20]

Negotiators. An employer engages in bad-faith bargaining if it selects as a negotiating team member an individual who is a member of the union's bargaining unit.[21]

Proposals. Failing to make counter-proposals,[22] failing to substantiate demands for substantial contract changes,[23] or making proposals late in the bargaining process[24] are evidence of bad-faith bargaining.

Tentative Agreements. Reneging on tentative agreements, like other forms of regressive bargaining (see discussion below), is usually proof of bad-faith bargaining.[25]

Unfair Labor Practices Outside of Bargaining. If a party commits separate unfair labor practices at or away from the bargaining table, it is evidence that the party is not bargaining in good faith.[26]

In most cases, it takes a lot for a labor board to conclude that bad-faith bargaining has occurred. Boards ask whether conduct is clearly illustrative of a desire to frustrate the process rather than to reach an agreement. For example, in one case a labor board found no bad-faith bargaining even where the employer canceled five bargaining sessions, reneged on a tentative agreement concerning a safety requirement, and withdrew salary proposals.[27]

A common form of bad-faith bargaining is referred to as "surface bargaining." Surface bargaining is where a party "goes through the motions of negotiations, but in fact is weaving otherwise unobjectionable conduct into an entangling fabric to delay or prevent agreement."[28] Labor boards often have to draw a line between surface bargaining and what they describe as "hard bargaining," which is not illegal. As put by Nebraska's Commission on Industrial Relations, "good-faith bargaining may be quite hard and still lawful."[29] The key question is one of intent. In a case involving a bad-faith bargaining charge against an employer, the NLRB phrased the analysis as follows: "From the context of an employer's total conduct, it must be decided whether the employer is lawfully engaging in hard bargaining to achieve a contract that it considers desirable or is unlawfully endeavoring to frustrate the possibility of arriving at any agreement."[30]

Regressive Bargaining.

Regressive bargaining occurs when a party does something to make a proposal or an agreement less attractive than it was.[31] Most commonly, regressive bargaining occurs when a party makes a new proposal that moves farther away from (rather than closer to) an agreement on an issue. It is also regressive bargaining for a party to escalate its demands on the way to interest arbitration.[32] Regressive bargaining can also occur when a party makes no effort to seek ratification of tentative agreements[33] or repudiates written or oral agreements made during bargaining.[34]

Usually, regressive bargaining is not, in and of itself, a *per se* unfair labor practice.[35] Instead, regressive bargaining is simply one of several indicators (albeit a very strong one) that a party is not bargaining in good faith.[36]

Under rare circumstances, a labor board will conclude that regressive proposals do not amount to bad-faith bargaining. For example, if a regressive position is the result of substantially changed economic circumstances or a novel decision rendered by a court or labor board, it will not necessarily result in a sustained unfair labor practice complaint.[37] Also, as the Massachusetts Labor Commission has held, the passage of time alone may in some circumstances explain a position that would otherwise seem regressive:

> Although it is undisputed that the Town adjusted its original total compensation offer to bargaining unit members during the January 10, 2005 negotiating session, this adjustment, in content, does not constitute regressive bargaining. Rather, the adjustment to the proposed compensation figure reflects the passage in time between the date the Town first made the offer in November of 2004 and January 10, 2005. The change reflects the expectation that the lapse of time reduced the number of snow and ice accumulations the Town would have to address.[38]

Changing The *Status Quo* During Bargaining.

One of the few *per se* unfair labor practices – where a labor board will not consider the totality of the bargaining process but instead will focus simply on whether particular conduct occurred – is where an employer unilaterally changes mandatory subjects of bargaining while negotiations are ongoing.[39] The topics that are mandatory for bargaining are discussed at length in Chapter 2 of this book. An employer's unilateral changes in mandatory subjects of bargaining are considered *per se* unfair labor practices if the union shows the following: (1) The employer took action to breach, change, or alter policy in the parties' written agreement or past practice; (2) the action was taken before the employer notified the exclusive representative and gave it an opportunity to request negotiations or bargain; (3) the change was not merely an isolated breach of the contract or practice, but amounted to a change of policy having a generalized effect or continuing impact upon terms and conditions of employment of bargaining unit members; and (4) the change in policy concerned a mandatory subject of bargaining.[40]

The obligation to maintain the *status quo* applies even after a contract has expired and before a successor agreement has been negotiated. It also applies to prohibit an employer from implementing tentative agreements before the entire contract is settled.[41]

Washington's Public Employment Relations Commission explained the purpose behind the *status quo* rule: "During contract negotiations, substantial changes to the terms and working conditions of employees without first bargaining to a lawful impasse has a detrimental effect on the terms and conditions of employment. This is true even where isolated instances of change occur because alterations of the *status quo* tend to create confusion and uncertainty regarding the floor for bargaining."[42]

In some states, there are some modest exceptions to the *status quo* rule. First, a change is permitted if both parties have specifically and unconditionally agreed to the pre-ratification implementation of the change.[43] Second, a change may be permitted in "extreme" situations where a party could engage in "unlawful abusive delay" of the interest arbitration process so as to prolong a beneficial *status quo*.[44] Lastly, at least from a theoretical standpoint, a unilateral change could be necessary owing to conditions beyond the employer's control, such as a change in external law.[45]

One area of frequent debate is how the *status quo* rule applies to wage adjustments after a contract expires. Labor boards agree that except in the most extraordinary of situations, the fact that an employer has provided across-the-board wage increases in the past, whether tied to the cost of living or not, does not obligate (or even allow) it to do so after a contract expires.[46] Step increases are another matter. Step increases involve another aspect of the *status quo* rule, one which recognizes the obligation for an employer to maintain the dynamic *status quo*. A basic explanation of the dynamic *status quo* is as follows:

> The "dynamic *status quo*" rule recognizes occasional circumstances when the *status quo* may not be static. For example, where a term of employment includes step increases for which employees qualify by length of service, a refusal to grant those step increases during bargaining is unlawful because payment of earned step increases is a term of the employment relationship and is the *status quo*.[47]

Most labor boards follow the dynamic *status quo* rule and require the continuation of step increases after the expiration of a contract.[48] A minority of states do not follow this rule, and find no obligation to grant step increases until a new contract is negotiated.[49]

Interest Arbitration Unfair Labor Practices.

Two other *per se* unfair labor practices relate to the interest arbitration process. One occurs when either party fails to comply with the terms of an interest arbitration decision.[50] The other *per se* unfair labor practice is when a party refers a non-mandatory subject of bargaining to interest arbitration.[51] If that occurs, the opposing party must immediately object to the consideration of the subject in arbitration or risk a ruling that it has waived the objection.[52]

Other *Per Se* Bargaining Unfair Labor Practices.

There are an assortment of other bargaining unfair labor practices that, depending upon state laws, may or may not be considered *per se* violations of the law. California's Public Employment Relations Board has provided this list of what it considers to be *per se* violations:

- Insisting on proposals that would require a union to forfeit its role as exclusive bargaining representative.[53]

- Refusing to provide necessary and relevant information upon request.[54]

- Refusing outright to meet or negotiate regarding a mandatory subject of bargaining.[55]

- Bypassing the representative and dealing directly with employees over negotiable matters.[56]

- Attempting to dictate who may serve as the opposing party's representative in negotiations.[57]

- Making post-impasse unilateral changes to subjects of bargaining not previously discussed or included in the employer's final offer.[58]

- Insisting to impasse on and/or imposing non-mandatory subjects of bargaining.[59]

- Insisting to impasse and/or imposing proposals whose provisions waive or limit the statutory rights of the representative and/or employees.[60]

- Imposing proposals to retain unfettered discretion over key subjects of bargaining, regardless of good-faith negotiations, where such implementation would be inherently destructive of collective bargaining.[61]

Direct Dealing.

The United States Supreme Court has long held that it is an unfair labor practice for an employer to bypass a union and deal directly with a represented employee concerning mandatory subjects of bargaining, such as wages and other terms and conditions of employment.[62] Courts have found that "direct dealing" is "inherently divisive" and has the effect of "undermining the authority of the…bargaining representatives."[63] Direct dealing exists where (1) the employer communicates with represented employees; (2) the purpose of the communication is either to establish a change to a mandatory subject of bargaining or to undercut the bargaining agent's role in negotiations; and (3) the communications are made without notice or to the exclusion of the bargaining agent.[64]

Direct dealing occurs in a wide variety of contexts in the public sector. In some cases, the direct dealing takes the form of the employer communicating directly with bargaining unit members or the union communicating directly with elected officials about the status of bargaining.[65] In other situations, a direct dealing violation results from the employer reaching an agreement with bargaining unit members. In each of the following cases, agreements between the employer and bargaining unit members were held invalid because of the prohibition on direct dealing:

- Negotiating directly with an employee for a grievance settlement after the union has accepted the grievance.[66]
- Requiring employees to sign financial statements that the wages listed on their pay statements were in accordance with a tentative agreement.[67]
- Entering into a "last chance" agreement with a bargaining unit member facing discipline.[68]
- Speaking directly with an injured employee about a reduced schedule after his anticipated return to work.[69]
- Forwarding a new drug and alcohol policy to employees and requesting their input.[70]
- Awarding signing bonuses to new employees.[71]
- Reaching agreements with employees as to new anniversary dates that would result in adjusted pay steps.[72]
- Entering into agreements with new employees that they would repay the costs of training if they left work for the employer.[73]
- Setting up a sick leave bank program.[74]
- Contacting laid-off employees to see if they were willing to take a pay cut if they were returned to work.[75]

Blocking Charges.

The usual use of the phrase "blocking charge" refers to a particular type of unfair labor practice charge filed while representation proceedings are ongoing (elections to decide which union should represent employees, or if any union should). The idea is that to preserve the "laboratory conditions" for a representation election, unfair labor practice proceedings should be resolved prior to holding the election.[76]

From time to time, parties to negotiations argue that the filing of an unfair labor practice charge should block the next stage in the bargaining process. The usual factual setting involves one party claiming that the other side is attempting to refer to interest arbitration a non-mandatory subject of bargaining, and is asking a labor board to block the interest arbitration hearing prior to resolution of the unfair labor practice.

Rules vary from state to state, but it would be an extraordinary result to see a labor board block an interest arbitration because an unfair labor practice complaint has been filed. Labor boards are clearly concerned with the possible misuse of the blocking charge option. Oregon's Employment Relations Board has noted that "we will not automatically stay an interest arbitration proceeding every time a party files a charge that raises scope of bargaining questions. We also note the potential for abuse if we were to give a party the power to unilaterally require the last-minute cancellation of a scheduled hearing by simply filing a complaint."[77] Wisconsin's Employment Relations Commission has pointed out that under a blocking charge approach, "any party interested in delaying the arbitration proceedings would have an unfettered opportunity to do so by simply filing a bad faith bargaining complaint and alleging that arbitration cannot proceed because impasse cannot be found until the allegations are resolved. Such a result would be at odds with that portion of state law that declares it to be the public policy of the State of Wisconsin that fair, speedy, effective procedures be available for resolution of labor disputes."[78] Washington's Public Employment Relations Commission allows blocking charges, but the only thing blocked from interest arbitration is the particular proposal claimed to be non-mandatory for bargaining.[79]

Remedies For Bargaining Unfair Labor Practices.

Where an unfair labor practice has occurred, a labor board has broad authority to craft remedies that will effectuate the purposes of the bargaining law. As a general proposition, "a properly designed remedial order seeks a restoration of the situation as nearly as possible to that which would have been obtained but for the unfair labor practice."[80] The most commonly-awarded remedies include the following:

Cease and Desist Orders. Cease and desist orders come in two forms. One version of a cease and desist order requires a party to stop doing something; for example, the order could require a party to stop making "end runs" around the other party's bargaining team, or could require an employer to stop threatening employees in retaliation for the exercise of bargaining rights.[81] The second form of cease and desist order deals with a party who has violated the law by not doing something, and therefore would require the offending party to affirmatively do something. For example, the order could require a party to cease and desist from refusing to sign a collective bargaining agreement.[82]

Posting. Many labor board decisions finding that an unfair labor practice was committed require the "guilty" party to post a notice that it committed the unfair labor practice and pledging not to do so again in the future. The purpose of posting is in one sense a public shaming – the notion that the public admission of committing an unfair labor practice will encourage compliance in the future.[83] Another purpose is more union-specific in that posting will "inform bargaining unit members of the employer's wrongdoing, and to assure bargaining unit members that they may engage in protected activity without fear of retaliation."[84] Increasingly, labor boards are requiring that posting be accomplished by email or through the employer's intranet.[85]

Restoration of the *Status Quo*. An employer that wrongfully implemented changes in mandatory subjects of bargaining will almost always be required to restore the *status quo* to the conditions before the change, and to make employees whole for all lost wages and benefits. The restoration of the *status quo* typically requires the payment of interest if employees suffered economic harm.[86] The obligation to restore the *status quo* can also include a requirement that the employer identify any negative impacts on wages, hours, and working conditions that may have resulted from the change in the mandatory subject of bargaining.[87]

Reinstatement of Withdrawn or Modified Proposals. If a party has wrongfully withdrawn or modified a proposal, a labor board has the authority to order the party to reinstate its proposal.[88]

Confirmation of Tentative Agreements. A labor board has the authority to compel a party to confirm a tentative agreement the party has tried to abrogate.[89]

Withdrawal of Proposals. If a party makes an illegal proposal, a labor board can require the withdrawal of the proposal.[90]

Rescission of an Implemented Final Offer. If an employer in a meet-and-confer setting wrongfully implements its final offer, a labor board is likely to order that the imposed offer be rescinded, and that employees be made whole for lost wages and benefits.[91]

Compliance With an Interest Arbitrator's Decision. If an employer fails to comply with an interest arbitration decision, a labor board may not only order that the decision be implemented, but can also award back pay and benefits for bargaining unit members affected by the non-compliance.[92]

Attorney Fees and Litigation Costs. In some states, the party losing an unfair labor practice complaint is required to pay the other party's attorney fees and litigation costs.[93]

NOTES

[1] *Fresno County In-Home Supportive Services Public Authority*, 39 PERC ¶ 133 (Cal. PERB 2015).

[2] *Muroc Unified School District,* Decision No. 80 (Cal. PERB 1978).

[3] *Carroll County Circuit Court Clerk*, 31 PERI ¶ 122 (Ill. LRB Gen. Coun. 2015); *Medford School District*, Case No. UP-77-11 (Or. ERB 2013).

[4] Section 447.203(17), Florida Statutes.

[5] *Clay County*, Order No. 13U-259 (Fla. PERC 2013).

[6] *State of Illinois*, No. S-CA-12-094 (Ill. LRB State Panel 2013).

[7] *Teamsters Local Union 444 v. Pasco County Board of County Commissioners*, 12 FPER ¶ 17041 at 68-71 (1985), *affirmed*, 505 So.2d 541 (Fla. 1st DCA 1987).

[8] *Laborers Local 996 and County of Woodford*, 8 PERI ¶ 2019 (Ill. SLRB 1992), *quoting Atlanta Hilton & Tower*, 271 NLRB 1600 (1984); *Jackson City School District Board of Education*, 32 OPER ¶ 92 (Ohio SERB 2014).

[9] *City of Winter Park*, 38 Florida Pub. Employee Rep. ¶ 360 (Fla. PERC 2010).

[10] *City of Lowell*, 28 MPER ¶ 62 (Mich. ERC 2015).

[11] *General Electric Co.*, 150 NLRB 192 [57 LRRM 1491], *enf.* 418 F.2d 736 (1964).

[12] *Stockton Unified School District*, Decision No. 143 (Cal. PERB 1980); *Lake County Circuit Clerk*, 29 Pub. Employee Rep. for Illinois ¶ 179 (Ill. LRB 2013).

[13] *Lackawanna County*, 45 PPER ¶ 18 (Pa. LRB 2013).

[14] *Tri-State Fire Protection District*, 31 PERI ¶ 78 (Ill. LRB 2014).

[15] *State of California (Department of Personnel Administration)*, PERB Decision No. 1249-S (1988).

[16] *Northern Cambria School Dist.*, 3 PPER ¶ 318 (Pa. LRB 1973).

[17] *Philadelphia Parking Authority*, 44 PPER ¶ 101 (Pa. LRB ALJ 2013).

[18] *Oakland Unified School District,* PERB Decision No. 326 (Cal. PERB 1983); *Lake County Circuit Clerk*, 29 Pub. Employee Rep. for Illinois ¶ 179 (Ill. LRB 2013).

[19] *Skagit County*, Decision 6348-A (Wash. PERC 1998).

[20] *San Ysidro School District*, Decision No. 134 (Cal. PERB 1980); *Washington County*, 2014 WL 3339216 (Or. ERB 2014).

[21] *Reading School District*, 44 PPER ¶ 108 (Pa. LRB 2013).

[22] *Oakland Community College*, 15 MPER ¶ 33,066 (Mich. ERC 2001); *Homer-Center School District*, 12 PPER ¶ 12169 (Pa. LRB 1981).

[23] *Town of North Kingston*, 2013 WL 5755149 (R.I. LRB 2013).

[24] *Carlisle School District*, 24 PPER ¶ 24168 (Pa. LRB 1993).

[25] *Charter Oak Unified School District*, PERB Decision No. 873 (Cal. PERB 1991); *Lee County*, 41 Florida Pub. Employee Rep. ¶ 342 (Fla. PERC 2015).

[26] *Beaumont Unified School District,* No. 429 (Cal. PERB 1984).

[27] *County of Riverside*, PERB No. 1715-M (Cal. PERB 2004).

28 *Muroc Unified School District*, PERB No. 80 (Cal. PERB 1978).

29 *County of Hall*, 2006 WL 5585903 (Neb. Cir. 2006).

30 *Atlanta Hilton & Tower*, 271 NLRB 1600 (1984).

31 *City of Redmond*, Decision 8863-A (Wash. PERC 2006).

32 *City of Norman*, Case No. 00421 (Okla. PERB 2006); *City of Clarkston*, Decision 3246 (Wash. PERC 1989).

33 *Seattle School District*, Decision 10037 (Wash. PERC 2008).

34 *County of Lee*, 31 Pub. Employee Rep. for Illinois ¶ 42 (Ill. LRB 2014); *Granite City Community School District No. 5*, No. 2002-CA-0014-S (Ill. LRB ALJ 2003).

35 *Chicago Local No 458-3M v. NLRB*, 206 F.3d 22 (2d Cir 2000)(NLRB precedent establishes the proposition that "regressive bargaining is not so harmful to the collective bargaining process as to require a general prohibition").

36 *County of Hall*, 2006 WL 5585903 (Neb. Cir. 2006); *City of Dallas*, Case No. UP-33-08 (Or. ERB 2009).

37 *City of Winter Park*, 38 Florida Pub. Employee Rep. ¶ 360 (Fla. PERC 2012); *City of Lawton*, 2010 WL 3939678 (Okla. PERB 2010).

38 *Town of Plymouth*, Case No. MUP-05-4391 (Mass. LRC 2006); *see Mead Corp. v. NLRB*, 697 F.2d 1013 (11th Cir. 1983).

39 *NLRB v. Katz*, 369 U.S. 736 (1962); *Dallas Police Employees Association v. City of Dallas*, Case No. UP-33-08, 23 PECBR 365, 378 n 7 (Or. ERB 2009).

40 *Natomas Unified School District*, 9 Pub. Employee Rep. for California ¶ 131 (Cal. PERB ALJ 2015).

41 *City of Princeton*, Decision No. 31041-B (Wis. ERC 2005).

42 *Asotin County*, Decision 9549-A (Wash. PERC 2007).

43 *City of Princeton*, Decision No. 31041-A (Wash. ERC 2005).

44 *Greene County*, No. 20030-D (Wis. ERC ALJ 1983).

45 *City of Brookfield*, 11406-A (Wis. ERC ALJ 2004).

46 *Chester Township*, 9 OPER ¶ 1341 (Ohio SERB ALJ 1992).

47 *Snohomish County*, Decision 1868 (Wash. PERC 1984).

48 *See, e.g., Ventura County Star-Free Press*, 279 NLRB No. 64 (NLRB 1986); *Regents of the University of California*, 22 PERC ¶ 29063 (Cal. PERB 1998); *City of Peoria*, 3 PERI ¶ 2025 (Ill. SLRB 1997); *New Horizons Community Charter School Board of Trustees*, 31 NJPER ¶ 149 (N.J. PERC 2005); *Snohomish County*, Decision 1868 (Wash. PERC 1984).

49 *State of Maine*, Case Nos. 03-13 and 04-03 (Me. LRB 2004).

50 *City of Long Beach*, 47 PERB ¶ 4591 (N.Y. PERB ALJ 2014).

51 *Washington State Ferries*, 2014 WL 4187470 (Wash. PERC 2014).

52 *Springfield Police Association v. City of Springfield*, Case Nos. UP-17/20-97, 17 PECBR 260 276-277, on *reconsideration* 17 PECBR 319 and 17 PECBR 368 (Or. ERB 1997).

53 *Kern High Faculty Assn. v. Kern High School*, 20 PERC ¶ 27007 (Cal. PERB 1995).

[54] *Stockton Unified School District*, Decision No. 143 (Cal. PERB 1980).

[55] *Dublin Professional Fire Fighters v. Valley Community Services Dist.*, 45 Cal. App. 3d 116 (1975).

[56] *City of San Diego (Office of the City Attorney)*, Decision No. 2103-M (Cal. PERB 2010).

[57] *Yolo County Superintendent of Schools*, Decision No. 838 (Cal. PERB 1990).

[58] *Lou's Produce*, 308 NLRB 1194, *enforced* 21 F.3d 1114 (9th Cir. 1994).

[59] *Chula Vista City School District*, Decision No. 834 (Cal. PERB 1990).

[60] *Rowland Unified School District*, Decision No. 1053 (Cal. PERB 1994).

[61] *Anderson Enterprises*, 329 NLRB 760 (1999).

[62] *J.I. Case Co. v. NLRB*, 321 U.S. 332 (1944); *Medo Photo Supply Corp. v. NLRB*, 321 U.S. 678 (1944).

[63] *NLRB v. General Electric Company*, 418 F.2d 736 (2d Cir. 1969).

[64] *Las Vegas Firefighters Local 1285 v. City of Las Vegas*, Item No. 786. EMRB Case No. A1-046074 (Nev. EMRB 2013).

[65] *Vandalia-Butler City School Dist. Bd. of Ed. v. SERB*, 1991 SERB 4-81 (Ohio SERB 1991).

[66] *Board of Education*, Case No. CE-05-551 (Haw. LRB 2004).

[67] *Village of Bath*, 45 PERB ¶ 3037 (N.Y. PERB 2012).

[68] *Washington State Patrol*, Decision 4757-A (Wash. PERC 1995).

[69] *City of Lowell*, 28 MLC 157, MUP-2478 (Mass. LRC 2001).

[70] *Findlay City School District Board of Education*, 5 OPER ¶ 5049 (Ohio SERB 1987).

[71] *City of Grosse Pointe Park*, 14 MPER ¶ 32051 (Mich. ERC 2001).

[72] *City of Fort Walton Beach*, 11 FPER ¶ 16240 (Fla. PERC 1985).

[73] *Town of Ludlow*, Case No. MUP-2422 (Mass. LRC 2002); *City of Pasco*, Decision 4197-A (Wash. PERC 1994).

[74] *Springfield School District*, 2005 WL 6711666 (Pa. 2005).

[75] *Frick, Vass, & Street Inc. and International Brotherhood of Painters*, 270 NLRB 459 (1984).

[76] *Community College District 13*, Decision 8118 (Wash. PERC 2003).

[77] *Benton County*, Case No. UP-36-02 (Or. ERB 2004).

[78] *Ozaukee County*, Decision No. 30561-A (Wis. ERC 2003).

[79] *Clark County*, Decision 11346 (Wash. PERC 2012).

[80] *Santa Clara Unified School District*, Decision No. 104 (Cal. PERB 1979).

[81] *City of Lowell*, 28 MPER ¶ 62 (Mich. ERC 2015).

[82] *Lee County*, 41 Florida Pub. Employee Rep. ¶ 342 (Fla. PERC 2015).

[83] *Federal Bureau of Prisons*, 67 F.L.R.A. 221 (FLRA 2014).

[84] *Gresham-Barlow School District*, Case No. UP-32-07 (Or. ERB 2009).

[85] *City of Haverhill*, Case No. MUP-13-3066 (Mass. LRC 2015).

[86] *Town of North Kingston*, 2013 WL 5755149 (R.I. LRB 2013).

[87] *Shoreline School District*, Decision 9336 (Wash. PERC 2006).

[88] *The Mead Corporation v. National Labor Relations Board*, 697 F.2d 1013 (11th Cir. 1983).

[89] *Seattle School District*, Decision 10037 (Wash. PERC 2008).

[90] *Ionia Public Schools*, 28 MPER ¶ 58 (Mich. ERC 2014).

[91] *City of San Ramon*, 39 PERC ¶ 92 (Cal. PERB ALJ 2015); *Southern Illinois University at Carbondale*, 31 PERI ¶ 98 (Ill. Educ. LRB 2014).

[92] *City of Long Beach*, 47 PERB ¶ 4591 (N.Y. PERB ALJ 2014).

[93] *Clackamas County*, Case No. UP-4-08 (Or. ERB 2010).

CHAPTER 12

INTEREST-BASED BARGAINING

Negotiation is a common experience in our lives. Depending upon our jobs and personalities, we may engage in negotiations once a week or multiple times a day. We negotiate with our children, our spouses, our employers, friends, businesses, and many others. Broadly speaking, negotiation is the process by which we discuss differences and attempt to jointly resolve them. Productive negotiations almost always involve the exchange of information, including facts and the reasons why each party desires a particular outcome.

Within the framework of public sector labor relations, there are two major negotiation styles, traditional bargaining (sometime called positional bargaining) and interest-based bargaining.

The debate over interest-based versus positional bargaining has waxed and waned several times. While there are still many interest-based bargaining advocates, the time and resources necessary for interest-based bargaining have definitely taken their toll on the use of the process. As economic times get better, it is likely that there will be a resurgence of attention on interest-based bargaining.

Definitions. If you ask an interest-based bargaining proponent to define traditional bargaining, you are likely to hear a fairly negative description. A common phrasing is that "Positional bargaining is based on fixed, opposing viewpoints (positions) and tends to result in compromise or no agreement at all. Oftentimes, compromises do not efficiently satisfy the true interests of the disputants. Instead, compromises simply split the difference between the two positions, giving each side half of what they want."[1]

A more neutral definition of traditional or positional bargaining is as follows:

> Positional bargaining is a negotiation strategy in which a series of positions, alternative solutions that meet particular interests or needs, are selected by a negotiator, ordered sequentially according to preferred outcomes and presented to another party in an effort to reach agreement. The first or opening position represents that maximum gain hoped for or expected in the negotiations. Each subsequent position demands less of an opponent and results in fewer benefits for the person advocating it. Agreement is reached when the negotiators' positions converge and they reach an acceptable settlement range.[2]

In interest-based bargaining, sometimes referred to as collaborate or integrative bargaining, the parties to the bargaining process begin by identifying their interests, desires, concerns and needs. Once these are identified, the bargaining teams consider various approaches to meeting all of their needs, and try to jointly select the option that works the best. There is an implicit notion in interest-based bargaining that the interests of the parties complement one another in that "both parties want the employer to excel at what it does."[3]

The "Bible" of interest-based bargaining is *Getting To Yes: Negotiating Agreement Without Giving In*, written by Roger Fisher and William Ury in 1991. *Getting To Yes* posits five advantages to interest-based bargaining:

1. Bargaining over positions is avoided;

2. People are separated from the problem;

3. Focus is placed on interests, not positions;

4. Options for mutual gain are invented; and

5. Objective criteria are used to select the appropriate resolution to an issue.[4]

A commonly-used example of how interest-based bargaining works involves two children and an orange. Both children want the orange. With positional bargaining, a likely solution would be to cut the orange in half. With interest-based bargaining, the children first discuss why they want the orange, and may discover that one wanted to eat the inside while the other wanted the peel to use in a cake. That discovery would produce a result that would benefit both children.

The Criticisms of Each System. Proponents of interest-based bargaining argue that the process produces better results, and that positional bargaining tends to result in compromise or no agreement. This chart sums up the view of positional bargaining held by advocates of interest-based bargaining:

Traditional Bargaining	Interest-Based Bargaining
The parties are adversaries	The parties are joint problem-solvers
Set sights on goal	Goal is prudent decision
Demand concessions	Work together to determine who gets what
Find out the exact point	Focus on the well-being/satisfaction/interests, not positions
Hoodwink, use tricks	Be open about interests
Insist on your point	Select objective criteria to take decision and go for multiple options
Apply pressure	Use reason and fair principle
Focus on success at the cost of other	Set sight on win-win solutions[5]

Proponents of positional bargaining have two arguments. First, they point to the time and expense involved in interest-based bargaining, each of which normally exceed that of positional bargaining. Second, they contend that interest-based bargaining proponents have created a fictional construct in their description of positional bargaining, and that any negotiator with any experience at all will identify interests, needs, concerns, and desires even in the most contentious positional bargaining. Using the interest-based bargaining orange as the example, positional bargaining advocates say that each child will inevitably say why it is they want the orange, and that it is overly simplistic to say that positional bargaining cannot satisfy the needs of both parties.

The Process of Positional Bargaining. The traditional bargaining process is described at length in the previous chapter. A shorthand description is that positional bargaining begins with a set of proposals, usually designed to present "best-case" scenarios for the party making the proposals. Once both sets of proposals have been exchanged and discussed, non-controversial issues are removed from the table through tentative agreements. More difficult issues may be subject to proposals and counter-proposals, usually with both parties moving closer to the other's position in the process. Eventually, remaining issues tend to be packaged into groups that usually offer something to each of the parties. If settlement is not reached, then whatever impasse resolution mechanism is in place is invoked.

The Process of Interest-Based Bargaining. The first step in the interest-based bargaining approach is the internal identification of the interests of each side. This identification is often done not just by the chief spokespersons for each side, but rather involves many members of both bargaining teams. Whoever is participating should have not only the authority to bargain, but also training in the interest-based bargaining process.

Next, a facilitator is chosen to aid in the process. The facilitator can be independently retained; if resources do not allow this, the position of facilitator can rotate between members of each bargaining team. It is the facilitator's job to coax out the parties' real interests, a process that may take many meetings as few of us readily reveal all of our interests immediately.

Interest-based bargaining then begins with a statement of the interests of each side. These statements should include not just why the needs are important to each party, but also how important they are. It is helpful at this stage to make sure both parties perceive the articulated interests in the same way, something often done by having each party verbally acknowledge and restate the interests.[6]

Whoever is facilitating the session usually records the interests or assigns another to do so. The recording is often done on large sheets of paper mounted on an easel, where the text is easily visible to all negotiators. When the session concludes, the recorded interests are transcribed and circulated, and become the basis for future discussions. At the end of each session, the parties try to agree on the topics for discussion at the next session.

The parties then move to attempting to frame the issues in a way that is non-judgmental and, if possible, presents a win/win solution. In doing so, the negotiators should look for general agreements in principle, particularly as to the interests each has expressed. At this stage, the parties begin to examine options for resolution, taking care to phrase those options in the context of the interests each has expressed. Package resolutions are discussed, and often multiple possible resolutions of the same issue are on the table at the same time. The parties look for "integrative solutions" that maximize gains and minimize losses on both of their parts. It is possible that subgroups will be created to address particular issues.

It is usually only when agreements in principle are reached that the negotiators put "pen to paper" and draft proposed contract changes. The process of reaching tentative agreements and the eventual ratification of the tentative agreements are much the same as with positional bargaining.

Is Interest-Based Bargaining For You?

The American Federation of State, County and Municipal Employees has a good checklist that helps assess whether a particular bargaining environment is ripe for interest-based bargaining:

- Does each party have the authority to bargain or will negotiated agreements be subject to further review by the executive branch? Legislative review of economic terms are often unavoidable.

- Do the parties have the ability to clearly and effectively communicate? Good communication is essential to the effectiveness of an interest-based process.

- Is training and facilitation available? Knowledge of the process and third party assistance are necessary for success.

- Are both parties willing participants in the process? Each party must be motivated to assume the behavior changes and risks associated with interest-based bargaining.

- Are the parties' expectations reasonable? Parties should not expect interest-based bargaining to result in an agreement superior to one that would be obtained through traditional bargaining.

- Does sufficient trust exist between the parties? Although Fisher and Ury argue that trust is not essential to the process, it is hard to imagine the process working in the absence of a mature relationship where the parties can rely on each others' word.

- Is the environment right for labor-management cooperation? An interest-based process cannot work if union or management leaders are openly hostile to the other parties' interests or in an unstable political environment.

- Is there internal consensus within the union and within management to engage in interest-based bargaining? Not everyone will agree that interest-based bargaining is appropriate. If there is substantial opposition to interest-based bargaining on either side, the process may be undermined. Similarly, if either party's decision-makers are experiencing significant challenges to their leadership, the process is not likely to work well.[7]

Some Last Words About Interest-Based Versus Positional Bargaining. Whatever else can be said in the debate about interest-based versus positional bargaining, one thing is clear – both parties need to use the same approach. If not, the early disclosure of information in the interest-based bargaining approach will merely provide a strategic advantage to the other party, who is engaged in more positional bargaining.

The Federal Mediation and Conciliation Service (FMCS) is a great resource on interest-based bargaining. Subject to availability and budget constraints, FMCS conducts free training on interest-based bargaining, and will even guide parties through the initial steps of the process.[8]

NOTES

[1] http://www.beyondintractability.org/essay/interest-based_bargaining/.

[2] http://www.au.af.mil/au/awc/awcgate/army/usace/negotiation.htm.

[3] http://www.afscmestaff.org/cbr/cbr495_1.htm.

[4] R. Fisher, W. Ury, & B. Patton, *Getting to Yes: Negotiating Agreement Without Giving In* (Penguin 1991).

[5] Eirene Rout and Nelson Omiko, *Corporate Conflict Management: Concepts and Skills* (Prentice-Hall 2010).

[6] http://www.maine.gov/mlrb/pom/ibbprocedures.htm.

[7] http://www.afscmestaff.org/cbr/cbr495_1.htm.

[8] http://www.fmcs.gov.

CHAPTER 13

BARGAINING IN HARD TIMES AND CONCESSIONARY BARGAINING

The economic troubles during the 2007 recession brought about the most difficult public sector bargaining ever. Where once negotiations focused on how much of a raise should be granted, questions became whether there should be any raise and, if not, whether and how much of a cut was needed. The problems posed by bargaining in hard times were often seemingly intractable, not readily subject to any traditional form of bargaining.

There are two contexts to concessionary bargaining. The first occurs when an employer is seeking a reduction in wages and benefits during the term of the contract. The second occurs when negotiations are being held on the terms of a new contract.

When Contracts Are In Effect.

Rescinding A Contract. When an economic crisis hits, the first question some employers ask is whether they can simply rescind or tear up a collective bargaining agreement. Though the standards vary from state to state, rescission typically requires the presence of fraud, a material misrepresentation, or a mutual mistake to a key contract item.[1] The mutual mistake must be to an item where the employer does not bear the risk of the mistake.

These are high standards to meet, and rescission is usually unavailable because of an economic downturn. Also, there is some authority for the proposition that, because of the constitutional "contracts clause" that forbids a governmental body from "impairing the obligation of contract," a public sector employer can never unilaterally rescind a contract.[2]

Reopening A Contract. An existing contract can be reopened for negotiations in only two ways: (1) If a clause in the contract allows for reopening; (2) if the state has a "financial urgency" statute; or (3) if both parties agree to the reopening. Contract clauses allowing reopeners in the event of an economic downturn are often tied just to the issue of wages, as in the following example:

> If the County's estimated general fund resources in the executive budget for any fiscal year falls fifteen percent (15%) or more below the estimated general fund resources in the executive budget of the immediately preceding fiscal year, any general wage increase provided by this agreement for the fiscal year for which such reduced revenue is projected shall not be implemented and negotiations over the terms of a substitute general provision for the affected fiscal year will commence on or before April 15 of the fiscal year preceding that in which the wage increase was to take effect.[3]

A few states have "financial urgency" provisions built into their collective bargaining laws. In Florida, for example, the declaration of a financial urgency allows the employer to unilaterally reopen a contract and provides an expedited negotiations process:

> In the event of a financial urgency requiring modification of an agreement, the chief executive officer or his or her representative and the bargaining agent or its representative shall meet as soon as possible to negotiate the impact of the financial urgency. If after a reasonable period of negotiation which shall not exceed 14 days, a dispute exists between the public employer and the bargaining agent, an impasse shall be deemed to have occurred, and one of the parties shall so declare in writing to the other party and to the commission…An unfair labor practice charge shall not be filed during the 14 days during which negotiations are occurring pursuant to this section.[4]

In the absence of either a "reopener" contract clause or a statute like Florida's, there usually is no employer right to reopen contracts. The employer can request that the union reopen the contract, but the union is free to decline.

How can the employer persuade the union to voluntarily reopen a contract? Employers who have had success in obtaining voluntary reopening of contracts have usually gone about the business quietly. They have approached unions privately, and have been willing to have discussions on a completely off-the-record basis. If an employer approaches the union with full disclosure of its financial condition and lays out the financial options it believes are available, it may be able to convince the union of the necessity of reopening the contract and making mid-contract concessions. The more an employer discloses about its financial condition, the more luck the employer will have in convincing a union to agree to mid-contract concessions. The more the employer refrains from threats and instead simply lays out the financial options it believes are available, and the more it engages the union in seeking alternative solutions, the more success it will have.

Furloughs. An option considered by many employers facing budgetary shortfalls is to furlough employees. Furloughs essentially involve adding unpaid days off into the employee's work schedule. Depending upon the employer's financial situation, a furlough program may add anywhere from one to upwards of twenty unpaid days off into the employee's schedule. With each day worth the equivalent of 0.38% of salary, only a few furlough days per year can be the equivalent salary savings of more than 1.0%.

As a general proposition, while an employer has the unilateral right to lay off employees, for a variety of reasons it may not have the right to furlough employees absent an agreement with the union.[5] From a contractual standpoint, furloughs may well violate the "wages," "hours of work" and "maintenance of benefits" clauses in a collective bargaining agreement. Even if a contract does not prohibit furloughs, the reduction in work hours and compensation resulting from a furlough would clearly at least impact mandatory subjects of bargaining, and could not be unilaterally implemented by the employer without bargaining.[6] As put by the Massachusetts Labor Commission, an employer would have to negotiate over the "manner in which those involuntary furloughs directly affect union members' hours of work and their wages."[7]

An employer might consider furloughs rather than simply laying off employees for two reasons. First, furloughs produce cost savings while leaving the work force intact. Productive employees at the bottom of a seniority list are not laid off, and do not begin job searches that potentially could result in their leaving the employer permanently. Second, furloughs can sometimes be scheduled on days when the employer's business is typically slower than others.[8]

Why would a union voluntarily agree to a furlough program? If the union is convinced that a financial crisis will cause layoffs and/or wage and benefit reductions, the union could see furloughs as an acceptable alternative for some or all of the following reasons:

- Furloughs keep the bargaining unit intact, and do not result in any bargaining unit members losing their jobs.

- As opposed to wage reductions, furloughs have no impact on the overtime rate and other salary-dependent benefits.

- As opposed to other forms of concessions, employees are not required to work while receiving lower compensation. Rather, the lower compensation is produced by employees receiving additional days off.

- Employees may be able to use vacation time on furlough days, eliminating or reducing any cuts in compensation.

- Furloughs do not result in the interruption of benefits such as health insurance, which might occur with layoffs.

- Furloughs are temporary, where other forms of concessions might be permanent.

Early Retirement Incentives. Another solution to a financial crisis is for the employer to offer early retirement incentives, or as they are sometimes known, an Early Retirement Incentive Program (ERIP). As two observers described, an "ERIP can be used to support a number of organizational objectives, including headcount reduction, replacement of higher salaried employees with lower salaried employees or to support plans or programs designed to further the organization's goals and missions."[9]

There have been a variety of ERIPs offered by employers, including:

- Adding a year or years to the service credits of employees electing to retire early. In this way, employees can receive a full retirement, and employers need no longer pay their salary (though the employer must make retirement contributions as if they were employed).[10] These additional service credits are often called "phantom" service credits, and almost always require the approval of the retirement system as well as the employer.[11]

- Post-retirement health insurance premium waivers for employees who are presently eligible to retire.

- Incentive payments to retirement-eligible employees who choose to retire.[12]

- A Deferred Retirement Option Plan, or DROP. Though DROP plans have various forms, the usual structure is that an employee who would otherwise be entitled to retire instead chooses to continue working. The employee's additional years of service are not taken into account for purposes of the normal retirement benefit. Instead, the employee usually has an additional amount of money deposited into an investment account during each year of additional service. Employees participating in a DROP program usually must agree in advance to a retirement date (often no more than five years in the future). When they finally retire, they receive both their pension and the funds in the separate account.

- Some combination of the above.

Common Contract Issues in Hard Times. Four issues dominate negotiations in difficult economic times: Wages, health insurance, pensions, and the duration of the contract. In addition, as economic concessions are discussed, unions may insist on gains in non-economic areas of the contract.

- **Wages.** The salary schedule is one of the first places financially-strapped employers turn when seeking cost reductions. Actual wage reductions tend to be fairly rare; much more common are freezes in movement between pay steps or temporary reductions in the pay steps of some or all employees. Unions tend to prefer concessions focusing on pay step movement and placement since, unlike wage reductions, pay step concessions are usually temporary in nature.

- **Health Insurance.** When economic times are difficult, employers focus more on transferring health insurance costs to employees. This cost transference can be accomplished either through benefit adjustments such as increased deductibles and higher co-payments for certain kinds of services or through employees paying a greater percentage of health insurance premiums.

- **Pensions.** It is no exaggeration to say that there is more of a focus today on pension costs than at any time in the last 30 years. Where employers participate in a state pension system, pension changes are brought about through legislative action. Where employers have their own pension systems, pensions are adjusted through the bargaining process. In either case, the focus is not just on the level of benefits (e.g., the pension "multiplier," retirement ages, and post-retirement cost of living adjustments), but also on the employee's premium contribution and the very structure of the pension program (defined benefit versus defined contribution).

- **Duration of contract.** The usual mantra is that employers are more interested in the stability of long-term contracts, while unions want the flexibility of shorter contracts and more frequent bargaining. During difficult economic times, these roles are often reversed, with employers wary of long-term financial commitments that may be impacted by economic developments, and unions seeking the shelter of long-term protections and contractual benefits for their members.

NOTES

[1] See Dominic O'Sullivan, Steven Elliot & Rafal Zakrzewski, *The Law of Rescission*, (Oxford University Press, February 2008).

[2] See generally *Fletcher v. Peck*, 10 U.S. 87 (1810).

[3] 2014-2018 Collective Bargaining Agreement, Multnomah County, Oregon and Multnomah County Deputy Sheriff's Association.

[4] Florida Statutes, Section 447.4095.

[5] *Oakland Unified School District*, PERB Decision No. 540 (Cal. PERB 1985).

[6] *King County*, 2010 WL 2553113 (Wash. PERC 2010).

[7] *Town of Weymouth*, 2013 WL 4027288 (Mass. LRC 2013).

[8] Employers have to be cautious about furloughing employees they treat as exempt under the FLSA. One of the requirements for an exemption under 29 U.S.C. §213(a) is that the employee receive the same salary in each workweek. That salaried status could be potentially jeopardized by a furlough program. One solution is that if an employer furloughs an exempt employee for an entire workweek, the employee's exempt status is not affected because no salary at all has been received for the week. Another potential solution is to reach an agreement in advance with a salaried employee for different salary rates for particular weeks of the year (those containing furloughs).

[9] http://www.ebglaw.com/content/uploads/2014/10/7328_article_1192-Implementing-Early-Retirement-Incentive-Programs-Heidi-Hayden.pdf. ERIPs are generally exempted from the age discrimination prohibitions of the Age Discrimination in Employment Act, 29 U.S.C. Section 623(f)(2)(B)(ii), though it would always be wise for an employer to do an ADEA analysis before adopting an ERIP.

[10] http://www.mass.gov/perac/docs/forms-pub/reports/valuation-reports/montagueval14.pdf.

[11] http://www.ct.gov/trb/lib/trb/formsandpubs/ERIPpacket.pdf.

[12] http://www.tampabay.com/blogs/gradebook/content/clock-ticking-pinellas-early-retirement-offer. In *Solon v. Gary Community School Corporation*, 180 F.3d 844 (7th Cir. 1999), some age-based incentive payments were held to violate the ADEA.

CHAPTER 14

SELECTING COMPARABLE JURISDICTIONS

Along with an employer's ability to pay, comparisons of total compensation usually play the most important role in public sector wage and benefit negotiations. The selection of comparable jurisdictions is by far easiest if the parties have historically agreed upon a certain set of jurisdictions in their prior negotiations or if an arbitrator has selected the comparable jurisdictions in the past. If either of these situations exist, the party seeking to add to or subtract from the traditional list of jurisdictions bears the burden of proving that the previously agreed-upon list is unsuitable.[1] While factors such as population change, annexations, mergers, and significant changes in demographic characteristics can suffice to justify a deviation from traditionally used comparables, usually fairly substantial evidence is necessary for a change.

If there are no pre-selected comparable jurisdictions, then each party must begin the somewhat daunting task of rationally selecting comparable jurisdictions. Unfortunately, few collective bargaining statutes provide any definition of comparability, and the term "comparable" is vague enough to invite just about every comparison possible. One can imagine thumbing through various Census Bureau data points about cities and coming up with a list of dozens of demographic indicia of comparability. As one arbitrator famously wrote:

> The notion that two municipalities can be so similar (or dissimilar) in all respects that definitive conclusions can be drawn tilts more toward hope than reality. The best we can hope for is to get a general picture of the existing market by examining a number of surrounding communities.[2]

A good starting point is to consider the purposes of total compensation comparisons. The whole idea behind compensation comparisons is that there is an employment market that exists, and that an employer's total compensation should be somewhere within the range of the market.[3] Defining the market usually means looking at similar employers, whether the term "similar" means solely the same size, or whether geographic considerations are considered as well.

The best way to assess whether another jurisdiction is similar is to look at its demographic characteristics.[4] Every public employer's service area has many different demographic characteristics; the Census Bureau alone collects information for cities and counties in dozens of data categories. Among these characteristics, two stand out as more important than the rest – population and geographic proximity to the jurisdiction under study. These two key characteristics are not only the most important, but their importance waxes and wanes in relationship to each other. The larger the jurisdiction, the less important proximity is in selecting comparator jurisdictions, and vice versa. For example, when Chicago is conducting a total compensation comparison, one would expect to see cities such as New York and Los Angeles on the list of comparable jurisdictions. However, when a small Chicago suburb is doing wage comparisons, one would not expect to see on the list any jurisdictions outside of the Chicago area, much less in another state, much less half a country away.

What follows is a list of the most commonly used characteristics, ranked roughly in the terms of how frequently they are used to select comparable jurisdictions.

Population. The resident population of a city, county or district is perhaps the most important factor in selecting comparable jurisdictions.[5] The Census Bureau provides official population figures every ten years, and also conducts a "Census of Governments" for years ending with a "2" and a "7" (every five years).[6] In addition, the Census Bureau provides annual census estimates which, though not as accurate as the periodic releases from the Census Bureau, are close enough for use in selecting comparable jurisdictions.[7] Most states also publish annual population estimates that supplement census figures.

The most common use of population is to look simply at raw population numbers. However, *population trends* and *daytime population* can also be important. Population trends show whether a jurisdiction is growing or contracting over time. One can plausibly argue, for example, that a city that has seen population growth of 40% over ten years should not be compared to a city whose population has shrunk by 20% over the same time period, even if their current population numbers are roughly the same.

Daytime population becomes important when a city serves as a population hub, attracting many more individuals during the day than it has residents. County seats are usually population hubs, as are large or medium-sized cities that are distant from other cities of their same size. If a city has a resident population of 75,000 and a daytime population of 125,000, something very different is occurring in that city than in another city of 75,000 which actually shrinks in size during the day. That difference between the cities impacts the need for and delivery of city services, the expenses of the employer, and the relative sophistication needed by the employees, all of which likely have an impact on total compensation.

Proximity. Comparator jurisdictions in closer physical proximity are very likely to be much more important in the bargaining process than those that are physically removed.[8] If there is an adequate number of comparators within the same county or within the same local labor market, then one should expect the comparability discussion to focus on those jurisdictions.[9]

Jurisdiction Type, and the Services Provided. Very important in the selection of comparable jurisdictions is that the comparators be the same type of jurisdiction and provide the same type of service. For this reason, it is unusual to see negotiators or arbitrators draw comparisons between cities and counties, or counties and special districts.[10]

This can at times pose difficulties in selecting comparable jurisdictions.[11] One arbitrator mused about this problem in selecting comparators to police officers working for a county "forest preserve" or conservation district:

> This case presents a unique twist on the usual police department interest arbitration, in that this particular bargaining unit's function is, while similar in some ways, distinctly different in others to those of traditionally-addressed municipal and county police departments, I would suggest. This record absolutely establishes that the Ranger Police Officers employed by the Forest Preserve District of DuPage County are eminently qualified in all areas of law enforcement, and perform, when called upon to do so, duties substantively similar in nature to those of other municipal agencies. However, as to the specific matter of external comparability, both the Union and the District expressly acknowledge the uniqueness of discrete forest preserve police jurisdictions, in that both "lists" of proposed external comparables (promulgated for purposes of analyzing salaries and other outstanding economic issues) are comprised exclusively of county "forest preserve" or "conservation" districts.[12]

Assessed Valuation of Real Property. For two primary reasons, assessed valuation of real property can be important in selecting comparable jurisdictions.[13] Most public employers depend to some extent on property tax revenues as an important source of income, and the assessed valuation of real property has a direct impact on property tax receipts. Also, the assessed valuation of real property, particularly viewed on a per capita basis, says something important about the relative wealth or penury of the jurisdiction.[14] Two cities can have the same raw assessed valuations, but because their populations are different, can have wildly different levels of assessed valuation per capita.[15]

Assessed valuation figures are almost always maintained electronically at the state level, usually by a state department of revenue or taxation. If the search for comparable jurisdictions spans state lines, keep in mind that the assessed valuation numbers in some states (California, for example) can be artificially suppressed owing to property tax limitation measures. If that difficulty is encountered, there either must be a rational adjustment to the figures or the use of assessed valuation to select comparators should be abandoned.

Number of Employees. The size of a department or number of employees in the job classification being studied is also a helpful measure of the similarity of different jurisdictions.[16] A county that has the same service population as a nearby county may superficially appear comparable, but looks less so if it has half as many deputy sheriffs, librarians, or teachers. Some arbitrators will also use the total number of employees (as opposed to those in a department) to select comparables.[17]

Other Measures of Comparability. The per capita and median family income of different jurisdictions says something meaningful about their character, and can be used to select comparable jurisdictions.[18] The number of square miles in a jurisdiction can be important, particularly in the fire service where square miles can be traced fairly directly to workload. The number of crimes can be the basis to distinguish between two law enforcement agencies.

Also important is whether the employees of the proposed comparators are unionized. Arbitrators are less likely to draw comparisons to non-represented employees, particularly where working conditions are concerned.[19]

Using Demographic Data. Once the parties have identified the demographic characteristics they believe are important, they then need to use the data to select comparable jurisdictions. Most commonly, parties use "comparability ranges."[20] For example, jurisdictions that fall within 50% of the target jurisdiction's population and assessed valuation could be identified as comparable. Usually, comparability ranges are percentage-based (for example, +/- 50%, or double and half the target jurisdiction's figures), though occasionally a party will use raw numbers to establish ranges (the target jurisdiction's population +/- 25,000).

Using different comparability ranges will often produce a different set of comparable jurisdictions. Whatever comparability range is used, it is important that the range be consistently applied throughout each of the different comparability criteria used, and that the range not be subject to attack as flowing from a result-oriented approach. For example, if a comparability range of cities within 62.5 miles of the target jurisdiction is used, it would certainly be subject to attack as being result-oriented, especially where an extremely low (or high) paying jurisdiction is just excluded (or included) on the edge of the comparability range. Similarly, if a party suggests a variance of 50% for assessed valuation figures, and uses a variation of 75% for the number of square miles, one could expect that party to bear an extremely heavy burden of showing why the comparability range is different from one criterion to the next.

There is no right answer to the question of what comparability range to use. Any of a variety of ranges can be appropriate given the particular circumstances in the target jurisdiction. For example, using a standard comparability range may produce too few comparable jurisdictions. Also, if the target jurisdiction is a city which is not only a manufacturing center but a county seat and has a resultant high level of transient population, then it may be appropriate to have a higher "upper range" than would otherwise be the case in order to take into account the peculiar nature of the target jurisdiction.

Probably the most popular comparability range is to vary the target jurisdiction's figures by a factor of 50%, and to require each comparable jurisdiction to meet the range for every demographic criterion selected.[21] The advantage of such a system is to establish a broad base of eligible comparable jurisdictions by allowing for the substantial variation of 50%, yet to winnow the number of potential comparables by applying the 50% range to each of the demographic criteria. With the addition of each criterion, more potential comparables will be eliminated, leaving a set of jurisdictions that have a good deal in common in an economic and demographic sense with the target jurisdiction.

If other than percentage variations are used for comparability ranges, the party doing the analysis must be prepared to justify how the ranges were established. For example, if a union argues for a population range of +/- 15,000 residents, then the union needs to be prepared to justify why 15,000 was chosen, and why 10,000, 20,000 or some other number was not used.

Statistical Means Of Selecting Comparable Jurisdictions.

Depending upon one's perspective, the techniques used to select comparable jurisdictions reached either their apex or nadir with the development of statistical methodologies for use in selecting comparables. Usually, such approaches entail multiple regression analysis, and require the services of an economist or statistician to perform and explain. Though there are a variety of statistical methodologies outstanding, most proceed from the same starting point and follow the same general route.[22]

The whole idea behind using regression analysis is that there is a meaningful relationship between certain demographic characteristics and wages. Intuitively, this makes sense. Looking at 100 or 1,000 cities, one would expect the larger cities and those with the highest assessed valuations would pay their firefighters higher wages. Regression analysis tests this supposition, looking at the relationship between the levels of presence of different demographic variables and wages. If a statistically significant relationship exists, then the economist can develop a formula that predicts what wages should be if a particular city followed the pattern displayed in the test jurisdictions. If the actual wages are higher or lower than the prediction, then there's an argument that wages should be adjusted to reflect the pattern.

Though the process makes a good deal of sense, multiple regression analysis has not been widely accepted as a way of examining total compensation. To begin with, regression analysis is difficult to explain, and bargaining teams and arbitrators are asked to digest what might be the equivalent of a college course in statistics through 30 or 60 minutes of explanation. Perhaps more importantly, by its very nature, the statistical approach only demonstrates an existing statistical relationship between the selected variables and wages;

it does not presuppose that the relationship is somehow causal, or that the relationship is one that <u>should</u> exist if all of the factors in a collective bargaining statute are followed. For example, it may well be that a city's predicted wage is quite low owing to sparse economic activity within its confines; however, if that same lack of economic activity leads to a higher crime rate which leads to a high level of police activities and thus to a higher level of exposure to danger on the part of police officers, saying that the predicted wage is the appropriate wage involves a leap of faith. Also, since the use of experts is usually necessary, the whole process tends to become much more expensive and legalistic.

NOTES

[1] *Yakima County*, PERC Case No. 17918-1-03-422 (Gangle, 2004); *City of Marietta*, 2007 WL 7562403 (Byrne, 2007).

[2] *Village of Streamwood & Laborers Int'l Union, Local 1002*, S-MA-89-89 (Benn, 1989).

[3] See Edward Benn, *A Practical Approach to Selecting Comparable Communities in Interest Arbitrations Under the Illinois Public Labor Relations Act*, Chicago Kent College of Law Institute for Law and the Workplace, Vol. 15 Lead Articles, Issue 4 (1998).

[4] *City of Bozeman*, http://erd.dli.mt.gov/Portals/54/Documents/Labor-Standards/dli-erd-ls099.pdf (Landau, 2003).

[5] *City of Hood River*, http://www.oregon.gov/ERB/awards/IA-01-14.pdf (Stiteler, 2014).

[6] http://www.census.gov/govs/.

[7] http://www.census.gov/popest/.

[8] *Township of Franklin*, 2004 WL 6012854 (Mastriani, 2004); *City of Mt. Vernon & FOP*, S-MA-94-215 (Briggs, 1995).

[9] *Macoupin County Health Department and AFSCME, Local 3176*, ILRB Case No. S-MA-08-103 at 15 (Hill, 2008); *Borough of Madison*, 1998 WL 35395347 (Weisblatt, 1998).

[10] *E.g., Whatcom County, Washington*, http://www.perc.wa.gov/Databases/IntArb/06094.htm (Snow, 1986).

[11] *Newark Housing Authority*, 2008 WL 8578879 (Mason, 2008).

[12] *Metropolitan Alliance of Police*, 2009 WL 8160974 (2009).

[13] *Macoupin County Emergency Telephone System Board*, Case No. S-MA-06-004 (Briggs, 2007).

[14] *City of Walla Walla*, Case No. 25787-I-13-627 (Latsch, 2014).

[15] *Clark County*, PERC Case No. 23615-1-10-559 (Lankford, 2012).

[16] *City of Belleville*, 2010 WL 6772784 (Goldstein, 2010).

[17] *Village of Beverly Hills*, 2011 WL 2468164 (Ott, 2011).

[18] *City of Wyoming*, 2013 WL 1558727 (Long, 2013).

[19] *Village of Stockbridge*, 2011 WL 2468165 (2011); *City of Portland*, http://www.oregon.gov/ERB/pages/awards/ia0603.aspx (Snow, 2004).

[20] *Jackson County*, http://www.oregon.gov/ERB/awards/IA-02-14.pdf (Blair, 2014); *City of Rochester Hills*, 2013 WL 2105951 (Long, 2013).

[21] *Wood Dale Fire Protection District*, 2008 WL 8578911 (Winton, 2008).

[22] See *City of Kennewick*, http://www.perc.wa.gov/databases/intarb/05380.htm (LaCugna, 1985).

CHAPTER 15

COMPARISONS OF WAGES AND TOTAL COMPENSATION

Once comparable jurisdictions have been selected, the next step is to make comparisons between the "target" jurisdictions and the comparators. This comparison is often the single most important factor in negotiations and interest arbitration,[1] and particularly so in relatively good economic times. In more difficult economic times, an employer's ability to pay may be weighed more than comparability.[2]

Most collective bargaining statutes call for two types of comparison – a wage comparison and a total compensation comparison. Some bargaining statutes lay out these comparisons only very generally. For example, New York's collective bargaining law only calls for a comparison of "wages, hours, and conditions of employment."[3] Oregon's statutes are a bit more specific, and require an arbitrator to examine the following in making an award:

> The overall compensation presently received by the employees, including direct wage compensation, vacations, holidays and other excused time, insurance and pensions, medical and hospitalization benefits, the continuity and stability of employment, and all other benefits received.[4]

Performing Wage Comparisons.

It is a deceptively simple proposition to measure "wages" in comparable jurisdictions. Questions immediately arise, such as what should be included in wages? What classifications should be studied? Where in the pay schedule should wages be analyzed?

What should be included in wages? Beyond simply the amount of salary stated in a collective bargaining agreement, there are three additional forms of compensation that could be considered "wages." The first is known as retirement "pickup," where a portion or all of the employee's required retirement contribution is paid by the employer. Though less in favor today than in the past (California has even outlawed it for participants in California's Public Employee Retirement Systems), retirement pickup still exists in many places in the country.

What has occurred many times in bargaining is that in lieu of a wage increase, an employer has agreed to retirement pickup. Employers have favored retirement pickup because unlike a wage increase, the amount of retirement pickup is not built into overhead and other salary-dependent costs. Employees have favored retirement pickup because the amount of pickup is usually not taxed in the same fashion as wages. Because retirement pickup is nothing but a substitute for wages, strong arguments can be made for including it in wage comparisons. This table is a simple example why:

City	Wage	Retirement Pickup	Comparison Wage
Asheville	$4,732	4.5%	$4,945
Columbus	$4,937	6.0%	$5,233
Junction City	$4,815	0.0%	$4,815
Salem	$4,910	6.0%	$5,204
Average	$4,849		$5,040
Springfield	$4,988	0.0%	$4,988
Comparison to Average	+ 2.88%		- 1.22%

Without retirement pickup in the mix, Springfield's wages would not only be 2.88% above the average, but would actually be the highest in the group. With retirement pickup included in the calculations, Springfield's wages would be 1.22% below the average.

A "deferred compensation match" should be treated in much the same way as a retirement pickup. A deferred compensation match occurs when an employer matches an employee's deferred compensation contribution, usually up to a specified percentage of salary. Like retirement pickup, deferred compensation matches are negotiated in lieu of salary increases, and could be considered wages.

The third form of compensation eligible for consideration as wages is premium pay received by all members of the bargaining unit. Some collective bargaining agreements call for premium pay for attaining a level of certification that actually is a minimum requirement for holding the job. For example, there are firefighter contracts calling for Emergency Medical Technician premium pay even though all members of the bargaining unit are required to possess an EMT certificate. If there is premium pay of this sort, it should arguably be considered a form of "wages" for comparison purposes.

What classifications should be studied? If possible, wage comparisons should be performed on all classifications within the bargaining unit. For large bargaining units – particularly "collector" units containing general municipal, county, state, or school district employees – it may not be feasible to collect comparison data for what might be dozens or even more than 100 job classifications. In that case, the usual approach is to base wage comparisons on the most populated job classifications in the bargaining unit and any other classifications targeted by either party for specific reasons (e.g., a turnover problem in a classification).

Even where wage data is collected for all classifications, it is still common for negotiations to end with the same wage adjustment for most if not all of the classifications in the bargaining unit. Variances from this "benchmark" approach usually only occur when wage comparisons for particular classifications have become skewed. For example, if prior bargaining has resulted in raises that were fixed dollar amounts and not percentages, the percentage wage difference between classifications can become compressed. This table is a simple example of wage compression resulting from a $100 raise being given to two classifications in each of ten years:

Year	Senior Clerk Salary	Clerk Supervisor Salary	Difference
1	$3,000	$4,000	33.33%
2	$3,100	$4,100	32.26%
3	$3,200	$4,200	31.25%
4	$3,300	$4,300	30.30%
5	$3,400	$ 4,400	29.41%
6	$3,500	$4,500	28.57%
7	$3,600	$4,600	27.78%
8	$3,700	$4,700	27.03%
9	$3,800	$4,800	26.32%
10	$3,900	$4,900	25.64%

Where on the pay scale should wage comparisons be made? There are several logical choices as to where on a pay schedule comparisons should be made. Perhaps predictably, arbitrators have been all over the map on the issue. Some use top step wages for comparisons. Others use the mid-point of a salary range,[5] the average wage in each jurisdiction,[6] or even entry-level wages.[7]

Absent unusual circumstances, the most rational comparison would be that of top step wages. In almost any bargaining unit, the largest grouping of employees will be at the top step of the pay scale, and employees generally remain at the top step longer than any other pay step. Retirement benefits are typically dependent upon top step wages as are some employer costs and employee benefits.

Some arbitrators do not even analyze actual wage figures, and are more interested in the percentage adjustment of wages in the comparables.[8] As the following table shows, using a percentage adjustment roughly the same as that in the comparables will have the effect of maintaining a jurisdiction's position with respect to the comparables:[9]

City	Year 1 Wage	Year 2 Increase	Year 2 Wage
Asheville	$4,029	3.00%	$4,150
Columbus	$4,938	3.25%	$5,098
Junction City	$5,029	2.33%	$5,146
Salem	$5,219	4.00%	$5,428
Average	$5,319	3.15%	$5,486
Springfield	$5,403	3.15%	$5,573
Comparison to Average	1.58%		1.58%

If one increases Springfield's wage in the table by 3.15% (the average increase in the comparable cities), the result is a new wage of $5,573, which precisely maintains the 1.58% differential that existed in Year 1.

What Should Be Included In Total Compensation Comparisons?

Most negotiators believe that total compensation provides "a more realistic pay comparison" than base wages alone.[10] A total compensation approach takes into consideration that employers and labor organizations often choose to stress different aspects of a total compensation package. One jurisdiction might choose to put money into premium pay while another might focus on base wages. A settlement might contain an additional holiday or reduced work hours, all of which have a cost to an employer and should be taken into account.[11]

Total compensation analysis smoothes out these variations and tries to get closer to the total cost of employing an individual. Ideally, the most thorough approach would be to look at the employment demographics of each member of a bargaining unit and then hypothetically ask "what would this employee make if she worked for the comparison jurisdiction?" To answer the question, one would need to know at least the date of hire (for vacation accrual purposes), the date of entry into the job classification (for employees who have been promoted), particular job duties (for premium pay purposes), education levels (for education incentive pay), certification levels (for specialty certification pay), and shift assignments (for shift differential pay) for each employee in the bargaining unit. Because it is so dreadfully laborious, this sort of specific total compensation comparison is rarely done and usually only with very small employers.

Instead, almost all negotiators settle for a rougher estimate of an employer's total compensation costs. The starting point is to include in total compensation those elements of the wage and benefit structure for which all employees are eligible. For example, all employees are eligible to receive wages, health insurance, retirement benefits, longevity pay, vacations and holidays, so the cost of each should be included in total compensation. Employees may also be eligible to receive education incentive pay and pay for different levels of state certification, so those costs should be included in total compensation. If all employees receive clothing, uniform or equipment allowances, the amounts should be part of total compensation.[12]

While this approach to total compensation does not take into account certain types of premium pay for which only certain employees are eligible (e.g., premium pay for assignment to certain duties), it does provide an accurate measure of the overall compensation paid to all employees.

How To Calculate Total Compensation.

Once total compensation components have been selected, calculating the value of the various compensation components is fairly straightforward. Commonly, total compensation is measured on a monthly basis, though some prefer annual or (more rarely) hourly comparisons.

Wages and Longevity. Wages and longevity pay are easily measured simply by calculating their values.[13] Since the employer's retirement contribution is an element of the total compensation analysis, retirement pickup and deferred compensation matches should not be included as "wages" for total compensation purposes.

Education Incentive/State Certification Pay/Other Premium Pay. Education incentive pay and pay for state certification poses a similar problem in total compensation analysis. No one education level "fits all" for total compensation purposes. To get a broader picture, comparisons should be drawn at all benefit levels of an education incentive plan. For example, if an education incentive plan has separate benefit levels for employees with two years of college and a bachelor's degree, then three separate total compensation comparisons should be done – for employees not eligible for education incentive and for the two levels of the plan.

A bit more complicated is the matter of pay for state certification. The tables on page 161 use a law enforcement bargaining unit to illustrate how to draw comparisons when premium pay exists for employees who receive certain types of state certification. Most state law enforcement licensing boards (often known as Peace Officer Standards and Training Commissions) issue at least three types of certificates, known as Basic, Intermediate, and

Advanced certificates. Simply receiving a POST certificate does not entitle an employee to additional pay unless a collective bargaining agreement calls for such pay. Frequently law enforcement contracts do call for this state certification pay, as do many fire contracts call for EMT certification pay and many teacher contracts call for different forms of certification pay. In the law enforcement example, an employee who has a bachelor's degree is usually eligible for an advanced POST certificate, and an employee with two years of college an intermediate certificate. As with education incentive pay, separate total compensation comparisons should be drawn for each level of state certification pay.

In addition to education incentive and state certification pay, total compensation analysis should take into account any incentive pay for which the vast majority of the members of a bargaining unit are eligible. For example, if an agency has a physical fitness program which calls for participating employees to receive incentive pay based upon performance, the physical fitness premium should be included in total compensation analysis. Similarly, some police agencies now pay a patrol officer premium to police officers. Since a substantial portion of the bargaining unit in such an agency would be entitled to receive the premium, it should be included in total compensation.

Retirement Costs. An important part in any total compensation analysis is the employer's cost of furnishing a retirement plan for employees. Since the amount of retirement pickup is not taken into account in calculating wage figures in total compensation analysis, the employer's total contribution (the employer's normal contribution plus any retirement pickup) should be used to derive retirement costs. Additionally, if the employer makes any contribution to the employee's deferred compensation account, either as an outright contribution or as a match to the employee's contribution, those costs should be included in total compensation as well.[14]

Because of practical difficulties, some negotiators do not include retirement costs in their total compensation comparisons. Those difficulties include:

- Retirement plan costs are in part a feature of the actuarial assumptions made by each retirement plan. That means that two retirement plans with identical benefit levels could have different employer contributions because of different assumptions made by actuaries as to factors as varied as the assumed future rate of return on investments, retiree life expectancy, and the anticipated rate of wage growth.

- Comparisons become hugely difficult when a retirement plan is in an underfunded or an overfunded state. Often, this means that the level of employer contribution has been adjusted to bring funding equilibrium, and that the contribution does not reflect the actuarial cost of the plan.

- Increasingly, public sector retirement plans have multiple tiers. Some tiers may be traditional defined benefit plans, others may be defined contribution or deferred compensation plans, and yet others can be a combination of the two. Accounting for multiple tiers across however many comparable jurisdictions have been selected can be arduous.

- Often, retirement issues are so complicated that they require an expert to unravel, adding to the expense of what might otherwise be routine negotiations.

Insurance Costs. The insurance figures used in total compensation calculations should be the employer's cost for providing the gamut of available insurance plans – health, dental, orthodontia, vision, life, disability, and prescription insurance. In calculating insurance costs, figures representing similar types of coverage in each jurisdiction should be used. The most appropriate figures to use in total compensation comparisons are those representing the employer's cost of providing coverage under the most commonly-used insurance plan in each jurisdiction.

One difficulty in comparing insurance costs is the product of the two common rate models for health care – tiered rates and blended rates. Tiered rates typically provide separate rates for at least three categories: employee only, employee and spouse, and full-family coverage. A blended rate is a single rate representing the average cost of health care for an entire group. Given these two rate models, care must be taken to make sure that the same types of rates are being compared in each jurisdiction. If there is a mix of tiered and blended rates, then an attempt should be made to gather whatever additional data may be necessary to convert a tiered rate into a blended rate, or vice versa.

Vacation. Providing employees with paid time off in the form of vacation leave represents a cost to an employer, either because the employer has to provide a replacement for employees utilizing vacation time or because the employer must have a higher-than-otherwise-necessary staffing level to accommodate vacation time off. Because of the cost of the benefit, it is appropriate to take vacation costs into account in total compensation analysis.[15] Vacation costs are easily computed by use of the following formula:

$$\text{Vacation Costs} = \text{Vacation Hours} \times \text{Hourly Wage}$$

Holiday Costs. Like vacations, providing time off on holidays to employees represents an expense, and so holiday costs should be included in computing total compensation.[16] The value of holidays can be calculated by using the same formula as with vacation.

$$\text{Holiday Costs} = \text{Holiday Hours} \times \text{Hourly Wage}$$

Calculating Total Compensation.

Choosing total compensation components is only half the battle. Unless total compensation information is going to be gathered for each level of tenure, negotiators must select where comparisons should be drawn. The most common "breaks" (at least in the public sector) in vacation accrual levels and longevity pay occur at five, ten, fifteen, twenty, and twenty-five years of service.

With these assumptions, the total compensation in a set of comparable jurisdictions can be calculated in a straightforward manner. Using the same law enforcement example discussed earlier in this chapter, the following fifteen combinations of tenure and incentive pay provide a good representative sampling of total compensation for a bargaining unit:

Tenure	Incentive Plan Participation
5 Years	No participation
5 Years	2 years college or intermediate certificate
5 Years	4 years college or advanced certificate
10 Years	No participation
10 Years	2 years college or intermediate certificate
10 Years	4 years college or advanced certificate
15 Years	No participation
15 Years	2 years college or intermediate certificate
15 Years	4 years college or advanced certificate
20 Years	No participation
20 Years	2 years college or intermediate certificate
20 Years	4 years college or advanced certificate
25 Years	No participation
25 Years	2 years college or intermediate certificate
25 Years	4 years college or advanced certificate

The following table is an example of how a completed total compensation study might appear:

Total Compensation
Five-Year Employee
(Two Years Of College Or Intermediate Certificate)

City	Wages	Education/ Cert. Incentive	Retirement	Insurance	Vacation	Holidays	Total Compensation
Asheville	$4,029	$201	$761	$1,529	$163	$293	$6,977
Columbus	$4,938	$148	$1,017	$2,092	$235	$293	$8,724
Junction City	$5,029	$0	$553	$1,740	$193	$348	$7,864
Salem	$5,219	$261	$1,260	$1,342	$263	$348	$8,694
Average	$4,804	$153	$898	$1,676	$214	$321	$8,064
Springfield	$5,103	$0	$765	$1,498	$216	$294	$7,877
Comparison to Average	6.23%		-14.77%	-10.61%	1.08%	-8.16%	-2.33%

A summary table can be helpful in recapping the total compensation status of employees of the target jurisdiction with respect to a set of comparable jurisdictions:

Summary Of Total Compensation Exhibits

Five Years Of Service

No Participation in Incentive Plan	-3.85%
2 Years of College/Intermediate	-3.53%
4 Years of College/Advanced	-4.51%

Ten Years Of Service

No Participation in Incentive Plan	-4.13%
2 Years of College/Intermediate	-2.32%
4 Years of College/Advanced	-5.22%

Fifteen Years Of Service

No Participation in Incentive Plan	-3.99%
2 Years of College/Intermediate	-4.11%
4 Years of College/Advanced	-5.04%

Twenty Years Of Service

No Participation in Incentive Plan	-3.22%
2 Years of College/Intermediate	-3.28%
4 Years of College/Advanced	-4.26%

Twenty-Five Years Of Service

No Participation in Incentive Plan	-3.53%
2 Years of College/Intermediate	-3.59%
4 Years of College/Advanced	-4.41%
Average	**-4.06%**

Where Should Total Compensation Be Set?

All things being equal, the usual aim in bargaining is to set total compensation at the point that will maintain the pre-existing relationship to the total compensation in the comparable jurisdictions.[17] That means that if a jurisdiction has compensated employees at the top or at the bottom of a set of comparables, the default is that the relative position of the jurisdiction should not appreciably change as a result of the bargaining or arbitration process.[18]

Of course, "all other things being equal" is rarely the case in bargaining. It may be, for example, that a city finds its compensation near the bottom of its comparables, but only because of a temporary downturn in the local economy. The bargaining process might well produce wage increases above those in the comparables in order to gradually regain the city's pre-downturn status. Conversely, it may be that a jurisdiction that has long paid the highest wages in the area can no longer afford to do so, and one would expect to see that jurisdiction's relative status to the comparables change.

NOTES

[1] *County of McHenry and Service Employees International Union, Local No. 3*, S-MA-12-001 (Fletcher, 2013); *City of Burnsville*, 1993 WL 13703287 (Lalor-Pribble, 1993).

[2] *City of Southfield*, 2013 WL 1558721 (Cheek, 2013).

[3] New York Civil Service Law, Section 209 (4).

[4] Oregon Revised Statutes, Chapter 243.746 (4)(f).

[5] *City of Chickasaw*, 1979 WL 430369 (Shearer, 1979).

[6] *City of Marietta*, 2007 WL 7562403 (Byrne, 2007).

[7] *Otoe County*, 1995 WL 17856455 (Neb. Cir. 1995).

[8] *Township of Rochelle Park*, 2004 WL 6012874 (Glasson, 2004).

[9] *City of Wyoming*, 2013 WL 1558727 (Long, 2013).

[10] *City of Canton, Ohio and Canton Professional Firefighters Association, Local 249*, 96 LA 259 (Duda, 1990).

[11] *Cass County Road Commission*, 2008 WL 8567921 (2008).

[12] *See, e.g., City of Bloomfield Hills*, 2009 WL 8153982 (2009).

[13] *Village of Stockbridge*, 2011 WL 2468165 (2011); *City of Kalamazoo*, 2007 WL 7562056 (2007); *Township of Lakewood*, 2007 WL 7562426 (Hundley, 2007).

[14] *Oakland County*, 2009 WL 8154001 (2009).

[15] *Township of North Bergen*, 1997 WL 34820422 (Tener, 1997).

[16] *Township of East Brunswick*, 2004 WL 6012871 (Mastriani, 2004).

[17] *City of East Orange*, 1998 WL 35395315 (Scheinman, 1998).

[18] *Jackson County Sheriff's Employees Association*, http://www.oregon.gov/ERB/awards/IA-02-12.pdf (Axon, 2013); *City of Trenton*, 1998 WL 35395340 (Scheinman, 1998).

CHAPTER 16

THE COST OF LIVING

One of the more important parts of any discussion of wages is the cost of living. As one arbitrator commented, "by including appropriate cost-of-living indices, the legislature gave its support to the philosophical proposition that real wages in the state should not be reduced by price increases beyond the employees' control."[1] Whether the cost of living is increasing as fast as 12-14% per year, as was the case in the late 1970s, or whether it is running at the 2-3% pace evidenced in the early part of the 21st century, it is no less important that cost of living analysis be accurate.

Wages, of course, do not run in lockstep with the cost of living. As one arbitrator phrased it, "It is ordinarily the case that in periods of very high inflation, salary increases tend to lag behind the rate of inflation. Conversely, in times of low inflation, when the cost of living is quite moderate, wage adjustments somewhat exceed the cost of living."[2] In addition, the cost of living is but one of many factors to be considered in bargaining, and has to be considered in the context of things such as the employer's ability to pay, comparable jurisdiction data, and the general economic climate.[3]

It can safely be said that there is no area in wage negotiations which has been more beset with misconceptions and misunderstandings than is the case with the cost of living. One frequently hears cost-of-living arguments from both management and labor representatives that, if not outright incorrect, are at least significantly exaggerated.

Part of the problem in making a cost-of-living analysis is that what is necessarily a very complex and difficult task – analyzing changes in the cost of living as they apply to the members of a particular bargaining unit – must be reduced to a simple, understandable, and hopefully fairly brief discussion. This can be done, though, and an effective cost-of-living presentation can easily be made even by an advocate unversed in economic principles.

Getting Started – The Types Of Cost Of Living Indices.

There are several major types of cost-of-living indices. The differences between the two most important in bargaining discussions relate to the type of "market basket" each index uses to measure changes in the cost of living. In each case, the market basket is designed to reflect the hypothetical average consumer's purchases of goods and services.

The first of the two major types of indices, known to economists as a Laspeyres Index, uses a "fixed" market basket.[4] This is to say the contents of the market basket are either not adjusted over the course of time, or are adjusted very infrequently. A Laspeyres Index uses the pattern of goods and services purchased in the base period, and then compares price changes for those commodities over time.

The most popular type of fixed market basket index is the Consumer Price Index (CPI), published by the Bureau of Labor Statistics (BLS) of the United States Department of Labor. As phrased by the BLS, the CPI is a "measure of the average change over time in the prices paid by urban consumers for a market basket of consumer goods and services."[5] The CPI does not include income or other taxes not directly associated with the cost of goods. The cost of more than 200 items which are surveyed by the CPI are grouped into eight major categories:

- Housing
- Food and beverages

- Apparel
- Transportation
- Medical care
- Recreation
- Education and communication
- Other goods and services[6]

On a monthly basis, the BLS samples the prices of about 80,000 items, using data collectors known as "economic assistants." Each component in the market basket is given a "weight," representing the percentage of the typical consumer's expenditures made on that component of the market basket. The CPI's weights were last determined during BLS's 2003-2004 Consumer Expenditure Survey.[7] Simplistically, when the prices for each component are multiplied by the weights for those components, the overall cost of the market basket is determined. That overall cost is then adjusted by the cost of a similar market basket in the CPI's "base year" of 1982-1984 to produce the CPI index number.

A second major type of index, known to economists as a Fisher-Ideal Index, contains a fluctuating market basket, designed to be adjusted over the course of time to reflect changes in consumer purchasing patterns. The most popular type of fluctuating market basket index is the Implicit Deflator for Personal Consumption Expenditures, known as the PCE Deflator, prepared by the Bureau of Economic Analysis of the United States Department of Commerce.

Over time, the PCE Deflator has risen at a rate about one-third percent less than the CPI. There are any number of potential reasons for this difference, including the different weights given by each index to expenditure components, the simple math of how Laspeyres and Fisher-Ideal indices are compiled, the fact that the PCE Deflator also looks at spending patterns of nonprofit institutions, the different way the indices treat seasonal expenditures, and many more. BLS itself believes that "there is no one 'smoking gun' that explains the discrepancy between the indexes. Rather, the overall discrepancy is the result of the accumulation of a number of small effects."[8]

Which Index Should Be Used, The CPI Or The PCE Deflator?

Though arguments can be made both pro and con with respect to each index, it is best to use the CPI. There is no doubt that the CPI is the most commonly-used measure of changes in the cost of living, and it is extraordinarily rare to find a collective bargaining agreement tied to the PCE Deflator. The CPI is frequently taken into account in the establishment of wages and benefits even where there is no collective bargaining agreement, and is used to index a wide variety of governmental payments such as pensions and welfare programs.

In addition, the CPI is published not only on a nationwide and regional basis, but it is also published for major metropolitan areas across the country. In contrast, the PCE Deflator has no regional or local indices. Finally, another advantage of the CPI is the groups of consumers studied by each index. Where the weights attached by the CPI to its various expenditure components refer to expenditures by a population of either urban wage and clerical workers or of all urban consumers, the PCE Deflator adds rural households to the groups studied, and takes into account expenditures by clubs, universities, hospitals, charities, and other social organizations. The increased group used by the PCE Deflator would appear to be a less appropriate one to use when measuring the wages of wage earners than would be the CPI's more narrowly-tailored groups.

The Bottom Line. The Consumer Price Index is the best available measurement of the cost of living.

Which CPI To Use – The CPI-U Or The CPI-W?

In 1978, the BLS created two separate Consumer Price Indices where there once was one. One is known as the CPI for All Urban Consumers, or the CPI-U. The other, the successor to the pre-1978 index, is known as the CPI for all Wage Earners and Clerical Workers, or the CPI-W.

In the past, there were significant differences in the measurements of housing costs used by the CPI-U and the CPI-W. For some time, the CPI-U utilized what is known as the "rental equivalence" measure of housing costs, while the CPI-W utilized an entirely different measurement of housing costs known as the "asset based" measure of housing costs. However, the BLS long ago changed the measure of housing costs used by the CPI-W to the "rental equivalence" measurement, leaving only one major difference between the two indices – the group of consumers studied by each index. The CPI-U views the purchasing and consumption patterns of "all urban consumers," and studies a group of consumers which includes retirees and consumers on fixed incomes (e.g. welfare recipients, Social Security recipients, etc.).[9] The CPI-U studies a group which includes approximately 87 percent of consumers.[10]

The CPI-W, on the other hand, studies a group comprised only of "wage earners," and excludes retirees and those who earn fixed incomes. The group studied by the CPI-W comprises 32 percent of all consumers, and includes only those households deriving at least 50 percent of their income from clerical or wage occupations. In addition, at least one of the household's earners must have been employed for at least 37 weeks during the previous 12 months.[11] Neither the CPI-U nor the CPI-W includes persons living in rural non-metropolitan areas, farm families, persons in the Armed Forces, and those in institutions such as prisons and mental hospitals.

Since employees in a public sector agency are by necessity "wage earners," the most appropriate index to use in public employee bargaining is the CPI-W. In the end, though, there's not much to argue about. Over the last 10 years, the CPI-W has increased 23.14%, ever-so-slightly faster than the CPI-U's 23.08%.

The Bottom Line. Unless there's a practice to the contrary, the CPI-W, which measures cost of living changes for wage earners, is the most appropriate CPI to use in public employee bargaining.

Which CPI-W to Use?

There are three broad types of CPI-Ws. The first, covering consumers throughout the country, is known as the "National" index. The second type includes the four broad regional indices, known as the Northeast, Midwest, South, and West indices. The third type of index covers major metropolitan areas, and measures changes in the cost of living in major cities in the country. The BLS publishes these metropolitan indices:

Index	States	Frequency
Chicago-Gary-Kenosha	IL-IN-WI	Monthly
Los Angeles-Riverside-Orange County	CA	Monthly
New York-Northern NJ-Long Island	NY-NJ-CT-PA	Monthly
Atlanta	GA	Even-numbered months
Boston-Brockton-Nashua	MA-NH-ME-CT	Odd-numbered months
Cleveland-Akron	OH	Odd-numbered months
Dallas-Fort Worth	TX	Odd-numbered months
Detroit-Ann Arbor-Flint	MI	Even-numbered months
Houston-Galveston-Brazoria	TX	Even-numbered months
Miami-Fort Lauderdale	FL	Even-numbered months
Philadelphia-Wilmington-Atlantic City	PA-NJ-DE-MD	Even-numbered months
San Francisco-Oakland-San Jose	CA	Even-numbered months
Seattle-Tacoma-Bremerton	WA	Even-numbered months
Washington-Baltimore	DC-MD-VA-WV	Odd-numbered months
Anchorage	AK	Semi-annually
Cincinnati-Hamilton	OH-KY-IN	Semi-annually
Denver-Boulder-Greeley	CO	Semi-annually
Honolulu	HI	Semi-annually
Kansas City	MO-KS	Semi-annually
Milwaukee-Racine	WI	Semi-annually
Minneapolis-St. Paul	MN-WI	Semi-annually
Pittsburgh	PA	Semi-annually
Portland-Salem	OR	Semi-annually
St. Louis	MO-IL	Semi-annually
San Diego	CA	Semi-annually
Tampa-St. Petersburg-Clearwater	FL	Semi-annually

A good adage is that where possible, the nearest metropolitan area index should be used. Since the cost of living in a proximate major metropolitan area is likely to reflect most closely the cost of living in the jurisdiction under study, the major metropolitan area index is best suited to evaluate the effect of changes in the cost of living on the bargaining unit being examined.

Whatever CPI is chosen, do not "index hop." If you have used one index in the past, stay with that index until compelling reasons exist for a change. If you frequently change indices in search of the index which is the highest or lowest of any one point in time, your entire presentation on the CPI will lack credibility.

Using The Consumer Price Index – Selection Of A "Base Year."

The next step in analyzing the cost of living is to select a "base year" from which to begin analysis of the cost of living. Normally, cost of living analysis is performed retrospectively, viewing changes in the cost of living from a fixed time in the past until the present. Since the relationship of wages to the cost of living frequently changes over the years, selection of the base year for analysis is one of the most important aspects of cost-of-living presentations. For example, if a group of employees received a raise 4.5% greater than the cost of living in 2014, selection of a base year prior to 2014 will necessarily show the employees worse off with respect to the cost of living than the selection of a base year after 2014.

As might be expected, there is no one best base year. Arguments have been made for all of the following:

- A base year representing the average date of hire for the members of the bargaining unit.

- A base year representing the start of the previous collective bargaining agreement.

- A base year representing the date of the last wage adjustment.

- A base year representing the passage of collective bargaining laws within the state.

- A base year representing the beginning of the collective bargaining relationship between the parties.

Though either of the first two options set forth above would seem to have the firmest foundation, whatever base year is employed must be rationally justified. There are few things as unpersuasive in CPI discussions as a base year selected for no reason at all, or worse, a base year selected because the resulting cost-of-living analysis is particularly beneficial to the party making the argument.

Should The CPI Be Discounted Or Augmented?

Though the issue had more importance when inflation was running at a high level, one still hears arguments that it is appropriate to make *ad hoc* adjustments to the CPI, either upward or downward, for certain reasons.

Arguments in Favor of Discounting the CPI.

There are three common arguments that the CPI should be discounted by some measure. It has been argued variously that:

(1) The CPI overstates changes in the cost of living because it does not adequately take into account that in inflationary times, consumers will substitute lower-priced goods for goods they previously consumed;

(2) The CPI overstates changes in the cost of living because it overstates the component of costs represented by housing costs; and

(3) The CPI overstates changes in the cost of living for workers covered by medical plans for which the employer pays all or part of the premium, and that the medical component of the CPI should therefore be discounted or excluded.

The Substitution Argument.

The first argument for discounting the CPI is that the CPI overstates the cost of living because it does not take into account what is known as the "substitution effect," where rational consumers will substitute goods with relatively small increases in price for goods with relatively high increases in price during periods of inflation. As has been noted by Janet Norwood, a former Commissioner of the Bureau of Labor Statistic (BLS), while the theoretical argument that the CPI fails to take into account substitution is absolutely correct, the conclusions to be drawn from the argument are uncertain:

> The economists in the BLS, of course, know that consumers shift their purchases in response to changes in relative prices. What we do not know, however, is whether such changes in consumption patterns result in a living standard that is higher or lower than in the base period. If the market basket were changed whenever prices were changed – without knowing whether the consumer is equally satisfied with the shift – we would not know whether a change in the index was caused by a change in prices or by a change in the market basket. Because a market basket change could amount to a change in living standards, those whose income payments are adjusted by the CPI would not be assured that the living standards would remain at the same level.[12]

As Norwood has also noted, the market basket (the hypothetical average consumer's purchases of goods and services) of the CPI is deliberately kept constant in an effort to ensure that fluctuations in the market basket do not involve adjustments in the standard of living:

> The Consumer Price Index is a good measure of the changes in purchasing power of the average family represented in the Index. The CPI is based on a fixed market basket…We keep the market basket constant deliberately because we want to keep fixed the living standard represented by that market basket.[13]

Thus, the basic difficulty with the substitution argument is that the argument really contends for a fluctuating market basket index – like the PCE Deflator – to measure changes in the cost of living. The argument is not so much one that certain adjustments for the substitution effect must be made to the CPI, rather it is that the CPI itself should not be used to measure changes in the cost of living. Once the decision to use the CPI has been made, an argument for discounting the CPI because of the substitution factor would appear to be automatically precluded.

Arguments concerning the substitution factor ignore the fact that in 1998, the BLS revised the CPI to include what is known as a "geometric mean indicator" in the formulas it uses to calculate the cost of living. Groups criticizing the CPI for ignoring the substitution factor had long advocated the use of the geometric mean indicator as a way of taking into account the substitution factor. The use of the geometric mean indicator has reduced the annual rate of increase in the CPI by approximately 0.2 percentage points per year.[14]

The Housing Component Argument.

The second argument frequently made – though not as often in recent years – for discounting the CPI is that the CPI overstates the importance of the rate of escalation of housing costs, or that the CPI's measure of housing costs does not adequately take into account consumers who rent houses. Often it has been argued that the CPI assumes that all consumers purchase a new home every month, every two months, or every year. All these arguments were and are wrong.

Since 1985, both the CPI-U and the CPI-W have used what is known as the "rental equivalence" measure of housing costs. As phrased by the BLS, "this approach measures the change in the price of the shelter services provided by owner-occupied housing. Rental equivalence measures the change in the implicit rent, which is the amount a homeowner would pay to rent, or would earn from renting, his or her home in a competitive market."[15] The BLS has revised the "rental equivalence" measurement of housing costs on several occasions. Most recently, in January 1999, the BLS made substantial revisions in the way it samples housing cost data and the manner in which it predicts housing costs.

The argument that the CPI's housing component overstates the actual costs of housing also suffers from a practical difficulty. Even if it is correct that the housing component overstates the percentage of a hypothetical consumer's budget expended on housing, then the argument must presume that the consumer has available to him or her "money on the margin" – that is, money which is not spent on the housing component which the CPI wrongly assumes is spent on the housing component. This money on the margin is spent somewhere, and is spent on other components of the CPI (the components of the CPI range from clothing to education to food). Unless and until it is determined on which components such money on the margin is spent, one cannot tell if the CPI overstates or understates the true cost of living. If the money on the margin is spent on components rising faster than the housing component, then the CPI can be said to understate the cost of living. If the money on the margin is spent on components rising slower than the housing component, then the CPI can be said to overstate the cost of living. However, until it is proven where the money on the margin is spent, any adjustment to the CPI owing to a purportedly incorrect housing component is extremely difficult to justify.

The Medical Component Argument.

With medical costs rising faster than the general CPI, it's not unusual to hear the argument that the CPI should be discounted because its medical component should not be considered. As the argument goes, the CPI overstates changes in the cost of living for workers whose employers provide prepaid medical coverage for employees, and this results in an upward bias for the CPI for workers who in fact are not required to "pay" their own medical expenses. The typical adjustment argued for is to calculate the CPI with the medical component omitted, and to use this as the appropriate CPI for workers with medical coverage.

There are two huge conceptual difficulties with this argument. First, the argument overlooks the fact that medical coverage furnished by the employer is part of the total compensation package paid to employees. Only if it could be shown that the employer and employee did not consider medical expenses as part of the overall cost package in past collective bargaining negotiations could it be considered appropriate to make any sort of adjustment to the medical component of the CPI.

Also, it has yet to be calculated what an employee does with the surplus monies not spent on the medical component (the same "money on the margin" difficulty with arguments about the housing component). Put another way, the fact that an employer may pay all or a portion of the costs of medical insurance means the employee has money to spend which he would otherwise spend on his own medical coverage. The question then becomes where the consumer expends this additional money and, more importantly, what the rates of the CPI increases were for those categories in which the employee's additional spending occurs.

Even if the argument that the CPI should be discounted because of its medical component clears these two hurdles, one must still remember that even with fully prepaid medical insurance plans, employees often bear at least a portion of medical costs. For example, if employees are required to pay deductibles, be responsible for co-insurance for major medical payments, provide a portion of the premiums for either employee or dependent coverage, or in any other way absorb medical costs, any adjustment to the CPI because of the medical component must bear these costs in mind.

Arguments in Favor of Augmenting the CPI.

Just as employers argue that the CPI has an upward bias, labor organizations have argued that the CPI has a downward bias, and actually understates changes in the cost of living. The two most common arguments for a downward bias in the CPI are as follows: (1) Since the CPI excludes most taxes and social security assessments from the scope of its coverage, and since these taxes have been increasing at a rate higher than the CPI, the net effect of the exclusion is to cause the CPI itself to have a downward bias; and (2) since other measures of housing costs show the CPI's housing component to have the lowest measure of housing costs, the effect of the housing component is to cause a downward bias to the CPI.

Both of these arguments suffer from the converse of the "money on the margin" problem set forth above. More specifically, if the CPI incorrectly assumes that consumers spend too little money in certain areas, what components of the CPI's market basket will provide the funds necessary to make the required purchase? Put another way, where will consumers forego expenditures in order to spend monies on taxes and more monies on the housing component? Again, with respect to both sides of the money on the margin argument, unless and until it can be proven how employees alter expenditure patterns in the face of either additional monies or insufficient monies, arguments for either discounting or augmenting the CPI should not be successful.

Adjustments to the CPI – A Conclusion.

While both management and labor advocates are fond of making arguments that the CPI should be either discounted or augmented owing to perceived flaws in the CPI itself, there has yet to be a convincing case made that any adjustments are appropriate. One thing is very clear – the party suggesting such adjustments should bear a strict burden of proving that the adjustments are necessary, and that the resulting figures provide a more accurate assessment of changes in the cost of living than the CPI itself.

The Bottom Line. There is no clear reason to adjust the CPI upwards or downwards, and no evidence as to how much of an adjustment would be proper.

Analyzing The Cost of Living.

After all of the preliminaries are complete (the cost-of-living index selected, the base year identified, and decisions made as to whether to discount or augment the index), the next step is to actually construct a cost-of-living presentation. This formula can be used to determine the "real wage" or "inflation adjusted wage" for each year in the cost-of-living study:

$$\text{Real Wage} = (\text{Actual Wage} \times 100)/\text{CPI}$$

The reason this formula multiplies the actual wages received by 100 prior to dividing the result by the CPI is because the CPI uses a base year of 1982-84, and a base year value of 100 (not 1). Thus, in order to arrive at a wage in terms of inflation adjusted dollars, one must adjust wages by the base year value of 100.

A simple example of how the above formula works is helpful. Let's assume you're comparing historical wages for a city in the Chicago area, and want to use the July Chicago CPI-W to measure inflation. The Chicago CPI-W in July 2014 was 223.96, and in 2015 was 221.82. Let's assume the actual wages paid to the bargaining unit were $4,500 in 2014 and $4,550 in 2015.

The first step is to calculate the inflation adjusted wage in 2014. Using the above formula, the inflation adjusted wages can be calculated as follows:

STEP 1
Real or Inflation-Adjusted Wage = $\dfrac{\text{Actual Wage} \times 100}{\text{CPI}}$

STEP 2
Real or Inflation-Adjusted Wage = $\dfrac{\$4{,}550 \times 100}{223.96}$

STEP 3
Real or Inflation-Adjusted Wage = $2,031

The next step is to calculate the inflation adjusted wage in 2015:

STEP 1
Real or Inflation-Adjusted Wage = $\dfrac{\text{Actual Wage} \times 100}{\text{CPI}}$

STEP 2
Real or Inflation-Adjusted Wage = $\dfrac{\$4{,}575 \times 100}{221.82}$

STEP 3
Real or Inflation-Adjusted Wage = $\$2{,}062$

A simple example of how the above formula works is helpful. Let's assume you are comparing historical wages for a city in the Chicago area, and want to use the July Chicago CPI-W to measure inflation. The Chicago CPI-W in July 2014 was 223.96, and in 2015 was 221.82. Let's assume the actual wages paid to the bargaining unit were $4,550 in 2014 and $4,575 in 2014.

Using the same formula, a more extended analysis of the cost of living can be performed over a lengthier time period such as a five-year period:

Year	Wage	CPI-W	Real Wage
2010	4450	206.30	$2,157
2011	4475	214.43	$2,087
2012	4500	215.69	$2,086
2013	4500	219.48	$2,050
2014	4550	223.96	$2,032
2015	4575	221.82	$2062
Change from 2010 to 2015			-4.38%

Regional Costs Of Living.

Particularly with larger employers that have no true demographic comparators in a state, arguments will be made that adjustments have to be made to account for regional differences in the cost of living. As the idea goes, a wage of $5,000 in El Paso may have considerably more purchasing power than the same wage in San Francisco, and that if one is to compare public sector wages in the two cities, one must take into account those regional cost of living differences.

It is difficult to find regional measures of the cost of living. There are dozens of cost-of-living calculators available on the Internet, and one can use these calculators to compare the cost of living in, say, El Paso and San Francisco. What is difficult is to find *accurate* and *theoretically sound* measures of regional costs of living, and Internet cost-of-living calculators fail either or both of these tests. Internet calculators also typically do not explain how their cost-of-living numbers are derived nor what formulas are used to produce results, making the use of their results difficult to justify in bargaining.

Spending ten minutes entering the same data into different Internet calculators will quickly produce varying answers as to the cost of living in two cities. Using the El Paso-San Francisco example, and assuming an employee earned $60,000 a year in El Paso, five popular Internet cost of living calculators produced these results as to what salary would be necessary in San Francisco to match the $60,000 buying power in El Paso. Note that no two of the numbers are the same, and there is more than a 7% difference from the lowest to the highest.

Calculator	Salary
Bankrate	$106,659
CNN Money	$107,793
NerdWallet	$109,957
PayScale	$105,000
Sperling's Best Places	$112,200

Better than – or at least more transparent than – the average Internet cost of living calculator is the Cost of Living Index maintained by the Council for Community and Economic Research, an index sometimes referred to as the COLI. COLI is prepared by using price data gathered by local participants in the study, with the price data then weighted by using BLS's 2004 weighting of different CPI expenditure components. Those using COLI should be aware of its limitations, including:

(1) By its terms, COLI tries to measure only "the cost of maintaining a standard of living appropriate for moderately affluent professional and managerial households,"[16] a pattern of expenditures not enjoyed by most public sector employees.

(2) COLI itself cautions against using the index other than as a broad tool, and comes with a fairly hefty disclaimer:

> Because the Cost of Living Index uses non-probability sampling techniques, however, the index numbers are approximations, rather than exact representations, of relative living costs. Any sampling procedure involves statistical error, which simply means that there is a certain probability that relative living costs really are higher or lower than the Cost of Living Index indicates. If sampling error were the only source of error in the Cost of Living Index, we could specify a confidence interval within which index measures could be presumed accurate. But in a project of this type, the potential for nonsampling error is great – and no way exists to calculate the likely magnitude of such error.[17]

(3) COLI does not take into account any taxes, and does so because "it feels the specifications needed to standardize tax-burden calculations would be so complex

that significant reporting errors would occur, diminishing the accuracy and reliability of the Cost of Living Index. The Committee believes a high-quality index restricted to the costs of consumer goods and services is far preferable to an index of dubious quality that includes taxes." The assumption that calculating taxes is too complicated is at least open to question since comparative tax burdens are frequently measured.

(4) COLI's methodology is based upon specific brand name products, a measuring yardstick that could fail to take into account promotional or advertising endeavors on the part of regional distributors of products, and the unavailability of certain brand name products in certain areas of the country.

(5) The database on pricing for the COLI is essentially compiled by volunteers belonging to different organizations and who may have different levels of training and instruction. The compilation of a comparative cost-of-living index by using this methodology, as opposed to the use of just one group of researchers (a methodology used by the BLS in compiling the CPI), has possibilities for error.

Those needing more sophistication in measuring relative differences in the cost of living have two additional resources. First, there are several national economic consulting firms, including notably Runzheimer International,[18] who prepare city-to-city and county-to-county price comparisons based on detailed models. A second alternative is to retain an economist to perform the analysis, though compiling a cost of living comparison is such a huge undertaking that the economies of scale might foreclose this option.

NOTES

[1] *City of Havre, Montana and IAFF Local 601*, 76 LA 789 (Snow, 1981).

[2] *City of East Orange*, 1998 WL 35395315 (Scheinman, 1998).

[3] *Township of Bernards*, 1997 WL 34820407 (Zausner, 1997).

[4] http://www.britannica.com/EBchecked/topic/331007/Laspeyres-index.

[5] http://stats.bls.gov/cpi/cpifaq.htm#Question_1.

[6] http://stats.bls.gov/cpi/cpifaq.htm#Question_1.

[7] www.bls.gov/cpi/cpi_riar.htm.

[8] http://www.bls.gov/ore/abstract/ec/ec020100.htm.

[9] http://stats.bls.gov/cpi/cpiovrvw.htm#item2.

[10] http://stats.bls.gov/cpi/cpifaq.htm#Question_1.

[11] http://stats.bls.gov/cpi/cpifaq.htm#Question_1.

[12] http://www.bls.gov/opub/mlr/1981/03/rpt1full.pdf.

[13] http://www.bls.gov/opub/mlr/1981/03/rpt1full.pdf.

[14] http://www.bls.gov/ore/pdf/ec990050.pdf.

[15] http://www.bls.gov/opub/btn/volume-2/pdf/owners-equivalent-rent-and-the-consumer-price-index-30-years-and-counting.pdf.

[16] https://www.coli.org/surveyforms/colimanual.pdf.

[17] https://www.coli.org/surveyforms/colimanual.pdf.

[18] https://www.runzheimer.com/Home.aspx.

CHAPTER 17

AN EMPLOYER'S ABILITY TO PAY

Always an important issue in bargaining, the question of an employer's ability to pay assumes a paramount role in tough financial times. When budgets are constricted, management and labor often never get far beyond the issue of ability to pay.[1] Neither do arbitrators. As the noted arbitrator Edward Benn commented in one case in dismissing an argument about which jurisdictions were comparable, "even assuming those jurisdictions are valid comparables, those contracts were not negotiated under the economic circumstances that have existed since these proceedings began in August 2008."[2] As pithily put by Arbitrator Christine VerPloeg, "This issue is self evident: It serves no purpose to issue an award that an employer cannot fund and thus could never agree to in collective bargaining."[3] Or as another arbitrator stated at greater length:

> Based on the evidence, the statute and for the reasons discussed above, I conclude that the Employer's Last Best Offer is in the interest and welfare of the public. While the Association's offer with respect to wages, insurance and term of agreement are superior, the Employer's inability to pay tips the scales heavily in its favor. I am particularly concerned about the impact on public safety should reductions in force be necessitated by payment of the Association's Last Best Offer. In a less uncertain time, with an ability to pay, the result would be markedly different.[4]

What is an inability to pay? Some state statutes are sparse on the issue, referring only generally to an employer's ability to pay.[5] Statutes in other states provide some more guidance. In Minnesota, for example, an ability to pay is defined as the "obligations of public employers to efficiently manage and conduct their operations within the legal limitations surrounding the financing of these operations."[6] Other states have statutes that are much more detailed, as in the case of the New Jersey interest arbitration law that requires an arbitrator to consider:

> ...[t]he financial impact on the governing unit, its residents and taxpayers. When considering this factor in a dispute in which the public employer is a county or a municipality, the arbitrator or panel of arbitrators shall take into account to the extent that evidence is introduced, how the award will affect the municipal or county purposes element, as the case may be, of the local property tax; a comparison of the percentage of the municipal purposes element, or in the case of a county, the county purposes element, required to fund the employees' contract in the preceding local budget year with that required under the award for the current local budget year; the impact of the award for each income sector of the property taxpayers on the local unit; the impact of the award on the ability of the governing body to (a) maintain existing local programs and services, (b) expand existing local programs and services for which public moneys have been designated by the governing body in a proposed local budget, or (c) initiate any new programs and services for which public moneys have been designated by the governing body in its proposed local budget.[7]

One can also turn to arbitration decisions for a ready definition of "ability to pay." Here is a good summary of prevailing arbitration sentiment on the issue:

> An inability to pay means "that the Union's offer would place such a heavy burden on the employer's finances that funds would have to be shifted from other services to pay the Union's offer," resulting – and this is the important point – in the elimination or harmful diminution of essential services, or extensive layoffs, or both.[8]

The Bottom Line. An employer's ability to pay focuses on the employer's financial ability to provide core services to the public.

The Most Important Financial Documents Bearing Upon An Employer's Ability To Pay.

There are two key documents that play a role in virtually any ability to pay discussion – the employer's budget, and the employer's most recent Comprehensive Annual Financial Report (CAFR). A budget is a projection of income, expenses, and their impact on assets. While budgets are financial documents, they are also political documents, and the projections contained in budgets can vary in minor or significant ways from what actually occurs as the fiscal year passes.

Employers have any number of reasons entirely unrelated to collective bargaining to budget in an accurate and conservative manner. For that reason alone, ability to pay analysis often relies heavily on the employer's budget. That does not mean, of course, that the employer's budget is the end of the inquiry. As one arbitrator noted: "A fixed budget does not provide an impossible barrier to funding economic proposals. Otherwise an employer's self-imposed budget would be able to eviscerate statutorily mandated collective bargaining."[9]

Where a budget is a projection, a CAFR is a look back at how prior budgets have performed. CAFRs consist of a series of financial documents compiled by the local governmental body and later audited by an accountant certified by the American Institute of Certified Public Accountants. CAFRs must be prepared in accordance with the accounting requirements of the Governmental Accounting Standards Board, or GASB.

The Twelve Questions To Ask About An Employer's Ability To Pay.

When thinking about ability to pay issues, it is helpful to pose a series of twelve questions that plumb the extent of the employer's budgetary difficulties. These are the sorts of questions that repeatedly occur in the bargaining process and, if arbitration is available, will be asked by arbitrators.

1. What About Total Compensation, Comparability, The Cost Of Living, And Other Factors?

Except in the most dire of times, ability to pay is but one of many things taken into account by negotiators and arbitrators. How the bargaining unit fares with total compensation, the cost of living, and a variety of other factors also bears on the question of the appropriate compensation adjustment. In normal economic times, ability to pay is likely to be treated with the same level of importance as these other factors. In difficult economic times, ability to pay can become paramount.[10]

2. What Are The Budget Impacts Of Compensation Adjustments?

There is an issue of relativity when one considers an employer's ability to pay. The expense side of the ledger of most public employer budgets is largely made up of compensation costs. If the bargaining unit represents a significant portion of the employer's workforce or if the proposed increase is significant, an inability to pay argument is more likely to be convincing. Conversely, if the bargaining unit is a smaller one or the proposed increase relatively minor, the employer's ability to pay is less likely to have an impact on the compensation adjustment.[11] And if the funds for the particular employees in question are paid by another governmental body such as the federal government, even a very weak economy may not support an inability to pay claim.[12]

But if there is not enough money, then the funds for a compensation increase can only come from cuts in programs offered by the governmental body. And this, say almost all arbitrators, amounts to an inability to pay that militates against the compensation increase.[13] Absent evidence of program cuts that will result from a compensation adjustment, ability to pay arguments resound less convincingly.[14]

3. Has Revenue Growth Matched Expenses?

The hallmark of an inability to pay claim is that revenue growth has been exceeded by expenses. If that has been the case, an employer's inability to pay claim will much more likely gain traction. If revenue growth has exceeded expenses, then it would be impossible for an employer to convince either a labor organization or an arbitrator that it has an inability to pay.

Employers with relatively healthy budgets often try to reframe the issue, asking not whether the employer *can* pay but rather whether it *should* pay. Or, as unions describe the same argument, employers display not an inability to pay but rather an unwillingness to pay. Arbitrators are usually unwilling to find a fiscally sound employer unable to pay a compensation increase that could be accommodated within its budget. As one arbitrator observed, "while it is not appropriate to cast judgment upon the City's decisions as to how it spends its money, its actions may be revealing and, indeed, provide evidence of ability to pay."[15]

4. How Have The Employer's Reserves Been Faring?

The amount of money held in reserve by the employer is an appropriate factor to consider in arriving at a wage settlement.[16] One arbitrator has even commented that it is impossible to assess an employer's ability to pay unless there is clear information presented on reserves.[17] Public employers have a wide variety of unallocated funds that can typically be used for any general fund purpose. Some reserve funds are specifically earmarked for purposes such as inclement weather, natural disasters, the potential for revenue shortfall, and other non-predictable drains on an employer's finances.

Ending fund balances – another form of reserve – are a necessary feature of a public employer's accounting system. Any governmental entity must have money left over at the end of a fiscal year in order to pay its bills at the start of the next fiscal year, when tax revenues may not be in the offing because of the tax cycle. Each one month of a fund balance is the equivalent of 8.3% of the budget. Though there has been much debate over how much of an ending fund balance is necessary (recommendations on fund balances range from 5% to 20%, for example),[18] there is little doubt that (1) employers have sought to increase fund balances above even these levels in the wake of the Great Recession; and (2) a decline in reserves significantly enhances an employer's inability to pay argument.[19] As one arbitrator observed:

> State-imposed reductions in the Board's budget and other deficits have forced the Board into a posture of spending down its contingency reserves, which are rapidly becoming exhausted, even with cost-cutting measures in place. Shortfalls must be covered, one way or another, and the costs associated with [the Union's proposal] add a burden that cannot be justified at this time.[20]

5. Have There Been Layoffs Or Program Reductions?

Layoffs and program reductions are the most convincing evidence of an employer's ability to pay. As one arbitrator described:

> For an interest arbitrator, no indicator of economic distress is more compelling than layoffs. The term "layoff" in this context has at least three distinct senses, which are all illustrated in the case at hand: the County's 2009 Executive Budget included the elimination of 390 "positions" – sometimes loosely referred to as "layoffs" – but the majority of those reductions were accomplished through attrition and leaving positions vacant. 126 existing employees received October 2008 notices of possible layoff at the turn of the year – a somewhat more concrete sense of "layoff" – and 63 employees actually lost their jobs on January 1, the most brutal sense of "layoff," sometimes referred to as "bodies out the door."[21]

6. Has The Pain Been Shared?

Notions of "internal comparability" play a role in ability to pay discussions. If the bargaining unit has been relatively exempt from layoffs and compensation concessions, at least as compared to the employer's other employees, then it will have a much more difficult time challenging an employer's inability to pay claim. Also, if a substantial number of the employer's other employees have accepted a particular concession such as furloughs, it will be all the more difficult for labor organizations to argue that some other result should occur.[22] Conversely, if a labor organization has made concessions in the recent past, it will be difficult for an employer to obtain additional concessions absent overwhelming evidence of financial distress.[23]

One arbitrator framed the issue in the following terms:

> The evidence presented by the County shows that it has laid off significant numbers of employees from departments whose operations are paid for by the County's general fund. The County laid off approximately 106 employees who formerly worked for County libraries, approximately 25% of the employees who formerly worked in the Assessor's Office, approximately 60% of the employees who previously worked in the County's Development Services Department, and approximately 50% of employees who worked in the County Clerk's Office. During that same time period, not one employee has been laid off in

the Sheriff's Office…Based on all these considerations, I hold that the County's proposals are the most reasonable in light of the stated criteria of reasonable financial ability of the County to meet the cost of the proposed contract.[24]

7. What Is The Community's Overall Economic Condition?

An employer's ability to pay is rarely considered in the abstract. Rather, the employer's budget should be considered against the backdrop of the community's economic condition. Relevant considerations include whether the local economy is growing or contracting, the degree of diversification in the economy, and financial information such as employment and unemployment rates, poverty rates, and median family income.

8. Are There Untapped Revenue Streams Available?

An employer's inability to pay argument is likely to be more persuasive if the employer has considered additional revenue streams and can legitimately say that other revenue sources are either unavailable or unlikely to be achieved.[25] This factor really has two components: (1) Whether the employer has exhausted all available alternatives for funding under its current financial structure; and (2) whether the employer has explored possible alternative forms of funding. As the authors of a monograph on ability to pay once wrote:

> The public employer must provide convincing evidence of an inability to raise the revenues necessary to pay for increased wages and fringe benefits… Such evidence should focus on a history of prior levy failures including any immediate past attempts and the margin of defeat. Also, the employer should present clear evidence of any other indications of the public's general willingness to provide the revenues necessary for a wage increase.[26]

While arbitrators consider potential revenue streams when considering an employer's ability to pay, it is rare to find an arbitration decision that actually rejects an inability to pay argument on the grounds that the employer could increase taxes. For example, in siding with an employer on an ability to pay claim, an arbitrator rejected the notion that a $0.10 increase in the average citizen's tax bill negligible, finding instead that:

> The problem is that [tax increases are] cumulative and on balance a recognizable impact will be felt. Counsel's *de minimis* argument on behalf of the union's final offer puts one in mind of the late Senator Everett Dirksen's remark on congressional funding – "A million here and a million there eventually adds up, and all of a sudden we're talking serious money."[27]

9. What Are The Revenue Projections For The Future?

Particularly when considering multi-year contracts, future revenue projections are critical in evaluating an employer's ability to pay. As noted by Arbitrator Joseph Daly, those projections can not only take into account direct taxing revenues, but also revenue sharing available from other governmental bodies:

> The current economic times are vastly different from the last time the contract was negotiated. The Union proposes increases in each category – wages, insurance and performance pay. But Minnesota is in a distressed

economic climate. There is negative impact on state funding aid and property taxes for [the employer]. These are hard economic times. While [the employer] at present may have some unreserved and undesignated funds in general funds, considering the likely upcoming local governmental assistance cuts and the continuing difficult economic times, the employer's [position] is fair and equitable.[28]

The words of other arbitrators are very much along the same lines, particularly in the last few years. As one arbitrator observed:

> The record documents that in FY 2008 the State of Connecticut experienced widespread financial difficulties with additional monetary problems predicted for the "out years." Testimony that serious financial problems have occurred and that more problems lie ahead was noted and credited.[29]

The Bottom Line. *The employer's revenues play two important roles in ability to pay analysis. Revenue trends have a significant impact on future compensation adjustments, and potentially untapped revenues may provide a source of funds for compensation adjustments.*

---

10. How Well Has The Employer Done At Budgeting In The Past?

An odd feature of inability to pay arguments is that employers who have done well at budgeting in the past and have managed to stave off financial problems are more unlikely to successfully make inability to pay arguments than employers with chronic (and perhaps self-induced) budget difficulties. It is probably scant comfort to an employer to hear words such as these from an arbitrator:

> The Arbitrator believes that the County has done an excellent job in managing County finances and has placed St. Clair County in a better financial position than many other levels of government. The County has shown that it can successfully balance the interests of the public and its employees. The County's cost-cutting measures and desire not to lay off County employees are admirable. However, the County has not convinced the Arbitrator that implementation of the Union's wage proposal would result in great economic consequences to the County.[30]

A key aspect of an employer's prior budget experience is the pattern, if any, in the employer's ending fund balances. Employers who routinely have larger-than-expected ending fund balances – whether through overbudgeting for expenses, underbudgeting for revenue, or both – can find it quite hard to make a convincing inability to pay argument.[31]

11. Are There "Me-Too" Implications To A Settlement?

The prevailing view is that ability to pay discussions cannot meaningfully happen without considering the impact of a similar settlement on other bargaining units with which the employer negotiates, or even upon unrepresented employees. An employer may be pressured, either directly or indirectly through the weight of habits of the past, to grant to all of its employees the same compensation adjustment it negotiates with one union. Though unions chafe at the notion, believing they are being required to negotiate not just for their members but for other employees as well, arbitrators tend to find the "me-too" implications of a settlement are a legitimate consideration.[32] As one arbitrator noted in an arbitration involving Oregon State Police:

> To allow one group of employees to avoid the full effects of the freeze could damage the morale of all other employees, as well as the credibility of their bargaining representatives. The impact it would have on future bargaining is unlikely to be salutary. Although OSPOA argues its members are "different" – because of the dangers of their job – and that other employees are unaffected by what is done for them, there is no evidence supporting that proposition.[33]

***The Bottom Line.** Compensation settlements are not considered in a vacuum, but are considered in the context of settlements with other labor organizations and adjustments to the compensation of non-represented employees.*

---

12. Did the Union Meaningfully Participate in the Budget Process?

Since most state laws mandate that the budget hearings of local governmental bodies be open to the public, a labor organization's participation, or lack of participation, in the budget process can impact the weight given to an inability to pay claim. Without participation in the budget process, a labor organization may be precluded from effectively arguing in favor of various revenue and expenditure alternatives in response to an employer's inability to pay case. If, on the other hand, a labor organization is able to demonstrate that it attended budget meetings, participated in those meetings in a meaningful way, and made suggestions at the time as to how to alleviate revenue shortfalls or excessive expenditures, then the labor organization's affirmative case on ability to pay should not be diminished, but should be considerably strengthened.

NOTES

[1] *City of Rockford*, 2010 WL 8317477 (Yaffe, 2010).

[2] *State of Ill. Dep't of Cent. Mgmt. Svcs and Int'l Bhd. of Teamsters, Local 726*, Case No. S-MA-08-262 (Benn, 2009), available upon request from the Illinois Labor Relations Board.

[3] *Saint Paul Principals Association*, BMS Case No. 10-PN-1074 (VerPloeg, 2011).

[4] *Marion County*, No. IA-14-08 (Fitzsimon, 2009).

[5] For example, New York's law only requires consideration of "the financial ability of the public employer to pay." Civil Service Law § 209[4][c][v][b].

[6] Minn. Stat. Sec 179A.16, subd. 7.

[7] N.J.S.A. 34:13A-16g (6).

[8] *City of Granite City and Granite City Firefighters Association, Local 253, IAFF*, ILRB No. S-MA-93-196 (Edelman, 1993).

[9] *Bend Firefighters Ass'n v. City of Bend*, IA-09-95 (Snow, 1996), available at http://www.erb.state.or.us/awards/ia0995.htm.

[10] *Shiawassee County Sheriff*, 2006 WL 6823208 (Long, 2006).

[11] *Horicon, Wisconsin Police Department*, Decision No. 33008-A (Knudson, 2011), available at http://werc.wi.gov/interest_awards/mia33008.pdf; *Minneapolis Professional Employees Association*, BMS No. 06-PN-30 (Kircher, 2006); *Township of Springfield*, PERC No. 2001-57 (Mastriani, 2001)("the employer can accommodate the cost impact of these salary terms without adverse impact").

[12] *State of Oregon, Military Department*, No. IA-03-10 (Boedecker, 2011), available at http://www.oregon.gov/ERB/awards/IA-03-10.pdf.

[13] *Association of Oregon Corrections Employees*, No. AI-13-03 (Wilkinson, 2004), available at http://www.oregon.gov/ERB/awards/Ia1303.shtml.

[14] *Lincoln County, Wisconsin*, Decision No. 33061-A (Strycker, 2011), available at http://werc.wi.gov/interest_awards/int33061.pdf.

[15] *City of Edina*, BMS No. 10-PN-1183 (Frankman, 2010).

[16] *City of Orting*, Case 26508-I-14-0645 (Elinski, 2015); *City of Eugene*, http://www.oregon.gov/ERB/awards/IA-01-15.pdf (Daly, 2015).

[17] *Village of Malverne*, No. IA2008-014 (Riegel, 2010).

[18] *Kitsap Transit*, Case 22135-I08-522 (Krebs, 2010), available at http://www.perc.wa.gov/Databases/IntArb/22135-I.pdf.

[19] *Lewis County*, Case 23148-I-10-544 (Latsch, 2011), available at http://www.perc.wa.gov/Databases/IntArb/23148-I.htm.

[20] *Board of Trustees of Community Technical Colleges*, available at http://www.the4cs.org/admin/Assets/AssetContent/629dedca-fcd8-4297-a1f9-312b494ee032/546bfa9e-94e2-495f-9d30-54cc81f55e47/deabc993-0c28-451c-ad77-8fe793f22851/1/CT-4C_s_DL_Int._Arb._final_3.pdf.

[21] *King County*, PERC Case 21957-I-08-0519 (Lankford, 2009).

[22] *State of Oregon, Department of Corrections*, No. IA-09-09 (Cavanaugh, 2010), available at http://www.oregon.gov/ERB/awards/IA-09-09.pdf.

[23] *City of Norton Shores*, 2013 WL 1558729 (Saltzman, 2013).

[24] *Jackson County Sheriff's Employees Association*, http://www.oregon.gov/ERB/awards/IA-02-12.pdf (Axon, 2013).

[25] *City of Syracuse*, PERB Case No. IA099-026 (Selchick, 2000)("Nor is the City in a position to raise property taxes to generate additional revenue"); *City of East Orange*, 1998 WL 35395315 (Scheinman, 1998)(City could not reasonably raise taxes).

[26] Timothy D.W. Williams, Marianne K. McCartney, John H. Abernathy, Martin P. Haney, Walter G. Ellis, *Ability to Pay: A Search for Definitions and Standards in Factfinding and Arbitration* (Univ. of Oregon Labor Education Research Center, 1984).

[27] *Essex County*, 1998 WL 35395336 (Light, 1998).

[28] *In re Law Enforcement Labor Services and Centennial Lakes Police Department, Minnesota*, BMS Case No. 09-PN-0840 (Daly, 2010).

[29] *In re State of Connecticut State Community Colleges*, http://www.the4cs.org/admin/Assets/AssetContent/629dedca-fcd8-4297-a1f9-312b494ee032/546bfa9e-94e2-495f-9d30-54cc81f55e47/6aa68b30-eb72-4381-860a-80ed0d5ad676/1/allied%20health%20reopener%20-small.pdf (Douglas, 2009).

[30] *County of St. Clair, Illinois*, ILRB No. S-MA-09-082 (Wojcik, 2009).

[31] *City of Sparks*, 2013 WL 4782260 (Halter, 2013); *Hudson Area Public Schools*, 2013 WL 1558726 (Kerner, 2013).

[32] *Int'l Ass'n of Fire Fighters, Local 3564 v. City of Grants Pass*, IA-02-00 (2000)(Brown, Arb.) available at http://www.erb.state.or.us/awards/ia0200.htm.

[33] *Oregon State Police Officers Association*, IA-15-03 (Brand, 2004), available at http://www.oregon.gov/ERB/awards/ia1503.shtml.

CHAPTER 18

THE "OTHER FACTORS" ELEMENT OF WAGE ANALYSIS

Though total compensation, ability to pay, and the cost of living are usually the three most important considerations in assessing wage and benefit adjustments, on occasion additional factors may be even more important. Collective bargaining statutes often explicitly recognize this fact. For example, Washington's public sector bargaining statute is not unusual in requiring an arbitrator to take into account "such other factors…that are normally or traditionally taken into consideration in the determination of wages, hours, and conditions of employment."[1]

Unfortunately, state legislatures have not been specific in defining what relevant "other factors" are, leaving the parties to argue about what other factors should be taken into account. The balance of this chapter discusses the types of considerations most commonly taken into account as relevant to the bargaining process.

Interests And Welfare Of The Public.

Of all of the other factors that are discussed in bargaining and arbitration, "the interests and welfare of the public" is perhaps the most bedeviling. Usually, the interests and welfare of the public is listed as an explicit factor in the state collective bargaining law.[2] In other places, the interests and welfare of the public is analyzed by the parties under the other factors element of a bargaining statute. No one quite seems to know what the phrase means, and many published arbitration opinions openly struggle with the concept.[3]

A starting point is to look at whatever other criteria are contained in the collective bargaining statute. If a legislature has specifically listed factors that should be taken into account, it is a basic rule of statutory interpretation that "interests and welfare of the public" must mean something else. For example, if a statute lists an employer's ability to pay as a relevant consideration, then interests and welfare of the public must mean something other than ability to pay (otherwise, the legislature would not have enacted both portions of the statute).

With that as a backdrop, arbitrators have cited the following in considering the interests and welfare of the public:

- The employer's desire to provide the appropriate level of governmental services and to provide those services in the most cost effective way.[4]

- The interests of the taxpaying public balanced against the promotion of labor peace.[5]

- The ability of the employer to attract and retain the most qualified employees.[6]

- Whether the award of a wage proposal would require layoffs or programmatic cuts.[7]

- The stability and morale in the workplace.[8]

- The operational efficiency of the employer and how the proposals of the parties impact that efficiency.[9]

- The ability to promote high-quality employees.[10]

Workload And Productivity.

Certainly one of the most common "other factors" taken into account when considering the determination of wages is that of the workload and productivity of the members of the bargaining unit.[11] Workload is perceived as important because factors such as workload and productivity have, in the words of most collective bargaining statutes, been "traditionally" taken into account in the setting of wages both in the public and private sector.[12] An unpublished fact-finding opinion by John Abernathy provides a good synopsis of the reasoning behind the use of workload and/or productivity in the "other factors" element of a statute:

> Turning to the question of whether productivity is an appropriate criterion for wage determination, this factfinder turned for guidance to standard references on wage determination. Professor John T. Dunlop, former Harvard economist and former Secretary of Labor, once stated: "The debate over wage rates in the public press and in proceedings between management and labor organizations has popularized economic analysis. There has come into use a limited number of clichés or standard arguments which are employed by the side that regards them as most effective at the time in winning the case. Illustrative of these phrases are 'comparable wages,' 'productivity,' 'cost of living' and 'ability-to-pay.'"
>
> Lloyd G. Reynolds, former Sterling Professor of Economics at Yale University, in discussing wages as a cost of production, stated: "...wages are important primarily as an element in production costs. The employer is interested in two things: How much it costs him to hire a man-hour of labor, and how much output he is able to obtain from this man-hour. It is not wages as such which matter, but wages in relation to productivity."
>
> The relationship between money, wage rates, productivity and unit labor costs has long been part of the concern of economists analyzing the behavior of the individual firm. For example, assume an employee who is being paid $10.00 per hour is producing 10 units per hour. In that case, the per-unit labor cost is $1.00. If wages and productivity both increase by, say, 50%, then unit labor costs remain the same. If, however, the rate of productivity increase exceeds the rate of wage increase, then, theoretically at least, the firm could decrease prices, or increase profits, or invest in more productive equipment or engage in some combination of price cutting, profit increasing or investing.
>
> At the macroeconomic level, the relationship between rates of changes in productivity and wages are frequently discussed as the basis of national economic competitiveness in international trade. In addition, the "wage guideposts" that were part of economic policy in the Kennedy-Johnson administrations were attempts to tie the wage increases in key collective bargaining situations to national productivity.
>
> This factfinder, therefore, concludes that even though productivity is not one of the factors named in the statute or in the rules as a factor that factfinders must consider in wage determination, it is one of the unnamed "other factors" that are normally or traditionally taken into consideration in the determination of wages.[13]

When presentations on workload and/or productivity are made, the differences between the two concepts should be carefully explained. Workload can be viewed as the job responsibility "inputs" into an employee's work life. Productivity can be described as the rate at which the employee disposes of the job responsibility inputs, or the relationship of the employee's output to the employee's inputs. Thus, workload can increase without a necessary increase in productivity, just as productivity can increase without a concurrent rise in workload.

As noted by Evan Berman in his book, *Performance and Productivity In Public and Nonprofit Organizations*, practical difficulty exists with measuring workload and/or productivity in the public sector.[14] Since much of the work done in the public sector is the provision of services, and since the concepts of workload and/or productivity applied to a service-oriented endeavor can be subjective in nature, measuring workload and/or productivity becomes quite difficult. One cannot measure if a social worker has become more productive solely on the basis of the number of cases handled by the worker – one needs to inquire further into the complexity and disposition of the cases, and the degree of satisfaction felt by the social worker's clients and supervisors. One can say generally that an agency is or is not providing first-rate service to citizens,[15] but that is hardly quantifiable.

In other areas of the public sector, some aspects of workload and productivity can be quantified. For police officers, for example, statistics can be amassed on the number of calls for service, arrests, citations, and incidents of self-initiated activities.[16] For firefighters, the number of aid and fire calls can be tallied, as can figures in other areas such as inspections. For teachers, measures of productivity are hugely controversial, but certainly ready measures of workload are class size and classroom hours. Similar quantitative measurements exist for the jobs of other public employees.

The Bottom Line. Workload and productivity have long been considered important factors in compensation negotiations, though they are occasionally difficult to measure for service providers.

Internal Comparability.

Internal comparability is the relationship between the compensation paid in the employer's various job classifications. It may be, for example, that a public employer has office assistants performing essentially the same tasks in a variety of different departments. Or it may be that there are analogous jobs, such as engineers working in different capacities. The analogies may be broader, as with comparisons between police officers and firefighters.[17]

While an employer's practices with its other employees is always relevant, there are limitations to the internal comparability argument. Different jobs within the employer's workplace may have entirely different market conditions demanding different wages and benefits. There may be working conditions in one bargaining unit that militate for or against a particular benefit, conditions that do not exist in other bargaining units. One arbitrator has cited this variability as a basic limitation of the internal comparability notion:

> Where the employees of a public employer have more than one bargaining unit and bargaining representative, inequities are inevitable. There are a number of variables which may produce this result. But these inequities are inherent in the system and are not, standing alone, an adequate basis for a major change in the *status quo* in one of the bargaining units. If the non-union employees feel disadvantaged, they have an option: organize. The turning question here

is whether there is a *quid pro quo* which is large enough to justify taking away from the police officers a benefit which they have had in the past. Using the common verbiage of collective bargaining, is it in the public interest to award the employer a "takeaway?"[18]

One of the most often discussed internal compensation relationships is that between supervisors and subordinates.[19] These comparisons can be simple, as in: "Supervisors receive two more vacation days than subordinates." However, supervisor-subordinate relationships are most meaningful when measured against external data. By way of example, assume that one is considering the wage structure in a police department, where sergeants have a wage 12% higher than police officers, lieutenants 18% higher than sergeants, and captains 22% higher than lieutenants. The disparity in the differentials is interesting, but not particularly informative. But if a survey of comparable jurisdictions shows the average officer-sergeant, sergeant-lieutenant, and lieutenant-captain differentials all to be 18%, then there are points to be made in bargaining.

When gathering information from comparable jurisdictions to aid in internal comparability studies, one must take care that the job descriptions for supervisors in the various jurisdictions are similar. Two positions titled "Wastewater Supervisor" (for example) can be quite different jobs in different jurisdictions. Also, care should be taken to make sure that the compensation plans in the comparables are roughly similar. In some jurisdictions, supervisors are not eligible for overtime; in others they may be able to collect overtime, but can do so only in the form of compensatory time off; while in yet others, overtime is paid in cash at the rate of time and a half. Distinctions such as these should be noted and shared with the other party.

Finally, a minority of arbitrators have observed that external comparability is more important in making wage awards and internal comparability more so in deciding benefit issues.[20] Most arbitrators follow a different approach and weigh the value of internal comparability the same whether a wage or benefit issue is being considered.[21]

Wage Increases For Other Employees.

Negotiators are also greatly concerned with issues of internal comparability of wage increases – how the wage increases for the particular bargaining unit match up against the wage increases paid to other employees of the same employer.[22] Particularly in times of constricting budgets and difficult economic conditions, there is a view that all employees should receive roughly the same compensation adjustments, whether up or down.[23] Others tend to treat some jobs – particularly public safety jobs – as *sui generis* jobs that should not be directly impacted by the wage increases given other employees.[24]

Also of interest are the wage increases received by employees working for other employers, both in the public and private sector.[25] As one arbitrator observed, the rates of wage changes in the public and private sector "are affected by the same national and local factors, such as the health of the economy, prevailing interest rates, status of unemployment, rate of inflation and the impact of tax legislation."[26] Some wage increase information must be gained through surveys; national wage increase figures are compiled by the Bureau of Labor Statistics of the United States Department of Labor.[27]

There can be limitations on the importance of wage increase figures from the private sector. Not only are funding sources completely different in the public and private sector, but the job markets themselves may have different patterns. In addition, it can be quite difficult to find private sector analogues to some public sector jobs:

> Although some private sector employees may be exposed to danger when intervening in disputes, notably in residential mental health facilities, or through exposure to hazardous working conditions, the knowledge of law and procedures, the emergency training, the street experience, and other attributes which enable a Police Officer to be ready, willing and able to protect the public in a variety of exigencies is unparalleled in the private sector. Other municipal employees do not carry weapons, are not subject to the same type of liability for a momentary lapse in judgment or performance, and do not deal with the types of stresses and unpredictable situations that bargaining unit Police Officers frequently confront, whether by stopping vehicles at night, intervening in domestic disputes, or responding to crimes in progress.[28]

The Level Of Turnover And Employment Application Rates.

Another of the "other factors" taken into account in bargaining is the ability of the governmental body to attract and retain qualified employees.[29] This consideration is often measured by voluntary turnover and, on the flipside, the number of employment applications received for the position in question.

If the employer has a very stable work force, without much in the way of voluntary turnover, then an argument can be made that the wage structure within the employer is at least satisfactory to those employees who choose not to seek alternative employment opportunities. Similarly, if there is no dearth of applicants for work in the job applications being studied, it can be argued that at a minimum the entry-level wage, if not the entire wage structure, is meeting market demands.

On the other hand, if the employer suffers from a high rate of voluntary turnover or if the number of applications is slipping over a period of time, then an argument can be made that at least the possibility exists that the wage structure is contributing to the problems of attracting and maintaining the highest caliber of employees in the target jurisdiction. When such data is viewed in comparison with similar figures from jurisdictions which have been determined to be comparable, these arguments may be strengthened. As one arbitrator analyzed it:

> The costs of a retention problem are not just monetary. Because the employer is losing its most experienced firefighters, there is also a cost to the safety of both the public and firefighters. Retention problems of this nature are unique to this employer. The president of the Tualatin Valley Fire and Rescue Department bargaining unit testified that in 15 years, TVFR has lost only two firefighters to other departments. The president of the Portland Fire Department testified that only one firefighter has left Portland Fire for another department in the last 15 years. The president of Clackamas County Fire Department testified that in the last 10 years, only three firefighters have left Clackamas Fire for other fire departments, and none of them left for economic reasons. Until the disparities and injustices in the wage scale are remedied, experienced firefighters will continue to leave this employer for other departments.[30]

There are several pitfalls to avoid when negotiators use turnover in employment application figures. With respect to turnover, one must be careful to use the figures only for voluntary, non-disciplinary, non-retirement, non-disability terminations of service. Turnover figures are especially persuasive if information can be developed as to the next jobs taken by employees voluntarily terminating their employment. For example, if the departing employees show a trend toward accepting the same type of employment with another employer with a higher wage scale, the turnover figures may take on added significance.

Similar caution must be taken with respect to information concerning the number of employment applications. Typically, applicants for a public sector job are required to undergo a thorough initial screening process after the applications have been received. Following this process, the employer then determines whether the applicants have sufficient qualifications to warrant the giving of a written test or employment examination. Only a portion of those who initially file applications with the employer may be invited to take a written test. Following a written test, those who score above a certain level on the test typically are required to pass an oral interview, followed by a background check, and, if relevant, a physical fitness examination. Only after this entire screening procedure is complete are candidates placed on a list of "eligible hires" who may be offered employment.

Given these levels of screening, when employment application figures are gathered from comparable jurisdictions, the figures that should be used are those reflecting the same stage of the screening process. It may be, for example, that one jurisdiction does not count an "application" until a written examination has been passed, while another jurisdiction would count every individual who initially applied for the job. A comparison of job application rates should take these variances into account.

The Bottom Line. The desirability of a job, as measured by turnover rates and the number of applications for vacant positions, is one of the factors that should be considered in wage negotiations.

Public Opinion.

In negotiations involving larger employers, public opinion surveys can play a role in the bargaining process. Such surveys generally measure the public's opinion either with respect to the level of satisfaction for the services being performed by the agency under study, or the public's attitude towards the wages and benefits of public employees.

The Local Labor Market.

What is going on within the local labor market often is a significant factor in bargaining. Jurisdictions that are truly comparable in the demographic sense may be geographically distant; the compensation settlements in the local area may thus have more of an impact on those in the comparable jurisdictions. To the extent that there are private sector jobs that are identical or analogous to the public sector job under consideration, local comparisons should look to the pay and benefit structure for those private sector jobs.[31]

NOTES

[1] RCW 41.56.465(1)(e).

[2] *E.g.*, Section 243.746 (4), Oregon Revised Statutes.

[3] *Lane County*, 2000 WL 36177793 (Downing, 2000)(lengthy discussion of arbitration opinions defining "interests and welfare of the public").

[4] *Township of Rochelle Park*, 2004 WL 6012874 (Glasson, 2004).

[5] *Borough of Cliffside Park and PBA Local 96*, PERC Docket No. IA-98-91-14 (Tener, 1999).

[6] *Borough of Keyport*, 2006 WL 6823294 (Glasson, 2006).

[7] *City of East Orange*, 1998 WL 35395315 (Scheinman, 1998).

[8] *City of Trenton*, 1998 WL 35395340 (Scheinman, 1998).

[9] *County of Hudson*, 2003 WL 26067480 (Hussey, 2003).

[10] *Borough of Ringwood*, 2006 WL 6823282 (Weisblatt, 2006).

[11] *E.g. City of Havre, Montana and IAFF, Local 601*, 76 LA 789 (Snow, 1991); *Public Service Electric and Gas Company*, 15 LA 496 (1950); *Pacific Gas and Electric Co.*, 7 LA 530 (1947).

[12] *Township of West Windsor*, 2004 WL 6012876 (Weisblatt, 2004).

[13] *Factfinding between City of Oregon City (Oregon) and Oregon City Police Officers Association*, (Abernathy, 1993)(unpublished opinion).

[14] Evan Berman, *Performance and Productivity In Public and Nonprofit Organizations*, (Routledge, 2006), http://www.amazon.com/Performance-Productivity-Public-Nonprofit-Organizations/dp/0765616084/ref=la_B001IXTVB2_1_7?s=books&ie=UTF8&qid=1429465659&sr=1-7.

[15] *Township of Franklin*, 2004 WL 6012854 (Mastriani, 2004).

[16] *City of Trentwood*, 2005 WL 6710754 (Keenan, 2005).

[17] *Township of Boardman*, 2004 WL 6012781 (Gardner, 2004).

[18] *City of McMinnville and McMinnville Police Officers' Ass'n*, IA 20-99 (Wollett, 2000).

[19] *Township of Franklin*, 2004 WL 6012854 (Mastriani, 2004).

[20] *Central Decatur Schools & Central Decatur Education Ass'n*, PERB CEO #127/3 (Scoville, 2004).

[21] *E.g., St. Louis County Corrections/911 Unit*, 2011 WL 2555253 (Remington, 2011).

[22] *City of St. Paul, Minnesota and City of St. Paul Confidential Employees Ass'n*, 101 LA 1205 (Jacobowski, 1993); *City of Southfield, Michigan and Command Officers Association of Michigan*, 78 LA 153 (Roumell, 1992).

[23] *City of Belleville*, 2010 WL 6772784 (Goldstein, 2010).

[24] *See, e.g.*, Hoover, Dowling & Bouley, *The Erosion of Police and Firefighter Wage Parity* (1996).

[25] *Monroe County, Wisconsin*, 113 LA 933 (Dichter, 1999); *Sibley County, Minnesota and Law Enforcement Labor Services, Inc.*, 111 LA 795 (Bognanno, 1998).

[26] *Union County*, 1999 WL 35113776 (Kurtzman, 1999); *see Township of Hanover*, 2005 WL 6710872 (Glasson, 2005).

[27] http://www.bls.gov/news.release/eci.toc.htm.

[28] *Cherry Hill Township*, 1996 WL 34548131 (Brent, 1996); *see City of Detroit*, 2013 WL 1558724 (Roumell, 2013).

[29] *Township of Rochelle Park*, 2004 WL 6012874 (Glasson, 2004).

[30] *State of Oregon*, No. IA-03-10 (Boedecker, 2011).

[31] *Ridgefield Park Board of Education and Ridgefield Park Education Association*, 68 LA 163 (Golob, 1977).

CHAPTER 19

INTEREST ARBITRATION

The most common model for public sector labor negotiations has the bargaining process for at least some employees ending in what is known as "interest arbitration." Interest arbitration is entirely different from grievance arbitration, where an arbitrator is asked to decide whether an employer has violated the terms of an existing collective bargaining agreement. In interest arbitration, the arbitrator is *setting* the terms of a new contract.

The interest arbitration model is most often used for public safety employees such as law enforcement and fire protection personnel, the rationale being that strikes by public safety employees pose too much of a risk to be countenanced, and that there should be some neutral system of resolving contract impasses. Interest arbitration is mandated at the state law level in most states in the Northeast, in the upper Midwest, and the Pacific Northwest. Interest arbitration can also exist as a local option in states where the state laws do not mandate it. Colorado and California are examples of states where individual cities have chosen to follow the interest arbitration model even though they are not required to do so as a matter of state law.

There are three types of interest arbitration:

- **Last best offer, issue-by-issue arbitration**. With this form of interest arbitration, often known as "baseball arbitration" because of its use in salary arbitrations for baseball players, the arbitrator must choose between the final offers of each party on whatever issues have been submitted to arbitration. For example, if the parties have sent 13 issues to arbitration, the arbitrator may choose the final offers of the employer on eight of the issues and the final offers of the union on the five remaining issues. The arbitrator is not free to reach a "middle ground" between the final offers of the parties on any particular issue; instead, she is required to select whichever of the final offers she believes is most appropriate.[1]

- **Last best offer, total package**. With this form of interest arbitration, the arbitrator must choose between the total packages of each party. If 13 issues have been sent to arbitration, then the arbitrator decides which of the two total packages is the more reasonable, and one side or the other wins its final offer on all 13 issues. It may well be that the arbitrator ends up awarding elements of a package with which she disagrees, but must award those elements of the package because the party's overall package is the more reasonable of the two.

- **Arbitrator discretion**. The most common form of interest arbitration gives the arbitrator the discretion to choose between the final offers of either party on an issue-by-issue basis, or to craft a position somewhere between the parties. For example, if the employer proposes a wage freeze and the union proposes a 4.0% increase, the arbitrator can award a freeze, 4.0%, 2.25%, or some other increase between a wage freeze and 4.0%.

Selecting An Arbitrator.

When picking an arbitrator, it is critically important to thoroughly research potential arbitrators of the dispute. This is the individual who will be deciding critical issues, and who will have the ability to issue an award that may involve millions or tens of millions of dollars. Like all of us, arbitrators have predilections. Some are more or less persuaded by particular arguments. Some have tendencies with respect to certain issues, whether those issues involve health insurance, overtime, wages, or other issues. Some have the ability to craft a decision that will articulately analyze matters in such a way that neither party will be interested in arbitration for many years; others manage to write a decision so badly that it virtually guarantees further conflict. You need to know these things, and 100 other things about potential arbitrators, before you select the person who will be setting wages and benefits for the bargaining unit.

> *The Bottom Line. The arbitrator has the authority to issue a decision that can have a huge impact on wages, hours and working conditions. Given that potential impact, there is no excuse for not thoroughly researching the track records of potential arbitrators.*

So how do you research an arbitrator? There are a number of different paths to take. You should consider following all of them.

- **Review The Arbitrator's Prior Decisions.** Many state labor boards publish on-line the decisions of interest arbitrators in the state. The national legal databases Westlaw and Lexis store some of the decisions of interest arbitrators, though they charge a fee to provide them. There are also fee-based arbitrator research services, such as arbsearch.com,[2] that will provide you with interest arbitration opinions.

- **Speak With Others.** There's little substitute for picking up a phone and calling people to ask about arbitrators. It's common for an advocate who sees a name she does not recognize on an arbitration list to call lawyers for both unions and employers to get their opinions about the arbitrator and the details of prior cases.

- **Use The Internet.** You can find interest arbitration decisions in a surprising number of sites on the Internet. Sometimes, the employer or union involved in the arbitration will post the decisions. On other occasions, a labor periodical might describe an arbitration opinion. On many occasions, you can find decisions on an Internet news site that collects articles published by newspapers and magazines. Once you see a reference to an opinion, track it down by contacting the employer or the union, and see if they'll send it to you.

Scheduling The Hearing.

It's almost a truism that interest arbitration hearings take longer than expected. Thinking you might be able to put on your case in a day, and the other side will take as long? Plan for three or four days of hearing, not two. The downside of scheduling too few days is heavy; with a busy arbitrator, it may be weeks or months before you can add an additional hearing day. The costs of scheduling too many days for the hearing are modest, particularly since you can make arrangements in advance with the arbitrator that if hearing days aren't used, the arbitrator will work on your case on those days, whether in "study time" or opinion drafting.

Developing Final Offers.

The rationale behind final offer arbitration is that it drives the parties to reasonable positions, narrowing the gap between them, thus making settlement more likely. There are no academic articles that actually prove this point, mind you, but it's a proposition that is widely believed. Here's Wikipedia's statement of the proposition:

> A primary purpose and effect of final offer arbitration is to encourage the parties to arrive at a settlement by introducing uncertainty into the arbitration procedure. Parties who fail to compromise during negotiations risk a total loss on some or all arbitrated issues under final offer arbitration. This uncertainty is considered a "cost" of arbitration that the parties can avoid by settling, even if the settlement is among the desired outcomes. By contrast, in conventional arbitration, parties are more likely to call on the arbitrator to decide disputed issues by crafting a "reasonable," middle-ground award. In addition to promoting settlement, use of final offer arbitration leads parties to adopt reasonable positions during the arbitration, because an unreasonable position will almost certainly be rejected in favor of a more reasonable competing proposal.

The due date for final offers is usually set by state statute or local ordinance, and is almost always relatively proximate (e.g., one week, ten days) to the first day of the arbitration hearing. Constructing a final offer requires work. Each party should be doing at least these things:

- Analyzing settlement trends for other public employees in the region.
- Taking into account the settlements the employer has reached with other unions.
- Researching arbitration trends on the issues being submitted to arbitration.
- Reading every word the arbitrator has ever written on the arbitration issues.
- Analyzing the cost of living, the employer's ability to pay, total compensation comparisons, and other arbitration criteria.

Ideally, a party's final offer will be just a hair more reasonable than the other party's, not giving away too little so that the offer won't be acceptable, but not giving away too much so that there won't be any money left "on the table."

If constructing a final offer requires work, constructing a final offer in a "total package" arbitration not only demands all the more work, but also is almost an art form requiring a carefully thought-out strategy. Let's say you have nine issues going to arbitration under a total package system. Two of the issues – say wages and health insurance – involve a lot of money. A third issue involves "medium money," not as much as a 1.0% adjustment in wages, but not relatively negligible either. A fourth issue is viewed by the employer as a core management rights issue, and by the union as an important working condition. The remaining five issues pale in comparison to the importance of the first four.

How will arbitrators evaluate the final offers on the package of nine issues? Regrettably, it's usually not the product of some sort of equation you could replicate in preparing for the hearing. Instead, arbitrators tend to balance the number of issues won by each party against the economic or other significance of each issue. Thus, if you end up on the losing side of wages, health insurance, and the management rights/working condition issue, you'll learn that it's possible to win six out of the nine issues and still have the arbitrator award the other party's final package.

What this tells you is that your final offer position on each of the issues in your package has to be crafted with the whole package in mind. For example, you may want to "move to the middle" on issues such as wages and insurance, but maintain an aggressive position on some of the smaller issues, hoping that the power of your position on wages and insurance will sweep your entire final offer to victory. Alternatively, you may want to shave your positions on wages and insurance to the edge of acceptability, saving your "move to the middle" for the smaller issues. Your decision on crafting your total package should be based upon one overriding concern – how to convince the arbitrator that your total package should be selected.

Key in this analysis is what you anticipate the other party's final offer will be. If you're the union, you can probably roughly anticipate the employer's wage and insurance proposal based on the settlements the employer has reached with other unions, or perhaps an ordinance setting the employer's total compensation philosophy. If you're the employer, you may be able to predict from the course of negotiations the issues the union simply has to win from its perspective, issues where its final offer might be more aggressive. From either side's perspective, consider whether there are drafting problems with the other party's proposal on one or more of the issues such that the arbitrator won't award the proposal simply from a language perspective. All of these things (and more) should be considered in constructing a final offer package.

The Interest Arbitration Hearing.

To people whose only exposure to litigation has been in court, interest arbitration hearings can seem like awfully strange creatures. In many cases, the evidence in interest arbitration hearings is presented through the mouths of the chief advocates for each side, who summarize massive amounts of information presented through documents such as budgets, collective bargaining agreements, total compensation surveys, annual reports, and data from agencies such as the Bureau of Labor Statistics. It's not unknown for all of the evidence to be presented by the advocate in one long presentation that sounds like a combination opening statement, testimony, and closing argument. Hearsay? No problem. Unauthenticated documents? No problem. Mixing opinion in with statements of facts to the point where you don't know where one ends and the other begins? No problem.

Of course, not all interest arbitration hearings are quite so loose from a procedural standpoint. But many are, and your bargaining team needs to be prepared for the possibility. You need to choose your advocate carefully. You need to make sure your advocate has at least these traits:

- **Credibility.** Much of your case may be presented by your advocate, not by witnesses. It's critical that your advocate have a solid reputation in the community for honesty.

- **Persuasiveness.** It will be your advocate's job to convince the arbitrator that your position is the correct one. An advocate who dryly reviews an employer's budget is not nearly as effective as one who extracts from the budget the salient points, brings them to life with examples, modulates her voice rather than speaking in a monotone, and who focuses all of her skills on persuading the arbitrator of the correctness of your position.

- **Flexibility.** It's true in litigation, but particularly true in interest arbitration – advocates need to be able to think on their feet. They have to be able to react, and react quickly, when the arbitration hearing takes an unexpected twist.

- **Numbers, Numbers, Numbers.** Interest arbitration is usually all about money. There will be debates about the cost of the parties' proposals, about the economic assumptions used in the creation of the employer's budget, about what health insurance trends may be two years from now, about the impact of federal budgetary policies on local governments, etc., etc. Your advocate needs to understand all these principles – better than the advocate for the other side – and needs to be conversant in how to use a spreadsheet, the basic tool for analyzing money issues in arbitration. Moreover, your advocate has to have the ability to do all of this "on the fly" in the middle of a hearing, often when a witness is testifying.

Consider an example of what can happen in an interest arbitration hearing. In a final-offer, total-package arbitration setting, one of the issues was health insurance. As the employer's health insurance expert was testifying in support of a premium-share formula that would have required union members to pay all premium increases above the cost of living, the union's lawyer was creating a simple spreadsheet. The spreadsheet showed the present cost of health insurance, and left blanks for the spreadsheet cells that would contain information on the cost of living and, most importantly, on the much-faster-growing medical cost of living. On cross-examination, the spreadsheet was displayed through a projector and the employer's expert was asked to help fill in the blanks of the spreadsheet and create the formula that would project what the cost-sharing arrangement would look like ten years in the future if the employer's proposal was adopted. The resulting spreadsheet – which the employer had now essentially constructed – showed that in ten years, the employer's formula would result in employees paying 63% of all health insurance costs. The result was that the arbitrator found the union's health insurance proposal more reasonable and awarded the union's total package proposal.[3]

The point of this anecdote is that your advocate needs to have the math skills necessary to challenge every number submitted by the other side in the arbitration process. Has the other party submitted a chart showing anticipated pension costs? Your advocate needs to be able to perform the calculations necessary to dissect the chart, figure out the formulas used in the chart, and point out any flaws in those formulas.

The Evidence You Should Submit In Interest Arbitration.

If you speak to arbitrators, you'll find more than occasional frustration with the evidence they're provided, or not provided, in an interest arbitration hearing. There are some basic pieces of evidence that should be submitted in pretty much every interest arbitration hearing. These include:

- The employer's budget, at least for the current year.
- The employer's most recent Comprehensive Annual Financial Report, or CAFR.
- The current collective bargaining agreement, and the proposals made by both sides in the arbitration process.
- All tentative agreements reached in the bargaining process.
- Source data from the Bureau of Labor Statistics on the cost of living.
- The collective bargaining agreements for each of the comparator jurisdictions. If some total compensation information isn't contained in the collective bargaining agreements, then you should submit the source data for that information. For example, health insurance premium rates are often not captured by a collective bargaining agreement. If that's the case, you'll need to obtain the "rate sheets" from the comparable employers.
- Any prior interest arbitration decisions between the parties.
- Any interest arbitration decisions involving other parties, but upon which one party in the current proceedings is relying.
- If productivity or workload are issues, any documents generated by the employers containing the source data.

You should also consider the format in which you'll be presenting this evidence. The record in interest arbitration hearings can usually be quite extensive. An increasing number of arbitrators and litigants prefer to submit evidence electronically. One flash drive can easily contain the contents of ten exhibit binders. Every exhibit should be presented in the form of a pdf file or, if helpful, as a spreadsheet. If you're submitting exhibits electronically, create an electronic index with links to each exhibit. That way, your arbitrator can easily call up Exhibit 131 (for example) simply by double clicking on the index entry.

The Use Of Experts In Interest Arbitration.

There are many highly-skilled experts in areas that arise in interest arbitration. Topics such as health insurance, pensions, municipal finance, and labor markets almost naturally lend themselves to expert testimony. Experts can be incredibly helpful and persuasive, but they can also be expensive. It is a safe assumption that by the time an expert witness sits down to testify at an interest arbitration hearing, his bill is already over $10,000, and probably much higher.

That suggests the first question should be whether you really need an expert witness. The expert witness calculus should consider things such as:

- Is this a topic that can only be explained by an expert witness?

- Do you have a good expert lined up? Does your expert have solid credentials, an unimpeachable reputation, a good working understanding of the facts and principles involved, and the ability to effectively communicate?

- Will your expert be better than those retained by the other side, or vice versa?

- How much will your expert cost?

Depending on how you end up evaluating these points, you may wish to consider approaching the other side to see if there's interest in a stipulation that no expert witnesses will testify at the interest arbitration hearing.

There are times when you'll have to use an expert witness. Perhaps your arbitrator demands more formal processes, and wants to hear evidence from witnesses rather than advocates. Perhaps the underlying issue is so important that you believe the expert will add the necessary gravitas to the hearing. If you're going to use an expert, try to pick one who is a good communicator. You need an expert who can reduce a complicated formula to English, and who can do so in an easy and non-pedantic manner. There are times, of course, where there are very few experts in a certain field, and you'll be stuck with an expert for whom communication isn't a particular skill. It will be your job to work even harder preparing the expert for the arbitration hearing, perhaps conducting a trial run-through of the expert's testimony before a panel of lay people who have no prior understanding about the subject of the expert's testimony.

If you can figure out who the other party's expert witnesses will be, research them. Even if you don't know precisely who the witnesses will be, be prepared to research them on the fly as they testify. It's a good idea to train one member of your bargaining team in how to conduct Internet research on an expert.

Technology – Use It Effectively.

Perhaps more than any other type of legal proceeding, interest arbitration hearings are particularly well suited to a technological presentation. Don't just submit reams of paper, make the information come to life. If the evidence is amenable to it, use charts, graphs, photographs, and other more visual formats to present the evidence. Short movies summarizing important things about the employer's operations or the bargaining unit can also be helpful. PowerPoint can be a wonderful or mind-numbing tool. Use it well, making sure you read several of the dozens of "Things To Do/Not Do With PowerPoint" advice sheets you can easily find on the Internet.

A good example of effective use of technology occurred in an arbitration several years ago between the Redmond, Washington Police Association and the City of Redmond.[4] One of the points the union was trying to make was that the City had a solid funding basis in the community. To be sure, that point could have been made by submitting Chamber of Commerce reports, property tax assessment data, and employment data. The police union, though, chose another route. Using Google Earth, it created a movie where the camera swooped down on the top ten private employers in Redmond, pausing while the camera displayed each employer's facilities and displaying a text box showing each employer's annual revenues, number of employees, and status in the industry, and then moving on to the next employer on the list. At the end, the camera was looking at the campus of Redmond's largest employer – Microsoft – and the point was made much more effectively than it could have been through hundreds of pieces of paper.

Recording The Hearing.

You need a record of your interest arbitration hearing. Courts will tell you that if there's no official record of the hearing, it's impossible for either side to challenge the arbitrator's opinion. The record doesn't need to be elaborate or expensive; audio recordings will suffice. My experience has been that having a court reporter prepare transcripts is an expensive proposition, and rarely adds much to the process since the "meat" in an interest arbitration hearing are the documents that are in evidence, not the testimony of witnesses.

After The Hearing But Before The Decision.

Let's say you've completed your arbitration hearing and you're waiting for the arbitrator's decision. You've got one more thing to do. Try once again to settle the contract. Both you and the other party now know more about each other's position than you ever did in negotiations, and each of you has had the ability to assess the strength of your own case and that of the other. That provides a wonderful opportunity for settlement, one not often explored.

If an arbitration panel has heard your case rather than a single arbitrator, you've got some special concerns. Typically, arbitration panels are made up of three members: A neutral arbitrator and appointees of management and labor. The panel will almost always meet after the hearing is closed, and will discuss tentative conclusions and the evidence. In real life, this means that the "partisan" panel members will want to take one more shot at convincing the arbitrator of the rectitude of their position.

You need to be prepared for this post-hearing lobbying process. In fact, you need to have prepared for it before you chose your appointee to the panel. Your appointee needs to be someone who at least matches the experience, ability, and skill set of the other party's appointee. The process can escalate to the point where both parties are appointing experienced (and expensive) labor attorneys as their panel members, if only to prevent the other party from gaining an advantage in the "second hearing." If you're in that situation, try to get the other party to agree to waive having "partisan" members of a panel and to go with a single arbitrator; failing that, attempt to obtain ground rules on the conduct of the panel post-arbitration.

The Finality Of The Arbitrator's Decision.

The very nature of interest arbitration means that the arbitrator's decision is usually final and binding. Some states – Alaska, for example – make the arbitrator's decision subject to funding by the governing body of the employer, but such statutory schemes are the exception rather than the rule.

What if the arbitrator got some facts wrong or misapplied the law? Following the lead of Supreme Court decisions going back more than 50 years, most courts will say that "final and binding" means precisely that. Courts will say that an arbitrator can be wrong on the facts, and wrong on the law, and still have her opinion upheld unless there's some evidence of fraud or that the arbitrator exceeded her jurisdiction.[5]

There is an emerging trend to watch out for with respect to the finality of interest arbitration decisions. Some states – New Jersey, for example – require arbitrators to analyze each of the criteria set forth by the collective bargaining statute for consideration by arbitrators. No matter whether you're in a state that has an explicit requirement that an arbitrator consider all statutory criteria, it's a good practice at the close of the hearing for both parties to request that the arbitrator do so. The last thing you want is an arbitration decision that gets overturned, requiring you to go through the whole process again.

What Will Likely Result From Arbitration?

It is an old adage that the parties neither get richer nor poorer in interest arbitration. Indeed, interest arbitration is a leveling process, designed to bring an externally-imposed sense of reasonableness to a bargaining process that has, for whatever reason, lacked reasonableness. Arbitrators usually try to award a result that the bargaining process *should have* produced, taking into account the employer's finances, the general economic condition, the cost of living, comparison wages, and the like.

Many interest arbitrators do not hesitate to say precisely this. Arbitrator Elliot Goldstein once wrote that "interest arbitrators are essentially obligated to replicate the results of arm's-length bargaining between the parties, and to do no more."[6] More than 65 years ago, Arbitrator Whitley McCoy wrote: "The fundamental inquiry, as to each issue, is: What should the parties themselves, as reasonable men, have voluntarily agreed to? The endeavor is to decide the issues as, upon the evidence, we reasonable negotiators, regardless of their social or economic theories, might have decided them in the give and take process of bargaining."[7] More recently, Arbitrator Harvey Nathan expounded at some length on the same topic:

> Interest arbitration is essentially a conservative process. While obviously value judgments are inherent, the neutral cannot impose upon the parties' contractual procedures he or she knows that parties themselves would never agree to. Nor is his function to embark upon new ground and to create some innovative procedural or benefits scheme which is unrelated to the parties' particular bargaining history. The arbitration award must be a natural extension of where the parties were at impasse. The award must flow from the peculiar circumstances these particular parties have developed for themselves. To do anything less would inhibit collective bargaining.[8]

As applied to individual proposals, this conservative principle of interest arbitration is often referred to as the "*status-quo* rule." One arbitrator has written that "among the settled principles in interest arbitration is that the systems or methodology the parties have negotiated and established for the operation of the terms and conditions of employment cannot be changed against the objections of the other party unless very good cause has been shown."[9] The longer the *status quo* has been in place, the higher the burden of proving that a change is appropriate.[10]

The *status quo* rule particularly applies in the area of proposed changes to contract language: "Arbitrators in 'interests' disputes normally allow a presumption favoring the *status quo* when considering a proposal that has not found prior acceptance in the parties' collective bargaining agreement or in other comparable settings."[11] As put by another arbitrator, "the party seeking to depart from the *status quo* must show more than that change is a good idea; it must show that the current conditions are 'broken' somehow."[12]

This is not to say that the *status quo* rule always results in the perpetuation of past practice in interest arbitration. It is possible to convince an arbitrator to award new contract language by showing that a problem exists that the proposal is designed to cure, that circumstances have changed since the prior practice came into being, that the evidence of comparability is overwhelming, or that a proposal is simply a "better idea" for how a situation should be handled.[13]

This is also not to say that the *status quo* rule does not have its detractors. A prominent Washington arbitrator, with almost 40 years of experience as both an arbitrator and the head of a state labor board, made the following comment about arbitrators who believe their awards should approximate what a settlement should have been:

> Interest arbitration is a statutory proceeding, not a forum for itinerant philosophers to dispense their own brand of industrial justice. None of [the interest arbitration awards relying upon this argument] provide any basis to add to or subtract from the criteria set forth by the Washington State Legislature in RCW 41.56.465.[14]

NOTES

[1] *City of Livonia*, 2013 WL 1558725 (Gravelle, 2013)(describing Michigan's last-best offer system).

[2] http://interarb.com/ADsearch/ADsearch?form=extended&qprev=.

[3] http://www.oregon.gov/ERB/pages/awards/ia0603.aspx.

[4] http://www.perc.wa.gov/databases/intarb/20138-I.htm.

[5] *Eastern Associated Coal Corp. v. United Mine Workers of America*, 531 U.S. 57 (2000), https://www.law.cornell.edu/supct/html/99-1038.ZS.html.

[6] *Metropolitan Alliance of Police,* Chapter 471, FMCS 091103-0042-A (2009).

[7] Whitley P. McCoy, in the often-quoted *Twin City Rapid Transit Company*, 7 LA (BNA) 845 (1947).

[8] *Will County Board and Sheriff of Will County*, S-MA-88-09 (Nathan, 1988).

[9] *Village of Lake in the Hills*, http://www.state.il.us/ilrb/subsections/pdfs/ArbitrationAwards/Lake%20in%20the%20Hills%20&%20MAP,%20S-MA-09-269.pdf (Nathan, 2010).

[10] *Pacific County*, Case 26447-I-14-0643 (Martin, 2015).

[11] *Pierce County Fire District 2*, AAA Case No. 75-390-0172-87 (Wilkinson, 1988).

[12] *Village of Romeoville and MAP*, S-MA-10-064 (Fletcher, 2010).

[13] *City of Medford*, http://www.oregon.gov/ERB/awards/ia-21-05.pdf (Skratek, 2008).

[14] *Cowlitz County and Cowlitz County Deputies Guild*, PERC Case 26333-I-14-0638 (Schurke, 2015).

CHAPTER 20

ON-LINE NEGOTIATIONS RESOURCES

Perhaps no area of public sector collective bargaining has changed as much as the availability of online resources. Information once cost thousands of dollars to amass, and months to gather, is now instantly available without cost over the Internet. Even the smallest of organizations can now have access to information that once was the province of organizations with greater resources.

We have compiled a list of the online resources that we have found to be helpful. There are many more web pages that could be of assistance; all it takes to locate them is time, energy, and imagination.

The Law.

Cornell University Law School has a well-organized on-line clearinghouse where one can find the constitutions, statutes and codes for all 50 states, as well as for the federal government, http://www.law.cornell.edu/statutes.html. The regulations issued by federal agencies such as the Department of Labor can be found at the Government Printing Office's web site, https://www.gpo.gov/, as well as through other sites. http://www.law.cornell.edu/cfr/.

The decisions of the United States Supreme Court can be found on the Court's web site, http://www.supremecourt.gov/. A wealth of information about the Supreme Court, including the briefs filed in cases as well as recordings of oral arguments, can be found at The Oyez Project, http://www.oyez.org/. The decisions of lower federal courts, as well as those of state courts, can quickly be located at Findlaw, http://caselaw.findlaw.com/. Findlaw, like the Cornell University law school webpage, is an excellent general legal portal for a variety of different sources of the law.

For many years, one of the most difficult things to find on-line were the codes for various municipalities and counties. Thanks to the Municode website, more than 1,100 local codes are now online, http://www.municode.com/. In addition, State and Local Government on the Net, http://www.statelocalgov.net/, is a broad portal to state and local government web pages.

Employment Law Newsletters and Blogs.

Employment law newsletters and blogs have proliferated in the last two years. Where once there were a handful, now there are hundreds. Among the best are:

- *Labor Relations Information System*, http://www.lris.com. A thrice-weekly free e-mail newsletter containing information about public sector wage settlements, court decisions, and statutory and regulatory changes.

- *Employment Law Information Network*, http://www.elinfonet.com/. Publishes a five-day per week free newsletter on private and public sector labor developments.

How To Negotiate.

There is seemingly no end to the advice contained on the Internet as to how to best negotiate. The more accessible web pages include:

- *Everyone Negotiates*, http://www.negotiatingguide.com/. Contains negotiating advice, and on-line tests of negotiating skills and style, books and audio materials, and a free monthly newsletter devoted to negotiations tactics.

- *Forbes*, http://www.forbes.com/. The Internet version of the popular business magazine has hundreds of articles on negotiations in its online archives.

- *The Harvard Business Review*, https://hbr.org/. Has dozens of free articles on negotiations tactics and strategy as well as materials that can be purchased.

- *How To Negotiate*, http://www.how-to-negotiate.com/. A blog devoted to the development of negotiations skills.

- *The Negotiations Experts*, http://www.negotiations.com/article/. A good collection of articles about effectively negotiating any type of agreement.

- *Top 10 Negotiations Tips*, http://meetingsnet.com/negotiating/tips/meetings_top_negotiating_tips_4/. A straightforward list of many of the important things to do (and avoid) when negotiating.

A greatly expanded list, together with many negotiations catch-phrases, can be found at *Changing Minds*, http://changingminds.org/disciplines/negotiation/tactics/tactics.htm.

Demographic and Economic Data.

From the standpoint of public sector negotiators, perhaps the greatest riches to be found on the Internet is in the area of economic and demographic data. Not that long ago, compiling this sort of information would require the services of an expert and the expenditure of a significant amount of money. Today, the information is not only available without cost, but is increasingly found on web sites with easy-to-use interfaces.

- *Census Bureau*, http://www.census.gov/. One could spend days on the Census Bureau's web site and not completely explore all the information helpful in the collective bargaining process. The Bureau compiles a Fact Sheet for every city and county in the country. The information on those Fact Sheets, including (among others) population, median family income, and home values, are useful in selecting comparable jurisdictions. Where some of the data on the web site are figures produced by the decennial census and can be dated depending upon when they are viewed, the Bureau also conducts an annual American Community Survey with more recent information.

- *Bureau of Labor Statistics*, http://www.bls.gov/. The BLS tabulates, among other things, the Consumer Price Index as well as information on the demographics of employment, safety, wages, earnings, and benefits. The BLS's web site is well laid out, and even a neophyte can determine the cost of living or the effects of long-term inflation in a particular area using BLS's cost of living calculator. Those interested in more detail will not leave unsatisfied; for example, information on the relative rates of change of different components of the CPI is easy to access.

- *Bureau of Justice Statistics*, http://www.bjs.gov/. An essential for negotiations involving law enforcement groups, the BJS web site contains crime and policing data allowing jurisdiction-to-jurisdiction comparison of matters such as officers per 1,000 population and relative crime rates. The BJS web site also contains information on more specific issues such as the relationship between law enforcement wages and levels of higher education.

- *Congressional Budget Office*, http://www.cbo.gov/. The CBO's web site contains the federal government's forecasts of changes in the Consumer Price Index and other key economic indicators.

- *Bureau of Economic Analysis*, http://www.bea.gov/. Economic trend analysis, including estimates of key aspects of the national and regional economy.

- *FedStats*, https://fedstats.sites.usa.gov/. The federal government's FedStats web site contains links to a variety of statistics collected by over 100 government agencies.

- *The Dismal Scientist*, http://www.dismal.com/. The British historian once referred to economics as the "dismal science." The Dismal Scientist web page is one of the best economics web pages on the Internet, containing an extremely thorough collection of economic indicators including ranking of states and metropolitan areas on 130 different statistical criteria.

- *Economagic*, http://www.economagic.com/. Economagic's web site contains over 400,000 data files, charting a wide range of economic time series data on such things as the Gross Domestic Product, changes in personal income, and interest rates.

- *EconData*, http://www.econdata.net. EconData has over 1,000 links to socioeconomic data sources, arranged by subject and provider, links to the Internet data collections, and a list of the ten best sites for finding regional economic data.

Regional Cost of Living Calculators.

If wage comparisons are made to jurisdictions that are geographically distant, it may be appropriate to make adjustments for regional differences in the cost of living. There are any number of "cost of living calculators" on the Internet. One should use these calculators with caution – few disclose their methodology, and one can enter the same figures into the calculators on different web sites and get wildly disparate results. Among the most popular of the calculators are:

- Bankrate, http://www.bankrate.com/calculators/savings/moving-cost-of-living-calculator.aspx.
- Sperling's BestPlaces, http://www.bestplaces.net/col/.
- MySalary, http://swz.salary.com/costoflivingwizard/layoutscripts/coll_start.asp.
- CNNMoney, http://money.cnn.com/calculator/pf/cost-of-living/.

Medical Information.

With medical and other insurance occupying an increasing amount of the total compensation package, it is important to obtain information about projected increases in medical care and about insurance trends. These websites all contain valuable health care information.

- *Kaiser Family Foundation*, http://www.kff.org/. The KFF web site – published by a foundation and not the HMO – provides historical and projected information on health insurance trends, including costs and benefit structures.
- *Health Affairs*, http://www.healthaffairs.org/. Health Affairs is the on-line version of the leading journal on health policy issues, and contains peer-reviewed articles on topics such as evidence-based health care and health care reform.
- *Health Policy Gateway*, http://ushealthpolicygateway.com/. Health Policy Gateway is probably the richest portal site for Internet links to health policy issues, covering dozens of topics from health care spending to health demographics to health care regulation and reform.

National Labor Organizations.

The websites for national labor organizations have some information that is useful in the collective bargaining process, though the amount of helpful information that is available outside of password-protected portals varies from organization to organization. Most of the web sites are focused on the organizations' structure, history, and activities, and contain only a modicum of information useful in the collective bargaining process.

- *The AFL-CIO*, http://www.aflcio.org/. Primarily general information about the AFL-CIO's legislative efforts, though the "Facts and Stats" database has interesting general information on topics such as worker safety and pension coverage.
- *American Federation of State, County and Municipal Employees*, http://www.afscme.org/. The "Collective Bargaining Tool Kit," containing everything from a compendium of state laws to tips on budget analysis, is one of the more helpful sections of any union or employer website.
- *American Federation of Teachers*, http://www.aft.org/. A well-designed web page

that, apart from AFT's annual Public Employee Compensation Survey, does not contain much information helpful to the collective bargaining process.

- *Combined Law Enforcement Associations of Texas*, http://www.cleat.org/. Since CLEAT largely operates in a non-collective bargaining environment, its web site does not contain much current information helpful to the bargaining process.

- *Fraternal Order of Police*, http://www.grandlodgefop.org/. The FOP has what is surely the most sophisticated collective bargaining-related applications on any union or management web site, including features that select comparable jurisdictions based on demographic characteristics, analyze total compensation, and calculate inflation-adjusted wages. However, those features are all behind a password-protected portal, and the rest of the FOP's web site is fairly standard for a labor organization.

- *International Association of Fire Fighters*, http://www.iaff.org/. The public sections of the IAFF's web site contain the usual fare for a union web site, with sections devoted to organizational structure, pending legislation, and the various programs offered by the organization.

- *International Union of Police Associations*, http://www.iupa.org/. The public portions of IUPA's web page, like the IAFF's, is focused almost exclusively on organizational issues and pending legislation.

- *National Association of Police Organizations*, http://www.napo.org/. Since NAPO is a lobbying organization rather than a true labor union, its web page is predictably short on collective bargaining information.

- *National Education Association*, http://www.nea.org. The public portions of NEA's web site are long on classroom issues such as lesson plans and educational strategies and shy on collective bargaining information.

- *Service Employees International Union*, http://www.seiu.org/. The "Members" section of SEIU's web site, which is not password protected, has some basic advice on employee rights issues such as the *Weingarten* rule.

National Employer Organizations.

- *Americans For Effective Law Enforcement*, http://www.aele.org/. There may be more freely-available content on AELE's web site than that of any other national organization. Though the user interface could use updating, the "Library" alone is worth visiting the web site, with hundreds of references to articles relevant to public sector negotiations. Several free periodicals offer updates on caselaw. Don't be deterred by the law enforcement-related name of AELE – most of the materials on the web site apply to all public sector employees.

- *National League of Cities*, http://www.nlc.org/. NLC has posted some valuable information about general economic conditions, located in the Research Reports section of its web site. The web site also contains legislative updates, and the Governance section of the web site contains some thoughtful publications on the upcoming challenges municipal governments face.

- *National Association of Counties*, http://www.naco.org/. The County Resource Center on NACO's web site contains some studies that are helpful in the collective bargaining process, particularly a study of health insurance trends.

- *National Public Employer Labor Relations Association*, http://www.npelra.org/. NPELRA is the largest organization representing employer labor relations professionals. To the extent its web page contains collective bargaining information, it is only found behind password-protected portals.

- *National School Boards Association*, http://www.nsba.org/. The NSBA's web page contains much more information on national legislative priorities than it does on collective bargaining issues.

News Article "Trawlers."

No organization about to embark on bargaining should be without at least one news article Internet "trawler." Trawlers set up user-defined searches of news sources, and produce results on a regular basis. A trawler can be set up so that each day one receives published articles on "the cost of living in Chicago," or "Long Beach budget," or "teacher or firefighter layoffs in New York." Many trawlers are now quite easy to use, and allow the user not only to define one or dozens of search strings, but also the frequency with which results are received. Among the best of the trawlers is Google News, http://news.google.com/, which touts itself as a "computer-generated news site that aggregates headlines from news sources worldwide, groups similar stories together and displays them according to each reader's personalized interests." Yahoo News also has a polished news trawler, http://news.yahoo.com/.

A

Ability To Pay
  Budget impacts 185
  Comprehensive Annual Financial Report 184
  Ending fund balances 186, 188
  Furloughs 186
  Layoffs 186
  Revenue growth 185
  Revenue projections 187
Arbitration Procedures
  As bargaining subject 16
Arbitrator Selection 205
Assessed Valuation
  Comparable jurisdictions 148
Attorneys
  Involvement in the bargaining process 64

B

Bad Faith Bargaining
  Authority of negotiators 116
  Surface bargaining 117
  Unfair labor practice 114
Bargaining In Hard Times 141
Bargaining Notes
  Ground rules 79
Bargaining Not Required Model 3
Bargaining Sessions
  Caucuses 95
  Delay tactics 117
  Frequency of 95
  Ground rules 79
    Audio or video recording 80, 103
    Cell phones 80
  Keeping records 101
  Length of 95
  Location of 95
  Note taking 79, 101
  Sidebar meetings 96
  Stages of 97
  Tentative agreements 98
Bargaining Team
  Characteristics of members 47
Bereavement Leave
  As bargaining subject 17
Binding Arbitration
  Defintion of 3
  Final offer, issue-by-issue 3
  Impasse 3, 29
  Interest and welfare of the public 195
  Preparation 43
  Total package 3
Blocking Charges
  Unfair labor practice 121
Brainstorm The Contract 60
Budgets
  Ability to pay 185
  Sharing information 87
Business Hours
  As bargaining subject 17

C

CAFR. *See* Comprehensive Annual Financial Report
Callback Pay
  As bargaining subject 17
Caucuses
  Ground rules 79, 95
Cease And Desist Orders
  Unfair labor practice 122
Cell Phones
  Ground rules 80
Clothing Allowance
  As bargaining subject 20
Collective Bargaining
  Attorney involvement 64
  Bargaining sessions
    Ground rules 77
  Interest and welfare of the public 195
  Pre-bargaining discussions 66
  Preparation 41
    Brainstorm the contract 60
    Comparable jurisdictions 61
    Constituent survey 59
    Negotiations binder 41
    Research bargaining history 60
    Writing proposals 59, 61
  Productivity 196
  Public opinion 200
  Sharing information 85
  Workload 196
Comparable Jurisdictions
  Assessed valuation of real property 148
  Contract language 61
  Demographic data 149

Determination of wages 198
Measures of comparability 149
On-line resources 220
Population 147
Proximity 148
Selection of 147, 150
Type of jurisdiction 148
Compensatory Time Off
  As bargaining subject 17
Complete Agreement Clauses 35
Comprehensive Annual Financial Report
  Ability to pay issues 184
  Interest arbitration 210
  Sharing information 90
Concessionary Bargining
  Furloughs 140
  Reopening a contract 139
  Rescinding a contract 139
  Retirement incentives 141
Consumer Price Index
  Cost of living 167
  CPI-U or CPI-W 169
  Housing component 173
  Medical component 173
  On-line resources 220
  Using the Index 171
Continuing Duty To Bargain 36
Contracts, Basic Rules
  Ordinary meaning of words 64
  Specific language 63
  Technical words 62
  Using Latin phrases 63
Contract Administration
  Sharing information 87
Cost Of Living
  Ability to pay 184
  Analysis of 175
  Consumer Price Index 167
  Fisher-Ideal Index 168
  Laspeyres Index 167
  On-line resources 221
  PCE Deflator 168
  Regional costs 176
  Using the CPI Index 171
Cost Of Living Index 177
Crime Statistics
  On-line resources 221

D

Defense Of Employees
  As bargaining subject 20
Deferred Compensation Match
  Total compensation 156
Demographic Data
  Comparable jurisdictions 149
  On-line resources 220
Determination Of Wages
  Comparable jurisdictions 198
  Internal comparability 197
  Retention of employees 199
  Workload and productivity 196
Direct Dealing
  Unfair labor practice 120
Discipline
  Sharing information 88
Discipline And Discharge
  As bargaining subject 16
Dress Codes
  As bargaining subject 20
Dues, Deduction Of
  As bargaining subject 16

E

Economic Data
  On-line resources 220
Education Incentive
  Total compensation 158
End Runs
  Defintion of 99
  Unfair labor practice 99
Equipment
  As bargaining subject 20
Experts
  Interest arbitration 210

F

Final Offer
  Interest arbitration 207
Fiscal Emergencies
  As bargaining subject 17
Fisher-Ideal Index
  Cost of living 168
Furloughs
  Ability to pay 186
  Concessionary bargaining 140

G

Good Faith Bargaining 115
Grievance Procedures
  As bargaining subject 16
Grooming Codes
  As bargaining subject 20
Ground Rules
  Bargaining notes 79
  Bargaining sessions 77, 79
  Breaches of 81
  Caucuses 79, 95
  Cell phones 80
  Negotiators 78
  Press releases 79, 99
  Proposals 78
  Recording sessions 80
  Sidebar meetings 96
  Tentative agreements 80
  Unfair labor practice 117

H

Health Insurance
  On-line resources 221
  Sharing information 87
Health Insurance Benefits
  As bargaining subject 20
History
  Researching bargaining history 60
Holidays
  As bargaining subject 16
  Total compensation 160
Hours Worked
  As bargaining subject 16

I

Impact Bargaining 15
Impasse
  Binding arbitration 3
  Meet and Confer 3
Information Sharing 85
  Budget information 87
  Comprehensive Annual Financial Report 90
  Contract administration 87
  Discipline 88
  Health insurance 87
  Promotions 88
  Retirement benefits 88
  Wage and benefit comparisons 86
  Work schedules 88
Insurance Costs
  Total compensation 160
Insurance Levels
  As bargaining subject 16
Interest Arbitration
  Arbitrator discretion 205
  Comprehensive Annual Financial Report 210
  Final offer 207
  Issue-by-issue 205
  Mandatory subjects of bargaining 15
  Recording the hearing 212
  Scheduling the hearing 206
  Selecting an advocate 208
  Selecting an arbitrator 205
  Status Quo Rule 214
  Technology, use of 211
  Total package 205
  Unfair labor practice 119
  Use of experts 210
Interest Based Bargaining
  Definition of 131
  Process of 132
Internal Comparability
  Determination of wages 197
Isssue-By-Issue Arbitration 3, 205

J

Job Security
  As bargaining subject 21
Jury Duty Pay
  As bargaining subject 20

L

Laspeyres Index
  Cost of living 167
Latin Phrases 63
Layoffs
  Ability to pay 186
  As bargaining subject 21
Leaves of Absence
  As bargaining subject 16
Longevity Pay
  As bargaining subject 17

M

Maintenance Of Benefits Clause
  As bargaining subject 36
Management Rights Clauses
  As bargaining subject 22
  Waiver by contract 33
Mandatory Subjects Of Bargaining 15
  Examples of 16
  Interest arbitration 15
Me-Too Clauses 107
Meals
  As bargaining subject 20
Meal Periods
  As bargaining subject 17
Meet and Confer
  Impasse 3
  Structure of 3
Merit Pay
  As bargaining subject 17
Mileage Reimbursement
  As bargaining subject 20

N

National Employer Organizations
  On-line resources 223
National Labor Organizations
  On-line resources 222
National Labor Relations Act 3
  Management rights clauses 22
  Waiver by contract 34
Negotiations Binder 41
  Content 103
Negotiators
  Authority of 116
  Ground rules 78
Nepotism Policies
  As bargaining subject 20
NLRA. *See* National Labor Relations Act
Note Taking
  Bargaining sessions 79, 101

O

Off-Duty Employment
  As bargaining subject 20
On-Call Status
  As bargaining subject 18

On-Line Resources
  Cost of living 221
  Demographic data 220
  Economic data 220
  How ti negotiate 220
  Law 219
  National employer organizations 223
  National labor organizations 222
  Newsletters 219
Other Factors In Collective Bargaining
  Employment application rates 199
  Interest and welfare of the public 195
  Internal comparability 197
  Local labor market 200
  Public opinion 200
  Turnover levels 199
  Wage increases for other employees 198
  Workload and productivity 196
Overtime
  As bargaining subject 17

P

Parity Clauses 107
Past Practices
  Changes in for purposes of collective bargaining 29
  Notice of change 31
  Requirements of 30
  Waiver of right to bargain 31
Pay Practices
  As bargaining subject 17
Pay Reductions
  As bargaining subject 17
PCE Deflator
  Cost of living 168
Pensions
  As bargaining subject 20
Permissive Subjects Of Bargaining 15
Population
  Comparable jurisdictions 147
Positional Bargaining
  Definition of 131
  Process of 132
Posting
  Unfair labor practice 122
Premium Pay
  Total compensation 156

Press Releases
  Ground rules 79, 99
Productivity
  Determination of wages 196
Prohibited Subjects Of Bargaining 15
Promotions
  As bargaining subject 20
  Sharing information 88
Proposals
  Calculating costs 71
  Estimating costs 74
  Ground rules 78
  Preparation 59
  Prioritizing 64
  Unfair labor practice 117
Public Opinion
  In the bargaining process 200

R

Recording Bargaining Sessions
  Ground rules 80, 103
Recording Interest Arbitration Hearings 212
Recordkeeping Of Negotiations 101
  Content 103
Regressive Bargaining
  Unfair labor practice 114, 118
Reopening A Contract
  Concessionary bargaining 139
Rescinding A Contract
  Concessionary bargaining 139
Residency Requirements
  As bargaining subject 20
Retention Of Employees
  Determination of wages 199
Retirement
  Sharing information 88
Retirement Incentives
  Concessionary bargaining 141
Retirement Pickup
  Total compensation 156
Revenue Growth
  Ability to pay 185
Revenue Projections
  Ability to pay 187

S

Safety
  As bargaining subject 16, 19

Selecting An Arbitrator
  Interest arbitration 205
Shift Trades
  As bargaining subject 18
Sick Leave
  As bargaining subject 16, 18
Sidebar Meetings
  Bargaining sessions 96
State Certification Pay
  Total compensation 158
Status Quo Rule
  Interest arbitration 214
  Unfair labor practice 119
Surface Bargaining
  Unfair labor practice 117

T

Tattoo Policies
  As bargaining subject 20
Tentative Agreements 98
  Ground rules 80
  Unfair labor practice 117
Total Agreement Clauses 35
Total Compensation
  Ability to pay 184
  Calculation 158, 160
  Holiday costs 160
  Insurance costs 160
  Premium pay 156
  Retirement pickup 156
  Vacations 160
  What is included 155
Total Package
  Interest arbitration 205
Tuition Reimbursement
  As bargaining subject 20

U

Unfair Labor Practices 113
  Bad faith bargaining 114
  Blocking charges 121
  Breach of ground rules 81
  Changing the status quo 118
  Delay tactics 117
  Direct dealing 120
  End runs 99
  Interest arbitration decisions 119

Regressive bargaining 114, 118
Remedies 122
Restoration of the status quo 122
Status quo rbargaining 117
Tentative agreements 117
Union Business
  As bargaining subject 16, 21

V

Vacations
  As bargaining subject 16
  Total compensation 160
Vehicles
  As bargaining subject 20

W

Wages
  As bargaining subject 16, 17
Wage And Benefit Comparisons
  Sharing information 86
Wage Comparisons 155
Waiver By Contract
  Collective bargaining 33
Waiver By Inaction
  Collective bargaining
    Past practices 31
  Results of 33
Working Conditions
  As bargaining subject 18, 19
    Off duty impact 20
  Disciplinary issues 21
Working Out Of Classification
  As bargaining subject 17
Workload
  Determination of wages 196
Work Schedules
  Sharing information 88
Work Shifts
  As bargaining subject 17